# Performance
# MANAGEMENT

Thank you for choosing a SAGE product!
If you have any comment, observation or feedback,
I would like to personally hear from you.

*Please write to me at* **contactceo@sagepub.in**

**Vivek Mehra,** Managing Director and CEO, SAGE India.

# Performance
# MANAGEMENT
## Toward Organizational Excellence

# 2
### EDITION

# T.V. Rao

Los Angeles | London | New Delhi
Singapore | Washington DC | Melbourne

*First published in 2004*
*Second edition published in 2016 by*

**SAGE Publications India Pvt Ltd**
B1/I-1 Mohan Cooperative Industrial Area
Mathura Road, New Delhi 110 044, India
*www.sagepub.in*

**SAGE Publications Inc**
2455 Teller Road
Thousand Oaks, California 91320, USA

**SAGE Publications Ltd**
1 Oliver's Yard, 55 City Road
London EC1Y 1SP, United Kingdom

**SAGE Publications Asia-Pacific Pte Ltd**
3 Church Street
#10-04 Samsung Hub
Singapore 049483

Published by Vivek Mehra for SAGE Publications India Pvt Ltd, typeset in 11/13 pts Adobe Caslon Pro by Zaza Eunice, Hosur, India and printed at Chaman Enterprises, New Delhi.

**Library of Congress Cataloging-in-Publication Data Available**

**ISBN:** 978-93-515-0730-7 (PB)

**The SAGE Team:** Sachin Sharma, Sanghamitra Patoway, and Rajinder Kaur

# CONTENTS

*List of Illustrations*                                      ix

*Foreword* by Vijay Govindarajan                             xi

*Preface to the First Edition*                               xv

*Preface to This Edition*                                    xxiii

*Acknowledgments*                                            xxix

1. Performance Management: An Overview                       1

2. Defining and Planning Performance                         30

3. Defining and Building Competencies                        54

4. Performance Analysis for Individual and
   Organization Development                                  75

5. Reducing Biases in Ratings and Managing
   Forced Distribution                                       103

6. Performance Conversations and Performance
   Review Discussions                                        132

7. Using Performance Management System Data for
   HR Decisions and Performance Improvements                 155

8. Best Practices in Performance Management                  173

9. Managing Motivation through Rewards and
   Recognition: Best Practices                               204

10. Lessons from Experience: A New Look at
    Performance Management Systems                           226

11. 360 Degree Feedback as a Performance
Management Tool                                           249

12. Performance Management through Assessment
and Development Centers                                  266

*Bibliography*                                                283

*Index*                                                       289

*About the Author*                                            299

# LIST OF ILLUSTRATIONS

**Tables**

1.1    Dyadic Performance Scores of Three Managers    27

4.1    Responses of 25 General Managers (Top Management Team) on Performance-related Questions    90

10.1    Suggested Components of Annual Performance Index to Be Made for Each Individual    242

10A.1    Differences between Performance Appraisal and Management    246

10B.1    Responses of Managers of Three Corporations on Performance-related Questions    247

10B.2    Wastage due to Lack of Proper Implementation of PMS by Various Categories of Managers in Four Organizations    248

**Figures**

5.1    The Normal Probability Curve    127

6.1    The Process of PRD    140

# FOREWORD

In a competitive world, every organization's performance depends on how well it can manage the present as well as prepare for the future. In a fast-changing world filled with technological innovations, speed, and scale working for the future requires selectively forgetting the past. What worked in the past may not work now and may not also work for the future. Corporations that do not change and innovate may not make it beyond a point of time. What is true with corporations is also true with individuals and teams. The only difference could be that individuals at top levels of management that constitute leadership team may have a lot more flexibility and freedom to change than those at the middle and lower levels. However, good corporations provide scope for everyone to have certain degree of autonomy to change and innovate.

The field of performance management is of interest to all. In the last few decades, it has over-focused on the past by limiting itself to performance appraisals. Appraisals deal with the past and are necessary, but planning deals with the future and is even more necessary. Over-obsession with the past and equating the entire individual's performance in a year to an inanimate number has brought in more issues in the corporate world and resulted in marginal improvements, if any, in performance than coming up with new performance strategies. Performance appraisal has most often resulted in pain as appraisal is always a painful process. In this book, T.V. Rao has shifted the focus from performance appraisals to management and incorporated performance planning, analysis, and development as critical components of it. The performance management system (PMS) has been made a future-driven exercise than merely a past-reviewing exercise. T.V. Rao rightly defines performance management to mean continuous improvements in performance of individuals, their teams, departments, and corporations. He also outlines that planning, analysis, review, coaching, and capability building are essential building blocks for good performance management.

As pointed out by the three box theory, actions that companies take belong to one of the three boxes: the first box is managing the present, the second deals with selectively abandoning the past, and the third deals with creating the future. All the three relate to performance management of organizations, their teams, various functions, and even individuals. The three box theory is equally applicable to various processes and systems. Box 1 is about improving current businesses; Boxes 2 and 3 are about innovation, breakout performance, and growth. Many organizations restrict their strategic thinking to Box 1, as leaders emphasize cost reduction and margin improvement in their current businesses. But strategy cannot be just about what an organization needs to do to secure profits in the short term. Similarly, limiting performance to short-term profits and goals is taking a very narrow view of performance. Such a narrow view may not facilitate innovations which are essential for competitive advantage.

If organizations do not plan their future well, appraising individual and teams' performances becomes a futile exercise. Performance management is about all the three boxes and not Box 1 alone. It must be about what a company needs to do to sustain leadership in the long term. Globalization is opening doors to emerging economies, most notably India and China, and billions of customers with vast unmet needs. Once-distinct industries, such as mass-media, entertainment, telephony, and computing, are converging. Rapidly escalating concerns about security and environment are creating unforeseen markets. More other subtle changes are important as well, such as the trend toward more empowered customers, the rising middle class in the developing world, and the aging population in the developed world. As a result of these forces, companies find that their strategies require almost constant reinvention because old assumptions are no longer valid, the previous strategy has been imitated and commoditized by competitors, or changes in the industry environment offer unanticipated opportunities. The only way to stay ahead is to innovate. It is the responsibility of executives to make money with the current strategy. That is the challenge in Box 1. It is also their responsibility to make up for the decay and commoditization of strategy. That is the challenge in Boxes 2 and 3, but too many companies ignore these boxes until it is too late.

I hope CEOs, CHROs, and other top level managers recognize the importance of the need to innovate, selectively forget the past, and plan for the future using their performance management strategies and practices outlined in this book.

I consider this a great pleasure to write this Foreword for my very dear friend T.V. Rao.

**Vijay Govindarajan**
Coxe Distinguished Professor at Tuck at Dartmouth
and
Marvin Bower Fellow at Harvard Business School
September 14, 2015

# PREFACE TO THE FIRST EDITION

In the summer of 1974, I was invited by Dr Udai Pareek to join him to study the performance appraisal system at Larsen and Toubro (L&T), India's premier engineering company, and make suitable recommendations. Both of us studied the system that had been developed by Dr K.K. Anand and was being implemented by Dr D.F. Pereira. The system required the appraisee to write about his accomplishments during the year and pass it on to his boss for appraisal. His boss then appraised him on a few qualities and passed it on to the personnel department. On the face of it, the form appeared to be good as it gave the appraisee the scope to record his accomplishments. Back in those days, such an appraisal system was unheard of; the appraisal system was built around annual confidential reports (ACRs) that determined the future of the individual.

Udai and I decided to seek the L&T managers' views on the appraisal system and suggest improvements based on the feedback. We had tremendous faith in the participative method of evolving human systems. We decided to interview the candidate, his appraiser (boss), and his subordinate. By the time we completed the study, we had received tremendous education about how a performance appraisal system (PAS) should be structured. The managers we interviewed taught us in simple terms a number of lessons on designing performance appraisals. One of the assistant managers I met was particularly impressive. He summed up what was needed to be done. I was very impressed with him and would not have been surprised if someone predicted back then that he would be the future chief executive officer (CEO) of L&T. His name is Mr A.M. Naik.

There was a lot of wisdom in what the L&T managers said from which I distilled a series of questions. Over the years, I have used these questions to educate people in simple terms about what an appraisal system should look like.

Here is an excerpt of how the conversation with the L&T managers went:

*TVR:* We are reviewing your appraisal system. We would like to have your suggestions. Please tell me what you think of your current appraisal system and what improvements you would like to see.

*L&T managers:* Professor, before you talk about a PAS, you should first clarify to the individual what you mean by his performance. Without telling him what he is expected to do, is it fair to appraise his performance? There is no "performance" in our performance appraisal system. If you want to call it a performance appraisal system, focus on performance and please tell every individual what he is expected to do.

*TVR:* That seems to be fair. Your current system does not tell you what you are expected to do. Is that what you mean?

*L&T managers:* That is right. Don't you agree that we should be told what we are expected to perform not at the time of appraisal but at the beginning of the year itself?

*TVR:* That is also fair. So, a good appraisal system should tell you in the beginning of the year what you are expected to perform during the year and the standards you are expected to show.

*L&T managers:* Second thing, Professor. If we are not doing well, is it not the responsibility of the boss to tell the subordinate so that he can correct himself and improve his performance?

*TVR:* Yes. That is also fair. You should be told by your boss how well you are doing. If you are doing well, you will continue to do well and if you aren't, then you will improve. What more?

*L&T managers:* Don't you think that the person who is not performing well should be told in the middle of the year itself rather than wait till the end? Is it not good for the company if the individual knows and improves himself in the beginning rather than wait for the end?

*TVR:* Yes, I agree. What more? What prevents you from telling your subordinates how well they are doing? Why do you need a system for it? Don't you think it is the job of a good manager irrespective of the system?

*L&T managers:* Yes, Professor. You are right. The trouble is that we are telling our subordinates what we think about their performance. But our bosses don't tell us. That is why we need a system to enforce our bosses to tell us frankly what they think of our performance—not at the end of the year, but in the early stages or at best in the middle of the year.

*TVR:* That is interesting. I have just interviewed your bosses and they are also saying the same thing. Which means there is some problem somewhere?

*L&T managers:* The problem is that we don't have it as a system. If you don't have it as a system, most managers don't even recognize that we are giving them feedback. Some managers don't give feedback but either reprimand or say good things about their juniors. You need to have a system. The solution is to make it mandatory. We give them feedback, but our subordinates don't see it that way as it is not formally done. It should be done systematically and formally, though in an informal atmosphere.

*TVR:* I agree. What more? How do you think you should be assessed?

*L&T managers:* Professor, each boss has limited time. If the span of control is about six to eight people, the boss gets to see each of his subordinates for less than 10 percent of his time. He only forms impressions. He often goes by what he sees or does not see. Don't you think it would be useful to give a chance to the appraisee to make a presentation about what he has done and what he has failed to do before the boss makes up his mind and assesses him?

*TVR:* Yes, that also seems to be fair.

*L&T managers:* Don't you think that the appraisee should know what exactly the assessment of his boss is, so that he can mend himself and improve? The forms should be property of the manager rather than the personnel department.

This is a sample of the conversation we have had with L&T managers in the mid-1970s. It was this amazing level of maturity shown by L&T managers that prompted Udai and me to develop an open system of performance appraisal for the first time in this part of the world. We were so excited by the opportunities provided by the system for development and learning that we made it an integral part of the human resources development system. For several years in L&T, it was referred to as HRDS rather than performance appraisal system.

The components of this system included:

1. Identification of key performance areas (KPAs) and setting objectives in the beginning of the year jointly by the appraisee. We introduced the term KPAs for the first time as a counter to key result areas (KRAs). KPA signified the inputs to be given by the candidate to achieve the output he is expected to give. Let the candidate plan what is in his control while focusing on the results he is expected to achieve.

2. Identification of attributes to be shown by all managers irrespective of the levels. (L&T identified creativity, initiative, and teamwork as the most important attributes to be shown by all managers and were included in all appraisals.)

3. Self-appraisal.

4. Performance analysis to identify factors facilitating and hindering performance and take corrective action.

5. Identification of training needs and preparation of development plans.

6. Assessment by the reporting officer and sharing the ratings with the appraisee to arrive at mutually agreed ratings. The discussion was expected to focus on performance and expectation gaps and help bridge them.

7. Performance counselling to help the individual learn from the senior and improve his performance.

8. Review by reviewing officer.

9. Development actions by the HRD department.

10. De-linking appraisal from performance rewards (separate forms are to be used).

This system was essentially perceived as a system meant to facilitate learning among the managers. It was envisaged that this system would clarify roles, focus more on performance and development, and strengthen dyadic relationships. Trust levels were expected to improve. Developmental needs would be identified clearly, communications both upward and downward would increase as seniors would get to know the difficulties of the juniors, and the juniors would know what their bosses expected from them. Thus, the system designed nearly 30 years ago at L&T is a great performance management system (PMS) and had all the components of the most modern appraisal systems.

There is everything good in the system we developed: performance planning, analysis, development, review, identification of development needs, participatory planning, culture building, competence building, upward appraisal (coaching was viewed as a two-way process and the meeting a learning opportunity for both the boss and the subordinate). L&T implemented it seriously. Mr H. Larsen, one of the founders of the company, was present along with Mr N.M. Desai when our report was presented and we proposed the establishment of a human resources development department whose main task was to plan, monitor, and manage the development of people. The open system of appraisal we recommended was at the heart of the HRDS. A train-the-trainer program was established to educate the senior L&T managers on counselling skills. Over 90 managers were trained and they, in turn, educated others. It used to be informally called the L&T University. A senior person such as Mr S.R. Subramanian was put in charge to implement the system.

Now I realize the truth of what many people said: "We were ahead of our times." Subsequently, most organizations evolved and implemented open appraisal systems similar to the one at L&T. The systems that have been evolved so far are so similar to the one we devised at L&T that we can say there has been very little development in the field of performance appraisal over the last 30 years. Many managers said in those days that it was an American system and the IIMA professors were trying to implement it on Indian soil. Little did they realize that it was a localized system that had been indigenously developed. The fact that it has survived for over 30 years with only marginal changes is itself an indicator of this.

Looking back, I now realize that we made one glaring mistake and have been stuck to it for the last 30 years. This was to call the system a PAS and not a PMS. The second mistake was not to emphasise adequately that the system was not owned by the HRD department, but by the managers themselves.

By calling it a PAS, we diverted the attention of the people from development to appraisal. Often people concentrated on an appraisal rather than a development system. Realizing this a decade later, L&T ECC revised the same system and removed the word appraisal from it. The system was called "PADS"—performance analysis and development system. Beginning with this in the 1980s, many organizations started changing the title. LIC introduced a work planning and review system (WPR), NDDB called it performance planning and review system, and so on. Some organizations such as SAIL continued to call it an appraisal system.

It is only in the last decade since the liberalization of the economy that we realized the big mistake we had been making all these years. There is a lot in a name. A name suggests and gives direction. The focus of the system is not on appraisal. Then why call it a PAS? Why do we pretend that it is meant to generate numbers and make a comparison? Appraisal is only incidental and, at best, it may be called an unavoidable evil. The focus is on performance improvements. The focus of the system is on learning, development, and improvement. Hence, it should be called a performance development system. As development is too narrow and the system and the term management include development, it is now more appropriately referred to as PMS.

Many will say what is there in a name. It is just old wine in a new bottle. Yes, the bottles make a lot of difference. In this era of packaging and consumerism, the bottle is important. The wine is great. It did not get the attention it deserved. Hence, let us package it after making marginal changes to keep up with the times and call it PMS. This book is, therefore, about the PMS and it deals with the old wine but it is much more refined. It contains all the experiences of the last 30 years. In earlier versions of the book—*Performance Appraisal: Theory and Practice and Appraising and Developing Managerial Performance* (AHRD and Excel)—I have included details of the performance appraisal systems of L&T, L&T ECC; State Bank of India; Voltas and SAIL and also described the implementation process followed in one of the companies. In this book, all these chapters have been eliminated. The chapter giving model appraisal forms has also been eliminated. In fact this book contains no forms. For good performance management, the forms are not important. The objectives are important, the focus is important, and the structure is important. This book is about the structuring of PMSs and their implementation. It incorporates the most modern 360 degree feedback systems and also talks about the ways and means of integrating it into PMS.

A number of chapters have been included dealing with implementation issues and highlighting the lessons learnt in the last 30 years. Arguments are offered to use rating-less appraisals and/or a combination of appraisals with 360 degree feedback.

The most recent experiences incorporating the PMS are highlighted: Infosys, Titan, TISCO, Bharat Petroleum, Dr Reddy's Laboratories, NOCIL, and the National Stock Exchange. All these organizations without exception have been using simultaneously the 360 degree feedback and are integrating the same into their performance management philosophy.

I humbly dedicate this book to Dr Udai Pareek and Dennyson Pereira, who laid the foundations for PMS, and the many managers of modern organizations struggling to manage their performance through a greater ownership of the appraisal system.

**T.V. Rao**

# PREFACE TO THIS EDITION

I have been writing about performance appraisals for more than 40 years. During the first few years, I wrote consultancy reports with Udai Pareek for various companies, including Larsen & Toubro, State Bank of India and its associates, Bharat Earth Movers, Crompton Greaves, and others in the private and public sectors. I joined one of the companies and helped it implement performance appraisal and human resource development (HRD) systems. My first book, *Performance Appraisal: Theory & Practice*, published in 1982, had become popular. The book was revised by the Academy of HRD in the mid-1990s and published in the late 1990s. It was a decade ago that I realized the big mistake we had been making over the years in continuing to use the term "performance appraisal," while our philosophy was to consistently use appraisals for development rather than control and rewards. I also realized that performance appraisal is an annual event while development is a continuous one. We also discovered that organizations that had tried new ideas promoted in appraisal were reporting limited successes, although there had not been any failures. Our successes and satisfaction levels were far below our expectations even when we took significant pains and tried our best to put in place the best possible systems. In most companies where we worked, we optimistically implemented new appraisals using statistics. However, when it came to Performance Coaching Sessions (PCS), as we called it earlier and subsequently replaced these with Performance Review Discussions (PRDs), implementation slowed down. Very few line managers and seniors seemed to conduct PCS or PRDs as we wanted or as they had agreed upon. Our own studies with many corporations indicated that the average time CEOs and MDs spent on PRD annually never exceeded an hour on an average, and, in most cases, this was limited to 20 minutes or 30 minutes. We felt that this time was just adequate to build a rapport and there were really no development-related discussions possible in this short duration. We always wondered why it was so difficult to conduct a PRD. In fact, we introduced the term

PRD, since we found that managers were uncomfortable with the term "counseling," which we first used in L&T. Instead, we started using the term "coaching" because it had become popular in the West and many people felt that it was better than the term counseling, which indicated to managers that they were required to counsel their juniors because there was something wrong with their performance. Our repeated explanation of the meaning of coaching—helping and influencing—did not make much of an impact. Everyone agreed about it in the classroom, but no one used it. It had a stigma.

The term "coaching" has been recently replaced by the term "performance conversations." The term conversation legitimizes managers' reviewal of their juniors' performance. They do not need to hold formal sessions to do this. They just need to have conversations.

In the same way, as we went on to implement various appraisal systems, KRAs became a controversial issue. Most people like the concept of KPAs in place of KRAs. We had differentiated KPAs promoted by the management by objectives (MBO) tradition from KPAs promoted by us since our L&T seminars in the mid-1970s. We used to maintain that KRA focus on results and KPS on effort. We realized that results were not in people's hands and they could not plan in a foolproof manner, and that they could focus on results it their activities and functions or performance were planned by them. Wherever we conducted PAS workshops, managers would appreciate the concept, but do nothing except to identify these when they suited their rating system and preconceived notions, rather than planning performance and getting role clarity managers. In the mid-1970s, the focus was on objectivity of appraisals to understand performers and their circumstances. However, understanding the circumstances never got the attention it deserved. Objectivity in ratings was focused. It was difficult to convince managers that an understanding of appraisees (performers), their mindsets, circumstances, competencies, and clarity were the essential components of a sound appraisal system. As the focus shifted to alignment of individual goals with those of the organizational goals, I never understood why we needed a system such as PAS to ensure alignment. It is the job of every supervising manager to help every employee plan and carry out work that is misaligned. However, it was needed to satisfy top management, which was finding that results were not up to expected levels. We slowly shifted the focus to performance planning. It is only in recent years that it dawned on us that time and talent management are closely linked and that KPAs and activities can only be carried out by proper planning. Hurconomics suggested how to value time. In Hurconomics, we discussed in detail returns on investment on performance management systems.

The focus of this edition is on the following:

1. Performance planning through activity planning and the hurconomics of planning.
2. Performance conversations supplementing or even substituting performance coaching.
3. Downgrading the importance of ratings and upgrading the need to moderate assessments and moving toward qualitative conversations based on number-based ratings.
4. Using performance analysis to develop individuals and corporations' organization development (OD).

If every corporation does the following four things well, it is likely to manage its performance well:

1. Help every individual perceive the importance of planning every minute of his/her time to utilize talent.

   • Recognize the linkage between time and talent management to plan one's time (hours, days, weeks, months, quarters, and years) well ahead and keep track of how one is using time and talent and not wasting either of these.
   • Help every individual to focus on what is expected to be done to get the desired team, organizational or individual results.
   • Recognize the linkage between one person's work and that of another, the department and the entire organization.

- Appreciate interdependencies and work on encouraging others do their work rather than prevent them from doing so and achieve results.

2. Help every candidate recognize that performance output is the result of competence, work-relarted efforts and circumstances, including organizational support, and in the case of performance improvement, individual effort and competence, which need to be understood and developed.

   - Recognize that performance analysis is a good tool to develop individuals and organizations.
   - Use it to diagnose and continuously remove blocks to higher performance rather than focus on who is blocking and playing the blame game.

3. Identify competencies required to perform each role successfully, particularly in technical, managerial and behavioral terms, and make employees understand, exhibit and cultivate these.

   - By defining competencies and using competency frameworks.
   - Using seniors as well as juniors as instruments of development.
   - Working and organizing platforms to develop competencies.
   - Using ratings as tools for provocation, expectation sharing, and measurement, and not for rewards and punishments.
   - Recognizing that people are facilitators of development through diagnosis, dialogue, knowledge-sharing, feedback, and supportive decision-making.
   - Engaging in performance-related conversations to delineate new activities and actions that can enlarge the effectiveness of individuals and their roles.
   - Identifying new areas and initiatives a role-holder can take.
   - Using tools such as upward appraisals, 360 degree feedback, Assessment and Development Centers (ADCs),

psychometric testing and others, and while providing feedback, recognizing talent and areas for development and preparing supportive action plans.

4. Recognize that all performance appraisals are largely subjective in nature and there can be no objectivity as long as people are involved in assessing each other, and also that it is futile to group un-groupables and use ratings and forced distribution methods. This can be achieved by:

   - Avoiding a focus on ratings and rewards associated with blind ratings.
   - Using forced distribution for specific purposes to make a point for a specified time and not as a part of the organization.

This book is largely devoted to the five points mentioned earlier and the chapters relate to them. Its focus shifts to talent management and development and through these to enhancement of performance. The various chapters focus on the fundamentals of PMS, which includes planning, analysis, review, and development.

Performance management is treated as a year-round and not an appraisal process or once in a quarter or annual exercise. It is considered everyone's job and not merely that of HR or the top management.

Performance is expanded to include individuals, as opposed to the individual, as role-holders, bosses, juniors, team members, team leaders, and employees. It is treated as multidimensional—technical, managerial, financial, behavioral, philosophical, qualitative, quantitative, and so forth.

**T.V. Rao**
October 17, 2015

# ACKNOWLEDGMENTS

- Steel Authority of India (Atul Srivastava, Executive Director) for their permission to reproduce two chapters from the book on "HR Best Practices," entitled: *HR Best Practices: Manufacturing Sector in India*, written by Nisha Nair, Neharika Vohra, T.V. Rao, and Atul Srivastava (New Delhi: Steel Authority of India).
- Indian Institute of Management Ahmedabad (IIMA) for permission to reproduce an article: T.V. Rao, "Lessons from Experience: A New Look at Performance Management Systems," *Vikalpa*, 33(3), July–September (2008), 1–15.
- Dr Anil Khandelwal, former CMD, Bank of Baroda, for giving me an opportunity to work as a part of the Khandelwal Committee appointed by the Ministry of Finance on HR in PSBs.
- Second Administrative Reforms Commission for giving me an opportunity to focus on PMS for civil services.
- Sachin Sharma of SAGE for driving me to work on and complete this edition.
- My wife, Mrs Jaya Rao, for letting me spend all the time due to her on this and other books.
- T.V. Rao Learning Systems Pvt Limited for all support to spend my time on this book.
- Executives of many organizations including: L&T ECC, IFFCO, SBI, NDDB, LIC, GIC, Crompton Greaves, SAIL, IIMA, EID Parry, Titan, Gulfar, GSPC, GSPL, NOCIL, HUL, National Stock Exchange, BPCL, BPL, BEML, Federal Bank, Reserve Bank of India; L&T, Voltas, Sundram Fasteners, TI Group, Crompton Greaves, Transpek Industries, IL&FS, Mahindra and Mahindra, Indorama, Indonesia, Gulfar, Torrent Power, CESC, Elite Core, Cadila Pharma, Vadilal Industries, IDBI Bank, UTI, CHR Oman, etc., who helped me over the last four decades to present and test out many ideas that got built in this book.

# 1

# Performance Management
## *An Overview*

## What Is Performance Management?

- Identifying KRAs and or KPAs.
- Assessing performance.
- Force-fitting people in different categories to distribute incentives and performance-linked rewards.
- A process in target setting.
- Assessing people with respect to their performance.
- Setting enhanced goals so that no one can achieve them and then justifying to people that they did not deserve anything.
- Annual appraisal of performance to make most people feel that they are average.

The above are a sample of answers given by different people to the question. All these are correct, but not complete. These are the ways most people experience or perceive the current performance appraisal systems, but it is not performance management.

Performance management is defined as "*doing all* that is required to *continuously improve* performance of every employee in relation to his/her *role, dyad, team and the entire organization* in the context of the *short and long term goals of the organization.*"

There are many things implied by this definition. The following are the most important components in this definition.

### DOING ALL THAT IS REQUIRED: WHAT IS REQUIRED TO BE DONE?

1. Defining Performance
   The first thing that is required to be done is to understand what should be done, that is, understanding the meaning of

performance. It means delineating the dimensions of performance in relation to a role, the expectations of seniors and juniors, the team and the organization as a whole. Organizational goals provide the context of delineating the actions that are required to be taken by each individual in relation to his/her role, by each person as an employee, as the boss of a team of employees, and so on. Doing all that is required for an employee in relation to his/her role means understanding what is required to be done, that is, defining performance for a given time period. The time period is normally a year and can be broken down into quarters, months, weeks, and days. The unit of this breakdown provides the details of activities that need to be done. The more concrete the activities and the more limited the timeframe the easier it is to carry them out. Daily listing of activities is the best way to ensure that they are carried out properly. Weekly listing dilutes them but at least the critical ones can be listed and efficient performance ensured. Monthly listing dilutes and quarterly and yearly listing still further dilutes such activities and moves from micro to macro action, from doing to achieving, and from activities to results. Therefore, the trouble with performance management begins with the way performance is understood. Most people understand it in the form of KRAs or KPAs, tasks, targets and results, since these are easier to list, understand and comprehend as there are only a few KRAs, targets, or tasks. So the trouble with performance management is in the beginning itself. We look at performance in terms of annual targets and key areas for delivering results or carrying out responsibilities associated with a role. Defining performance in terms of KRAs, tasks, and targets is misleading and only states intention at best, and not the desired actions.

A good definition of performance states what exactly a role-holder is expected to do for management to recognize that he/she is "performing" or "doing a good job," and demonstrating a "good performance." The term "good" is relevant here, since all organizations are concerned about good performance and not an average one. *The starting point of performance management, therefore, is defining or delineating performance in actionable terms, or activities that are visible and observable to be carried out by the role-holder during a given period of time (normally a quarter or an year) in detail, is exhaustive and includes all his/her actions and activities, or at least the significant ones.*

- *Dyadic Performance:* Such activities may include responsibilities as a boss, as a team member, and as an organizational citizen. These activities may always be not covered under the role definitions or job descriptions. For example, as a senior, activities every reporting officer or boss is required to engage in may be listening to and understanding the difficulties of juniors and solving their problems; giving clear instructions about the work to be done; providing feedback on a daily, weekly or monthly basis to improve performance; and recognizing and appreciating juniors who exceed expectations, innovate, take initiatives, save costs, or achieve new goals.

- *Team Performance:* The activities that are required to make each team achieve its goals are called team performance-related activities. These may include "helping other members of the team as and when required," or 'understanding the needs of dependent members and providing inputs required on time and of quality," or "contributing to teamwork by understanding team needs by participating in team meetings and supplying the information required." These activities cannot be defined exhaustively and may depend on the nature of teams and their functions in different organizational contexts.

- *Organizational Performance as a Whole:* Every individual as an organizational citizen is expected to exhibit certain behavior or activities. These include coming to work on time, fulfilling routine tasks, and following the organization's discipline at one level and values at another. Organizations keep stating their values and competencies from time to time. They also develop their own competency frameworks to prepare for their future and also to promote the career and leadership development of their employees. Where values and competency frameworks are defined, they are translated into actionable terms through behavioral indicators and key performance indicators. These constitute a part of the performance of every employee and expected levels are defined from time to time.

2. Planning Performance

The next action required is to plan performance. The performance of an individual in relation to his/her role, dyad, team, and organization needs to be planned. Actions that are required to ensure dyadic, team, and organizational performance may be the same all throughout the year, but those required for specific roles may change from time to time, depending on the nature of the job and its challenges. Therefore, it is important to plan for the year, quarter, month, week, and day. While the time unit of planning is left for every individual organization, debarment, and the individual, some amount of common understanding is required. All the activities (or at least the critical ones) required to be performed need to be recognized and planned in terms of the way in which these need to be carried out.

In a year, there are 365 × 24 hours = 8760 hours. Every employee is expected to normally work any where between 2000 to 2400 hours (250 days × 8 hours to 300 days × 8 hours or 240 days × 10 hours, and so forth). We will take this hereafter as 2000 hours for organizational work-related activities that provide resources to employees for them to spend the rest of the time fruitfully. Performance planning in organizational context deals with how an individual is expected to use these 2000 hours to enable his/her organization to achieve its goals. Performance planning encompasses the activities that need to be carried out by individual employees by virtue of their roles and organizational requirements. Normally, what is planned are KPAs or KRAs. Around 40 to 60 years ago, the concept of KRAs was introduced by Peter Drucker and other management experts to ensure that people achieved the results they are expected to achieve. Results can be targeted, but what is planned at the individual level include the input. The result is normally the output of activities engaged in by a number of employees. For example, selling a number of products, generating revenue at a certain level, or minimizing costs to a certain level are all consequences of the work of a number of employees and cannot be done by an individual. Therefore, performance planning should focus on what the individual is expected to do, rather than on what he/she is expected to achieve. The results are non-negotiable. Organizations set these parameters for their survival and growth. Individual goals and activities can be intermediate ones and need to be planned to ensure that larger outcomes or results are achieved.

Thus, performance planning means planning the inputs in terms of activities or categories of activities (functions, KPAs or tasks) with time lines and expected outcomes. It is useful to maintan performance indicators to signify what is good performance in an activity, task, KPA or KRA. Planning time and observable activity is desirable in performance planning. Until time and actions are planned, performance planning is not complete. Until this takes place, shared, and mutually agreed upon, dyadic performance cannot be completed. Shared understanding of activities and a time plan, therefore, constitutes performance planning.

This requires time, effort, and the right attitude. It is not a great skill if these are not in place.

3. Performance Planning Process

This process should involve the individual and the reporting manager jointly discussing what is expected from the former (performance dimensions, activities, standards, inputs, etc.) and the latter (support and so forth) in the coming quarter/ year, andplanning to improve their performance or setting realistic and challenging goals. This process and the time spent on it are more important than whether the component is called a KPA or KRA. However, given the choice between the two, KPAs are to be preferred over KRAs, since the latter relates more to the effort(s) put in by an individual instead of the desired output. Some of the issues that are raised by executives in this context include whether it is possible to plan managerial performance, whether a manager's job can be quantified, and whether it is necessary to have role clarity as an objective since most managers are expected to have a clear concept about their jobs and cannot afford to be ambiguous.

The extent to which executive performance can be planned depends on a number of factors, such as the nature of the job, organization, and so forth. Some jobs are difficult to plan completely because the executives holding them are only required to simply execute their bosses' instructions or those of other departments, and consequently, their performance is determined or at least planned by others. Some other jobs are relatively easier to plan due to a high degree of autonomy. However, irrespective of the nature of a job, it is possible to plan some part of it. For example, even when a manager is required to blindly implement another person's instructions, he/she can plan for improved implementation (speedy, effective, qualitative, and so forth.) in some areas. This is where the concept of "continuous improvement" is clearly illustrated.

Similarly, quantification is difficult in some jobs and some components of every job. Therefore, it is not necessary to quantify every KPA/KRA/task/target. However, the effort should be toward achieving some form of quantification. Where quantification is very challenging, a common understanding between the reporting manager and performer on this issue may itself provide the desired role clarity.

When sufficient role clarity already exists, most organizations have found that the use of KPAs/KRAs/tasks/activities/targets as part of their performance management systems improves "role clarity" substantially. In fact, some organizations have even revised their selection/promotion procedures after such role clarity exercises.

Executives in organizations often ask about what is the best way of identifying KPAs and targets. Quite often, the KPA identification exercise, and consequently performance planning, is postponed due to lack of clarity or competence in identifying KPAs. There is no ideal way of identifying KPAs and not much expertise is required too. KPAs/KRAs/tasks/activities/targets are vehicles used for detailed performance planning and to achieve role clarity. Detailed performance planning at the beginning of the year helps organizations analyze their performance objectively at a later stage. It also helps them plan strategies to develop/improve their executives' performance. If the reporting manager and performer are able to sit together and spend some time discussing and sharing expectations, and then put down in writing the significant expectations they have agreed to meet in the coming year, the exercise can be considered complete. The time they spend together is an indicator of the extent of their sharing. *If they finish their discussion in 15 to 20 minutes, it is more likely that they have done a superficial job. Performance planning requires time and planning to the satisfaction of the reporting manager and performer.*

4. Planning Performance on Attributes/Qualities/Traits/Competencies

The components of many performance management systems include identification, planning, assessment, and development of critical attributes (qualities, competencies, traits, etc.) that need to be demonstrated by an executive on the job. In the past, appraisals used to be "trait-based." Most organizations, realizing the extent of subjectivity involved in trait-based appraisals and recognizing the need to promote performance-related rather than merely trait-related orientation, have started using a mixture of KPAs and attributes/qualities for assessment. Some give equal weightage to performance and attribute parameters. Some others determine the weightage to be given to attributes, as against KPAs, based on the level of seniority in their organizations—the greater the seniority, the greater the weightage given to attributes.

Attributes, as a part of the performance management system, help in reinforcing the behaviors/qualities/competencies that are required or are to be developed by the executives.

There are many ways of identifying attributes and including these in formats:

• Leave it to each reporting manager–performer pair to identify the qualities an individual is required to exhibit on the job. This identification is done through a discussion conducted every year. Some organizations adopt this method. The disadvantage of this process is that there is no standardization in attributes, and hence the use of data for later HR-related decisions becomes difficult, since different pairs of managers and performers may use different terminologies for the same behavior/qualities. The advantage of this process is that it forces the reporting manager–performer pair to reflect, discuss, and share their views with each other.

• The organization undertakes a competency mapping exercise, either internally or with the help of consultants, the outcome of which is a well-defined competency model (for example, an organization-wide, functional competency framework) with proficiency levels and behavior indicators clearly identified. This provides a ready-to-use list of attributes that are critical for each level or group of positions, and can be directly incorporated in organizations' performance management systems and appraisal formats. Some organizations may specify competencies based on levels or functions and others give the option to the employees and their managers to select the relevant competencies from a list of competencies.

- The top management identifies some characteristics the organization values in its employees (for example, loyalty, teamwork, initiative, etc.) and incorporates them in the performance management system, with detailed explanations.

Whatever the methodology used, there are likely to be some common attributes. Irrespective of the way the attributes are identified, a common experience with most organizations is the neglect in providing a clear picture or outline of these attributes. *Both the performer and reporting manager should have a shared understanding of what each quality means, how important it is for the performer's current role or for the organization, and how high quality can be exhibited and assessed (performance standards) in a given job.* This is possible only through some discussion between the performer and reporting manager periodically or at least once a year along with the performance planning exercise.

5. Analyzing and Reviewing Performance for Continuous Improvements
The next part of performance management is performance of these activities. Individuals should keep a record of their activities. Where the PMS is IT-based, every individual could keep a record of his/her activities completed and the details of these. How will organizations know how well or bad individuals have performed? This is achieved through monitoring and review.

Completed activities do not necessarily indicate that they meet the quality, speed, time, extent of contribution to results, and other required dimensions. Therefore, there is a need for a review of the extent to which and the way in which activities are carried out. This review is conducted through an assessment of the key performance indicators for each KPA, KRA or task, the extent to which targets are achieved, and so forth.

This is achieved by the process of performance analysis and review, which are based on the performance equation.

Performance analysis should be based on the dimensions of performance planning. Work completed or performance during the year should be broken down into various KPAs/KRAs/tasks/activities/targets. Performance should be analyzed using the following questions under each KPA/KRA/task/activities/target:

- How is the individual's actual performance in relation to the set KPAs/KRAs/tasks/activities/targets?
- Does it fall short? If yes, by how much?
- Does it exceed set expectations?
- Is it to be considered outstanding/excellent more than expected/as expected/less than expected?
- What are the factors that contributed to his/her achievement?
- What factors (competence, motivation, hard work, specific ability, etc.) helped the individual do whatever he/she has done?
- What were the factors relating to his/her subordinates that helped her/him?
- What factors relating to the superior or the superior's superior helped her/him?
- What factors relating to organizational support and policies helped her/him?
- What factors were responsible for failures, if any, or what factors prevented the individual from doing better?
- What factors were attributable to the superiors/organization/general environment?
- Which of these factors could have been influenced by the individual and how?
- Which of these could have been influenced by the reporting manager and how?

Performance analysis consists of answering the questions mentioned earlier in relation to each KPA/KRA/major task/target/activity/function. It is desirable that the performer and reporting manager do this independently. Normally, the performer has more data than the reporting manager. An independent analysis and subsequent exchange during the performance review discussion is educative for both. *This is the most time-consuming part of appraisals and if done properly can help achieve a variety of objectives.*

- Self-appraisal: Development or change only takes place if the individual is interested in it. Such a desire is normally an outcome of self-review or reflection. Self-appraisal or self-assessment as a component of a performance management system aims to promote such a review and sets the stage for development. In addition, it is an opportunity for the individual to recall and list his/her accomplishments and failures during the performance period, and analyze the extent to which he/she is responsible and the other factors that contributed to their success or failure.

  Some organizations do not recognize the value of the objective of self-appraisal. They simply ask the performers to write down the tasks and targets assigned to them and indicate their significant achievements in relation to these. This is not sufficient. *The most important part of self-assessment is the process of review and reflection through a performance analysis.* Such performance analysis should be done both by the performer and the reporting manager separately and exchanged during the course of performance review discussions.

- Performance Conversations (PCs) and Performance Review Discussion (PRDs): *A number of objectives can be achieved through performance analysis conducted a little in advance. Performance analysis helps in making the review discussion more fruitful. A review discussion aims at ensuring that the reporting manager and the performer understand each other better by communicating to the individual an analysis of his/her performance. It is in this discussion that the reporting managers should* compliment individuals on their accomplishments and good qualities. They should:

i. Understand and appreciate individuals' difficulties and make action plans for the future with a view to help them.

ii. Understand the individual's perception of the situation and correct some perceptions, if necessary.

iii. Help them recognize their strong points and weak points.

iv. Communicate the reporting manager's expectations to the individuals.

v. Identify developmental needs of the individual and chalk out a course of action for meeting these needs.

Such a discussion would bring the performer and reporting manager closer. Therefore, it should be conducted in a congenial atmosphere, which encourages two-way communication between the individual and his superior. *Every annual review discussion, if properly conducted, may require about three to four hours. Short review discussions are indicative of lack of respect on the part of the reporting manager for the performer, or lack of commitment of the organization to development-oriented appraisals.* It is also necessary for organizations to make available meeting/discussion rooms for reporting manager–performer pairs to conduct annual review discussions. In the absence of such space for review discussions, employees should be given the freedom to use the company guesthouse or any other place that is convenient for such review discussions. Some organizations have the practice of declaring a particular month or fortnight as an appraisal month/fortnight and expect the reporting managers to conduct their reviews during this period. If an employee is not in his/her seat on any day during this month, it is assumed that he/she is busy with his/her appraisal and review discussions.

• Performance is discussion around performance: This includes discussions on KRAs or activities, standards, competencies facilitating factors, blocks to be removed, or any aspect of performers or their seniors. Such conversations are intended to serve a variety of purposes. These include continuous communication and empowerment by providing each other with information, review, and learning from their experiences, prevention of failure by enhanced planning and support for success, mid-course corrections, an understanding each other and enablement of individuals' capabilities.

Such conversations may be formal or informal and may range form meetings of five to ten minutes to half an hour or an hour. Where longer conversations are required, it is useful to plan them n advance. Informal conversations go a long way in creating mutuality and strengthening dyadic relations.

6. Developing Performance through Individual Development Plans (IDPs) and Training
A well-designed performance management system provides ample opportunities and windows to identify the development needs or requirements of an employee or individual. At the very beginning of the financial year, the performance planning and goal setting process can be used to identify if there are any areas that need reinforcement. It is important to identify the "competency" or "capability" a performer needs to develop in order to perform a given task better. Many employees are quite aware of their strengths and areas of improvement with respect to their roles, and hence, they are well equipped to identify training assistance required during the year. Reporting managers can help them by sharing ways and means by which their specific competencies can be improved or developed. Identifying training needs at the beginning of the performance period is very beneficial and a proactive move to ensure success in the goals set. It is not advisable to wait for non-achievement of goals (based on year end review) and then start arranging for training. This approach to identification of training needs is more of a post mortem and not a productive approach.

Thereafter, individual development needs can also be got from the performance analysis. Individuals' development or training needs should be in terms of their competencies rather than on training program titles. *There are many ways in which employee development can be planned, for example, on-the-job coaching by superiors, external training, field visits, job rotation, visits to other departments, discussions with others who have done a good job in the past, etc.* It is useful to keep these avenues in mind and make joint recommendations, which may be worked out during review discussions. The following points should be kept in mind:

- Individual performers should be the initiators of the statements of their developmental needs. This ensures commitment of the performer to his/her development.
- A statement of the development needs by a reporting manager or performer does not automatically ensure that the organization will take care of it, because the organization might have some constraints or some other priorities.
- An individual in the HRD department/training team/ learning and development team should consolidate and follow up on the employees' developmental needs.
- It is useful to inform every employee once a year about the action that could/could not be taken by the HRD department on his/her developmental needs.
- It is also useful to have committees of line managers to review the developmental needs of all employees and work out strategies and plans to address these.

7. Assessing, Rewarding, and Recognizing Performance to Enhance Performance

The following will enhance performance:

- Planning Removing obstacles
- Multiplying facilitators or enhancers
- Increased competencies
- Increased efforts

Recognition and rewards improve the work effort as well as the desire to learn and multiply competencies.

Managing recognition without de-motivating some people is a critical competence organizations need to develop. Forced distribution of ratings makes many people depressed rather than encouraged. Managing ratings for motivation is an important issue. Ratings should help to enhance performance enhancements rather than in de-hancements.

## PMS and Its Many Dimensions

Raman Dutta is 17 years old and is studying in St. Xavier's High School. He is in the XIIth standard and will appear for the Board examinations in the science stream in March next year. He did well in his Xth Boards. He aims to join one of the leading engineering colleges and specialize in IT. Last year, the cut-off for admission to the top college was 89 percent. Raman decided to work hard and secure at least 95 percent to ensure a seat in one of the prestigious colleges. He decided on the following strategy:

Focus on science and mathematics as they are scoring subjects. Solve as many previous Board examination papers as possible. Get a private tutor to help him improve in mathematics. Work hard. "That should get me 95 per cent marks."

His dad, Roshan, an HR director, asked him to draw up a more comprehensive strategy. He asked Raman to convert the strategy into an action plan for the year. The first step would be to identify the key performance areas.

When Raman asked his father what these key performance areas were, he explained: "Key performance areas are those where you need to focus if you have to get your target result of 95 per cent marks in the Board exams. This will give some idea of the effort you need to put in to achieve the result. The result is not negotiable; without 90–95 percent marks, you will not get admission into your dream college. You should simply ask yourself, 'What should I do different to get 95 percent? Or, what more should I do to get 95 percent? Or, what new activities should I undertake? The answers to these questions will give you your key performance areas. They help you to plan and give a sense of direction to your work. They help you to remain focused all through the year. Now, decide what inputs you need to make to get 95 percent in the examinations.'"

Raman replied: "I should work hard, solve all the previous examination papers, attend classes, clarify doubts, and keep learning."

"Excellent," said his father. "These are the key performance areas. Now list them one by one and see if the list is exhaustive."

Raman started listing them; on reflection, he added a few more. The final list read:

1. Attend classes regularly. (I must attend classes as a lot of things are discussed and there are good teachers in my school. However, I can afford to skip the chemistry class as the teacher does not explain anything properly. As a result, I often get the feeling that I am wasting my time.)
2. Study hard at home.
3. Seek the help of a tutor to clarify doubts.
4. Solve question papers of the previous years.
5. Do reference work in the library.

Roshan's dad saw the list and said, "This is great. Now estimate how much of your time goes into each of these activities on a daily or a weekly basis and then set targets for each activity. Your targets should be such that if you fulfil them you will get closer to your goal of 95 percent. There is no guarantee but it is an assumption based on your previous record as well as intuition." Raman set targets in each of the areas with the following reasoning: "I have to spend eight hours a day for attending classes in school. I cannot avoid this as I need to have good attendance. Besides, most of the teachers are good and they teach well. I learn a good deal in school and therefore it is important that I attend all the lectures and clarify my doubts." He set his KPAs and targets as follows:

## KPA 1: LEARNING FROM CLASS TEACHERS

Activities: Attending classes—articipating laboratory experiments, clarifying doubts with teachers, going prepared to classes, completing homework given, meeting teachers outside class in case of additional doubts and clarifications.

Targets:

1. I will go prepared to every single class.
2. I will read in advance all that I am required.
3. I will listen to all lectures attentively.
4. I will not miss a single lab experiment.
5. I will not return home without clarifying all doubts and things that I don't understand.

(Time involved: eight hours a day and an additional 30 minutes on an average for clarifying doubts outside the class.)

## KPA 2: WORKING HARD AT HOME

Activities: To study in a concentrated manner all that he needs to at home.

Targets: I will put in at least five hours of study every day, two hours in the morning and three hours in the evening. On holidays I will work on an average about eight hours a day in addition to coaching classes.

(Time involved: five hours a day on class days and eight hours on holidays.)

## KPA 3: COACHING CLASSES

Activities: Attending coaching classes in mathematics and chemistry; solving all previous Board examination papers; clarifying doubts with coach.

Targets:

1. I will attend coaching classes twice a week and put in my best effort to understand everything I am told.
2. I will solve Board examination papers of the last five years and those of other state boards of the last three years.

(Time: Two hours a day and twice a week, and travel time an additional two hours.)

## KPA 4: EXTRA STUDIES

Activity: To go beyond what is asked to study in the class or by the coach; visiting the library and reading new books; studying about new advances in science.
Targets:

1. I will visit the library on a regular basis and consult at least one new book a week.
2. I will take tips from my seniors who passed with high marks whenever they come on vacation (one hour a day).

Raman worked out his schedule as follows:

On class days: 5 am to 7 am homework and study preparation for class; 8 am to 4 pm attending classes; 4 pm to 5 pm library and clarification of doubts; 5.30 pm to 7.30 pm coaching classes (twice a week); 8 pm to 11 pm study at home.

This is the way in which Raman has planned his daily schedule and is confident of achieving 95 percent marks. However, he is under no illusion that this will guarantee such a result. The final result depends on a number of factors such as the type of questions set (because some years papers are difficult and some other years they are too easy), the relative performance of other students and schools, the nature of corrections of papers that year, etc. He is clear that things will work in his favor if he does his job well, and even if things do not work out he will have the satisfaction of having done his best.

Raman discussed his KPAs and targets with his father and requested him to keep warning him whenever he slipped. He also requested his dad to suggest any improvements that could be made as they went along in order to keep him focussed. In the long run, Raman wants to be an entrepreneur. He wants to become a national hero. Dr Abdul Kalam and Narayana Murthy are his role models. He has invented a portal and successfully launched it to make cheap food available for college students. He has also prepared a directory of coaching classes for students and put this up on the portal. He wants to serve the student community.

However, for the present, getting good grades in the Board exam is his immediate goal.

# What Is Performance? Dimensions of Performance Management

The case of Raman is a good example of performance management. I have always wondered why managers who have been through all this in school resist systematic planning and monitoring of their performance. Performance management involves thinking through various facets of performance, identifying critical dimensions of performance, planning, reviewing, and developing and enhancing performance and related competencies. It is simple, commonsensical and enjoyable. Performance has many dimensions:

1. Output or result
2. Input
3. Time
4. Focus
5. Quality
6. Cost

Performance is what is expected to be delivered by an individual or a set of individuals within a time-frame. This can be stated in terms of results or effort, tasks and quality, with specification of conditions under which it is to be delivered.

## RESULTS AND OUTPUT

The most acceptable and visible as well as measurable dimension of performance is result or output. It describes the consequence of input in a summary form, or a final or semi-final product form or service form. It describes the standard. It is easily measurable. For example, getting 95 percent is the result. Salary figures, customer numbers, financial targets, production targets, completion of tasks to meet deadlines, etc are all stated in result/output form. Sometimes these are also called key result areas.

Raman could have aimed at increased learning as a final output. However, increased learning is not easily measurable. Final percentage of marks in an examination can be taken as a good indicator of learning. In addition, marks constitue a good record and are acceptable as a relatively objective measure of performance. Normally, all performance management starts with this final targeted performance. It is to achieve this performance output that performance activities need to be planned. They are the input to be provided by the individual.

## INPUT DIMENSION

The input dimension deals with activities or tasks to be accomplished by the individual. The nature of activities to be undertaken by the individual, the time-frame, the quality of input to be given, and so forth, constitute the input dimension.

Performance can be managed better if the nature of input required to be provided can be envisaged without mistake, planned properly, and implemented.

It is here that performance equation comes into the picture. Performance equation indicates that any individual's performance is a function of three sets of factors—ability or competence to perform various tasks that lead to performance, motivation to carry on each of these tasks or work effort to carry out the tasks and the organizational support one gets to carry out these tasks. If any one of these is inadequate, the performance is bound to be poor.

In this equation, performance is the output and work effort is the input, and ability and organizational support are the intervening variables. They can also be considered as the input variables. If the input (ability, work effort or motivation and organizational support) is inadequate, the performance is also likely to be insufficient.

The various dimensions of performance include the following:

## TIME DIMENSION

Another dimension of performance is time. Performance can be defined for a task, a day, a week, a month, a year, or for life. The period set for performance is important. Time for information technology organizations is limited to a quarter or a three-month period. Performance may also be defined by tasks or projects and not time. Time may become the target.

In the case of Raman, the time dimension is one year. It can also be divided quarterly. A quarterly time-frame helps mid-course corrections and ensures long-term performance.

Normally, individual performance is judged in relation to a role over a short period. We normally talk about how well an individual has done in a given role over a period of two or three years. While organizations are interested in performance, they are more concerned with an individual's performance in a financial year or parts of a year. Some organizations that are project driven (for example, in the IT industry) are interested in an individual's performance in a project as well as in a role. For example, an organization may want to know how the employee has handled a particular project as project manager.

*Thus, in the context of organizations, performance management is time-bound as well as role-specific.*

---

## Lifetime Performance

The other day, a friend of mine (aged 62 years) remarked that he had achieved whatever he wanted to in management. "I am now completing two more books and am reasonably well known in my field. After I complete these two books—one on the Fourth Eye and the second on Corporate Greatness—I am planning to change my profession." He said he had achieved enough in this profession and would like to try out something else. He also remarked that he had done reasonably well in life as well and had created a niche for himself and felt that he should be happy and concentrate, if he so chose, on academics.

My friend was appraising his own performance as well as mine. Performance here spans an entire lifetime. The same performance can be contextual; it can be limited to appraisal of how well one has written a book or how well one has performed in a particular role assigned to him/her in a particular year or place.

Note that in the case of Raman Dutta, we have not assessed him at all in relation to his life's ambition and also on the work done by him outside studies. This is because our perspective was limited to that year and Board exams, and not his performance in relation to life.

Getting the individual to give his/her best in a given role during a given period of time is a performance management issue.

*Performance of an individual in an organizational setting may therefore be defined as the output delivered by an individual in relation to a given role during a particular period under the set of circumstances operating at that point of time.*

Performance management attempts to ensure use of various interventions so that the individual delivers maximum output under given circumstances. The output may include changing the circumstances or turning every circumstance to one's advantage in order to deliver maximum output. However, maximum output is a relative term and is defined or determined by the following considerations:

1. Previous performance of the individual on a similar task under similar circumstances
2. Performance of any other comparable individual or a standard available at that time, including the maximum performance of another individual with whom competition is being set
3. Estimated performance of the individual specified in advance, taking into account his/her capabilities and capacity limitation and the constraints imposed by the situation

Thus, in order to manage performance, one has to have an idea of the expected level of performance, the circumstances, the kind of support needed, the previous performance level of the individual or similar individuals under similar circumstances, etc.

In most cases, such data is not easily available to managers. While it is not very difficult for operators and other blue collar workers (whose physical labor can be measured), it is difficult to set standards for and measure managerial performance. This is because managerial performance is highly interdependent, dynamic, and difficult to isolate.

## FOCUS DIMENSION

Performance also has a focus dimension. The focus can be on anything. For example, Raman could have focused on learning or on marks. Similarly, in defining the performance of a sales executive, the focus of performance can be on market share, profits, new areas covered, or some of these or most of these.

The focus of performance can be on many other dimensions. It could be on quality, cost, or financial dimensions.

## INPUT–OUTPUT RELATIONSHIPS

An important issue to be understood in performance management is the input–output relationship. Let us take the case of Raman. Assume that Raman has done all that he had decided to do. He attended all classes, put in all the extra work required, listened attentively in class, clarified all his doubts, solved all previous papers, and in addition, did some extra things. At the end, he got only 85 percent marks instead of the targeted 95 percent. How do we rate his performance?

You may choose one of the following:

1. Average or OK
2. Excellent, since he had done more than what he originally planned to do
3. Not good as he got a far lower percentage than what he aimed for

If a person is contracted to provide certain input with the assumption that these will lead to the targeted outcome or result and he/she gives more than the required input, how can we call the performance anything less than good or excellent? If he/she did not achieve the desired result, it may be because of various factors. His/her competencies may be limited or the person may not be examination-wise. His/her memory may be weak or home environment may not be conducive, which may affect his/her results in spite of the hard work. The examination papers that year may also have been tough. What if 85 percent is in that year's top 10 and the person still gets admission into a good college? If in reality 85 percent is poor and he does not get admission, what good does it do if he/she is rated excellent in performance input, but the result and its consequences are disastrous?

There are no easy answers to all these questions and that is what makes performance management complex. It has been treated lightly by experts, CEOs, manager,s and HR professionals.

*Treating such a complex issue in a simple manner and reducing performance management to a simple form-filling exercise is the biggest mistake managers have made in the past.*

This book is meant to present various facets of performance management and also assign performance appraisals their right place. Performance appraisals cannot be treated as performance management, which consists of the following:

1. Defining performance, taking into account all the complexities mentioned earlier (KPAs, tasks, etc.).
2. Planning performance in terms of input, output, conditions under which these take place, etc. (objectives, activities, targets, etc.).
3. Measuring performance and understanding the limitations in measuring performance.
4. Analyzing performance and understanding what caused it or contributed to it. Positively? Negatively? Identifying development needs and support requirements from the analysis.
5. Developing capabilities to perform or the capability to provide inputs and have the competencies to convert the inputs into desired output.
6. Monitoring and reviewing this (performance review discussions, and so forth).
7. Recognizing various dimensions of performance and rewarding it where appropriate.

The various chapters in this book deal with these aspects of performance.

## SOME NEGLECTED DIMENSIONS OF PERFORMANCE MANAGEMENT

### Dyadic Performance

In the past, performance management was limited to individuals. We have behaved as though it is each individual's business to be a good performer. We have ignored the role played by the boss or the subordinate (to represent the two with equal status, we use the term "dyad") in determining performance. In fact, a two-person performance is also performance. Just as a teamworking in any department is expected to deliver results, we also expect each dyad to provide certain input and deliver results. For example, in the case of Raman, his mother, father, brothers and sisters have a role to play in his performance. This is normally neglected and less talked about. In organizations, a manager and his boss together constitute a dyad and each have some responsibility to provide inputs. As dyadic performance contributes substantially to an individual's performance and deserves attention.

In measuring dyadic performance, two types of measures are possible—outcome measures and process measures. Outcome measures take into consideration situational variations and are based on assumptions. Process measures deal with interpersonal processes. They include the extent to which each person is a source of motivation to the other person, the extent to which joint effort yields results that are higher than the sum of individual efforts, and the extent to which there is mutuality, help, synergy and learning, and so forth.

### A Measure of Dyadic Performance: Process Parameters

Use the following items of a questionnaire to measure dyadic performance. Collect data from each of the pairs of supervisors or managers. The sum of the scores will give the dyadic performance index.

1. I enjoy working with this person.
2. He provides me the guidance and support I require to do my job well.
3. He provides the information and support I require to do my job well.
4. He is a great motivator. I feel motivated to work with him.
5. He gives me feedback that is empowering.
6. He complements and supplements my efforts.
7. We work well as a dyadic team.
8. I get a lot of clarity about my job and what is expected out of my job from him.

Consider manager X, who has a motivating value uniformly with each one of his six subordinates (dyads). If we rate the motivational value he has on a 5-point scale and assign 5 to each, then he has a 30 point score on his dyadic performance. (His average dyadic performance with respect to his subordinates is 30 divided by 6 = 5.0.) Another manager Y has a good equation with three of his subordinates (performance value = $3 \times 5 = 15$ points), a demotivating influence on one of his subordinates (performance value = 0 or even negative—we ignore the negative for the time being), and he has an average motivational influence with the other two (performance value = $2 \times 3 = 6$). His total dyadic performance value is 21 (15 + 6 + 0) and the average is 3.5. Consider another manager Z, who motivates only one of his five subordinates, while the other four avoid him and consider him of no help. He has a total dyadic performance score of 5 and an average of 1.

Thus, X, Y, and Z have different levels of performance in terms of their dyadic performance vis-à-vis their subordinates. Now consider their dyadic performance with each of their bosses. X and Y have one boss each. X has a very productive relationship with his boss and a dyadic performance rating of 5 while Y has a somewhat strained relationship with his and has a rating of 2 on a 5-point scale. Z has two bosses and he has a very productive relationship with one of them and a poor one with the other (value = 5 with one and 2 with the other, averaging 3.5).

X has three colleagues (peers) who depend on his work, Y has three colleagues who also depend on his work and Z has five colleagues who depend on his work. Let us assume that the average dyadic performance scores of the three are 4.0 for X, 4.0 for Y, and 2.5 for Z with respect to their colleagues. The totals are as follows in Table 1.1.

Table 1.1 indicates the total overall dyadic performance scores of the three managers. We have, however, assessed them only on relationships (how motivating each has been). This is only one dimension of dyadic performance. The areas of performance can be expanded to include a variety of other dimensions, such as support provided, problems solved, ability to provide technical guidance, autonomy, etc. These parameters may vary from organization to organization and are significant determinants of individual performance in terms of output.

This is what needs to be identified and measures developed. This area has so far been highly neglected. Performance management therefore has other connotations for developing dyadic performance.

## TEAM PERFORMANCE

Team performance has been widely recognized. However, it is most often mixed with individual performance. For example, general managers and unit heads are normally assessed for their

| TABLE 1.1 | | | |
|---|---|---|---|
| **Dyadic Performance Scores of Three Managers** | | | |
| | Manager X | Manager Y | Manager Z |
| Dyadic score with | | | |
| Subordinates | 5.0 | 4.25 | 1.0 |
| Seniors (boss) | 5 | 2 | 3.5 |
| Colleagues | 4 | 4 | 2.5 |
| Total dyadic score | 14 | 10.25 | 7.0 |

*Source:* Author.

performance in terms of the number of units produced, sales figures achieved, products manufactured, profit made, etc. These are treated as individual accomplishments while in reality these are group performance indicators. In the recent past, internal customer satisfaction surveys, departmental surveys and employee satisfaction surveys have been treated as team performance indicators. A lot more thought is needed and a chapter is devoted at the end of this book to this.

## Who Manages Performance?

The answer is obvious. The performer or the candidate whose performance is being planned, analyzed, assessed, developed, and so forth. It is he/she who manages his/her performance. It is a mistake to think that the primary responsibility for managing the performance of a person lies with his/her boss.

A boss is an important instrument in managing performance. He/she has the responsibility to ensure that it is defined, planned, analyzed, measured, reviewed, and developed. He/she is a partner in this, but it is the performer who has to manage his/her performance. The roles of the performer and the boss are highlighted in various chapters.

## Role of Appraisals in Performance Management

Performance management is a continuous process. Appraisals are periodic activities. Management is a dynamic process while appraisals are static. Appraisals are a part of performance management. If management involves improvement, the moment an employee is assessed there is an appraisal taking place. Therefore, without some form of appraisal management becomes difficult. Appraisals do not mean reducing the performance of individuals and dyads or teams to a 5-point scale or a number. It is this reduction of annual performance into a number and equating one number with another that has created havoc in managing performance or in appraisals. Numbers generated from the appraisal process are not comparable across functions, levels, departments, and organizations. This is because the scales are not calibrated and equated. Some use liberal scales, some conservative ones, and some no scales but merely feelings. It is this lack of calibration and treatment of the incomparable as comparable that has created chaos.

Performance management with performance appraisal should lead to increased performance. However, in most organizations, performance appraisals lead to decreased performance. This usually happens when appraisals are linked to rewards and fewer people are rewarded than those expecting them. Those who are not rewarded are demotivated. If their number exceeds that of those who actually get rewards, the net outcome of performance appraisal may be negative. If people continue to perform in spite of appraisals and do not have a positive attitude to them, it means that the organization is spending too much psychological energy.

The effort should be to make the performance management process effective and productive by using appraisal systems. Appraisal systems help managers manage their performance. They should be seen by line managers as aids to performance management. Managers should not be overwhelmed with appraisals and appraisal outcomes, and ignore the most important aspects of performance management—performance improvements and competency building. This happens when their concerns are focused on appraisals rather than on improvements or on ratings and rewards rather than performance enhancement and development. They need to learn to enjoy the performance management process when it takes place around the year and is not blocked by appraisals, which occur once in a while. Performance management systems with an appraisal component built into them should result in improved performance and more motivated and competent individuals.

# 2

# Defining and Planning Performance

## Performance Equation

*Individual Performance = Ability × Motivation × Organizational Support + Chance Factors*

*Ability is competence—technical, managerial, human relations, and conceptual and abstract thinking. It is reflected through knowledge, attitudes, traits and qualities, values, and skills.*

*Motivation is reflected through hard work, commitment, and other such behavior on the job.*

*Organizational support is the extent to which a person receives support from his/her boss and others in the organization to do his/her work well.*

Performance = Competence × Commitment × Culture that is supportive and enabling + Chance factors

The equation as mentioned earlier means that any individual's performance on a given job for a particular period depends upon his/her ability or competence multiplied by motivation or work effort or commitment further multiplied by organizational support or a culture of empowerment and support.

A brief explanation of each of these factors is given as follows:

The equation requires that performance to be defined. Without a definition, it cannot be measured. Normally, we define performance in terms of KPAs or KRAs. However, KPAs or KRAs do not constitute performance, but are merely performance, result, or responsibility areas. Any performance measurement requires an exact statement of "what the performer is expected to do." It is also useful to state "what the performer is expected to do and to achieve." If achievement is a group goal, it should be clarified. If it is totally related to what the individual alone does, it can be stated. In many cases, it is not possible to state what the individual is expected to achieve. Normally, result or achievement goals are group or team goals. It is easy to understand this if we look at sales and marketing goals. Achieving a sales target of x amount is an individual goal for the salesperson. However, achieving the sales target of x amount is a group goal for the area sales manager (ASM) who supervises a large number of salespersons, and his/her target is an addition of all the individual targets of salespersons in his/her territory or area. Some organizations add a little more—that the ASM should achieve something more than the added sales targets of all those whom he/she is supervising. However, the tasks and activities of the ASM may be substantially different than those of his/her salespersons. For example, he/she may contact customers or dealers much less and his/her tasks may include appointing new dealers who can help him/her achieve sales targets, guide salespersons, maintain MIS, and keep contacting high-value dealers and customers to achieve additional targets in his/her territory. The KRA or KPA (achieving sales targets) for a salesperson and an ASM may appear similar, but his/her targets and activities are different. When we define performance, it is important to include in detail all the activities the performer is expected to undertake as well as the results he/she is expected to achieve.

Performance management involves managing all aspects of the performance equation:

1. Defining and clarifying what constitutes performance.
2. Providing context for performance, environmental changes, and expectations.
3. Ensuring that the required competencies are identified, available, and developed.
4. Ensuring motivation and commitment—communications and measuring scales.
5. Ensuring organizational support.

Performance management is all about managing this equation and is a continuous process. A well-designed PMS system takes into consideration all the aspects of performance, as outlined in the equation. While designing a good system is important, its implementation is equally important. Most systems fail because inadequate efforts are made to ensure implementation. A good PMS starts by defining and planning the performance for a given period. The following sections explain the need for this and elaborate on the mechanisms for planning performance. The subsequent sections deal with the other parts of this equation—competencies, motivation, and organizational support.

Competencies are developed through planning, delineating competency indicators, and reviewing individuals' performance on the job while they are working to achieve their goals or are carrying out their performance-targeted activities. Periodic analysis of the performance of individuals and teams and taking corrective action when required ensures that their motivation is maintained. Moreover, it needs to be ensured that organizational support is provided to help them achieve their targets.

## Why Performance Needs to Be Planned?

Planning for performance is the first step in performance management. As mentioned in the first chapter, an employee is expected to spend about 2,000 to 2,400 hours a year working for the organization. That works out to about 166 to 200 hours a month. If a person's cost to the company is ₹400,000 annually, his/her per hour cost will be ₹200 and he/she will be expected to deliver an output ranging from three to 10 times his/her cost to the company. This means that the opportunity cost of an employee drawing a salary of ₹4 lakh annually ranges from ₹600 to ₹2,000 an hour. If the employee costs ₹40 lakh, his/her opportunity cost per hour to the company will be ₹6,000 to ₹20,000. Even if we take the minimum, the per-hour cost to company of an ordinary manager is likely to be ₹1,600 and above and the opportunity cost will be ₹16,000 and above. Given this kind of a cost, imagine the benefit the organization will derive if the individual becomes aware of how he/she uses his/her time and tries to ensure that the input he/she provides yields the desired output. Thus, performance planning is a simple way of ensuring that the employee gives quality input that will ensure the output expected from him/her. Planning gives a sense of direction and ensures good economics for the company. In addition, it ramps up the contribution of the individual and enhances his/her self worth. An individual who adds value to the company on a continuous basis enhances his/her own worth in many ways.

Indian managers are excellent in managing crises. They are equally good in creating them. While each executive emerges as competent in handling the crisis created by others, little does he/she realize the role he/she plays in creating a crisis for others. Organizational life is full of inter-dependencies; the effective performance of one manager may depend on the task performance of another. Managers waste a lot of time negotiating with each other, managing each other, sorting out their ego problems, and so on. Crisis management also keeps the manager constantly powerful as he/she can break all the rules, use up organizational resources, cut the chain of command, undermine the autonomy of subordinates, and show his/her bosses that he/she is doing a lot of work. Crisis management is a good way to cover up one's own inefficiencies and postpone less enjoyable and non-tangible things, such as planning and development. The crisis management competence of Indian managers is so powerful that it is very difficult to get them to plan their performance or the performance of their subordinates, which is probably the solution to this problem.

Performance planning fixes accountability, sets role boundaries, helps better time management, and requires time at least once a year. It also helps the manager to understand and analyze his/her contributions and increases his/her responsibility for continuous performance.

## WHAT IS PERFORMANCE PLANNING?

Performance planning may be defined as a systematic outlining of the activities that the manager is expected to undertake during a specified period so that he/she is able to make his/her best contribution to developmental and organizational outcomes. The activities thus outlined are indicative of the nature of contributions the manager is expected to make to the departmental goals. They also provide a framework for performing the role. They denote how the manager is likely to spend his/her time during the year. They also indicate the quality, magnitude, and variety of contributions he/she is expected to make. They set directions for time management. They establish what could be expected by all those whose contributions are based on their contributions and what is expected from those whose contributions become inputs for this manager's work. Performance planning also indicates the relative emphasis to be placed by the individual on different activities he/she undertakes during the year.

## WHOSE PERFORMANCE IS TO BE PLANNED?

It is often said that the individual's performance cannot be planned and it is the department or organization's performance that can be mapped out. The author would like to argue that it is easier to plan an individual's performance rather than that of an organization. This may be true for several reasons. Every individual manager understands the reality and circumstances within which he/she is expected to perform. Individual performance is subject to fewer uncertainties than that of an organization. Organizational uncertainties are a sum of the uncertainties faced by each employee and those arising from the external environment. Not all managers are required to deal with the external environment. Most individuals can plan their performance with some understanding of internal uncertainties. Unfortunately, managers seem to magnify the uncertainties within the organization and feel each one of them will affect their performance. Hence, they argue that performance cannot be planned. This is simply a good escape mechanism.

Organizational plans can at best be goals to strive for. Individual plans should be the actions expected to be undertaken by each manager with the hope of achieving organizational goals. Organizational goals, corporate plans, mission statements, annual operating plans, budget statements, and performance guidelines issued from the CEO's office from time to time provide the perspective and framework required to determine the departmental goals and thus provide the context for an individual performance plan. However, individual performance plans do not have to wait every year for the creation of such a context as only marginal changes are expected from year to year with some exceptions.

It is, of course, ideal if these guidelines are available before the individual plans his/her performance. However, in the absence of such guidelines, groups of managers can sit together and set new goals for their department in the context of the previous years' performance and their knowledge of the current situation. They first need to raise a few questions: How did we perform last year? What influenced our performance? How can we improve? What new challenges can we undertake? How is the situation going to be different this year? How do we intend to improve our quality and quality of outputs? What new process, technology and systems do we want to introduce this year? Organizations should set their goals and plan their strategies. Departments and other sub-systems should delineate their roles and plan their contributions. Individuals should plan their performance. Ideally, the sequence should be from organization to department to individual. This helps in several ways. However, one should not wait for the other indefinitely. Lack of information on organizational plans and strategies should not prevent departments and other sub-units from planning improvements and individuals from planning their performance.

It is often argued that the organizational plans should follow individual plans. This goes against reality in Indian organizations. First, it does not make sense to consolidate individual plans to make departmental goals and then determine organizational goals. It is difficult to do so. Second, participative management cannot be stretched to such an extent.

## PLANNING INDIVIDUAL PERFORMANCE

Annual performance management exercises provide good opportunities for performance planning. These provide many ways in which individual performance can be planned, some of which include:

1. Task analysis and/or activity analysis;
2. Key performance areas (KPAs);
3. Key result areas (KRAs);
4. Task and target identification;
5. Activity plans/action plans; and
6. Goal-setting exercises.

There are only subtle differences in the six methods mentioned above. All these methods emphasize to some extent the key tasks the individual is expected to perform as part of his/her role during the year. Some of them emphasize a detailed analysis and listing of all activities (task analysis or activity analysis), others emphasize the outcomes or results expected or targeted by the individual (KRAs, goal-setting exercises). A few others emphasize the planning part of the work (activity plans) and some others emphasize the performance or what the individual is expected to do (KPAs).

The distinctions are smaller if we treat each of these as different ways of planning performance. Any of these could be used and there is no standard technology available for each method. What is important is that the individual should be able to plan his/her work and, as a result of that, should have greater clarity of the activities in which he needs to put in more effort.

The author feels that the Key Performance Area approach is best suited for the purpose of planning as it emphasizes individual performance and also gives scope for quantification.

## KPAs AND PERFORMANCE PLANNING

Identifying KPAs and setting quantifiable targets wherever possible is the only one way of planning one's performance. Some organizations stress on increasing objectivity in ratings through KPAs. The author is of the view that increasing objectivity depends on a

number of factors. KPAs help in reducing subjectivity but sometimes not in very visible ways. Objectivity in appraisals is difficult
to achieve and ratings will always have limitations, as explained
in subsequent chapters. Hence, organizations would do better by
trying to inculcate a planning orientation and role clarity through
KPAs than by improving objectivity.

A lot of managerial time is wasted in the goal-setting process if
it aims at objectivity and some ill-feeling may also be associated
with it. On the other hand, if KPAs or target setting are viewed
as performance planning, role clarity, and direction-setting mechanisms, the numbers assigned to weightages take on a different
meaning.

There is no well-tested technology to identify KPAs. If the following questions can be answered positively after the exercise, one
could say that KPAs have been well identified:

1.  Do the KPAs and targets emphasize/indicate what the
    manager (performer) is expected to do by himself/herself
    (rather than what his/her department, subordinates, and
    so forth, are expected to do)?
2.  Together, do they cover a large part of his/her job and
    include all significant contributions expected from his/her
    role?
3.  Do they indicate the priority areas of work for the per-
    former during the year?
4.  If all KPAs are well done, can the performer be labelled as
    a good performer?
5.  Are the set targets challenging and stretch the capabilities
    of the performer moderately rather than being routine?
6.  Are they comprehensive?
7.  Do they specify the standards of performance expected
    from the performer?
8.  Do they take realistically into consideration the condi-
    tions under which the performer is expected to function
    during the year?
9.  Do they satisfy both the performer and reporting manager?
10. Has adequate time been spent on the process of identify-
    ing KPAs and gaining role clarity?

All these questions cannot be answered by looking at the written KPAs on a piece of paper. The performer and reporting manager are the best judges on these.

## Need for Clarity of Roles and Functions in Modern Organizations

Any organization interested in its growth has to be dynamic. Dynamic organizations are always looking for growth opportunities, creating challenges for themselves and making an impact on their environment. Such an organization has to have a certain amount of flexibility in its own internal organizational structure, roles, and role relationships. Thus, dynamic organizations are continuously in a process of change either in response to their own needs and growth plans or in response to the environmental changes. These changes impact the roles—particularly the managerial roles—in any organization. For example, the role of banks today is substantially different from the role they played about 20 years ago. Having taken up agricultural development and lead bank roles, working with government agencies, supporting small-scale industries, and participating in the industrial development of backward areas, the role of branch managers and other officers today has become much more complex and demanding than in the past. The rising expectations of a variety of clients and the changing industrial relations scene have imposed additional demands on branch managers and other officers. Many organizations have witnessed a similar change in the roles of managers. For example, the role of personnel managers in most organizations has been changing as new demands are being created due to changes in the environment as well as growth of organizations.

The nature of managerial roles is such that it is neither possible nor desirable to rigidly define all the tasks and functions associated with it. In fact, effective managers are constantly creating new tasks and functions for themselves around the roles assigned to them and top management of organizations would do well to encourage such dynamism.

In order to help people to develop various capabilities, a clear understanding of the different functions associated with their roles and the capability requirements need to be clearly understood. Performance review along these dimensions is likely to be more meaningful and helpful for development. The concept of key performance areas explained below intends to serve this purpose.

## KPAs AS MECHANISMS OF ROLE CLARITY AND DEVELOPMENT

*Key performance areas may be defined as the important or critical categories of functions to be performed by any role incumbent over a given period of time.* These categories of functions should be defined so that the performance of any employee can be assessed meaningfully for any given period of time. In addition, these functions should specify what the employee would be doing rather than what results are expected from him/her. Some examples of KPAs are:

| | |
|---|---|
| For a Sales Officer | 1. Contacting potential customers |
| | 2. Market survey for new products |
| | 3. Attending to customer complaints |
| For an R&D Manager | 1. Identifying product improvements |
| | 2. Development of new products |
| | 3. Testing samples |
| For an Accounts Manager | 1. Budget preparation |
| | 2. Payment of bills to suppliers |
| | 3. Developing a system of computerization |
| For a Branch Manager | 1. Balancing of ledgers of a bank |
| | 2. Public relations |
| | 3. Recovery of sick accounts |
| | 4. Mobilizing new deposits, and so forth |

As the samples (mentioned earlier) indicate, KPAs are broad categories of functions to be performed by any employee in relation to his/her job. Normally, KPAs can be obtained from job descriptions if these are elaborate and extensive. However, job descriptions in most organizations are usually very broad and sketchy. Even if they are supplied to new incumbents, they may not be able to get a complete picture. Moreover, for reasons mentioned earlier in this chapter, the nature of jobs may be changing. Hence, it is desirable to have periodic exercises in identifying performance areas for each role and KPAs for each person in relation to his/her role. The following process is recommended to identify key performance areas in the context of the performance management system suggested in this book.

## IDENTIFYING PERFORMANCE AREAS FOR A GIVEN ROLE (EXISTING)

1. A group of four or five persons may be involved in this process. Once these KPAs are identified, it could form a basis for any role incumbent to identify his/her own KPAs in that role. This group should consist of mainly two categories of people—those who are performing that role at present and those who performed that role in the past and are supervising others performing that role now. This group is constituted to list all the tasks associated with that role and then classify them into meaningful categories. Those who are currently involved in performing the role are likely to give exhaustive information about the tasks they are handling. Those who are supervising them will be able to provide guidance and, in the process, may sharpen their own understanding about their subordinate's role, the relationships with them, and their obligations to the role incumbent.

2. In some cases, the same role (or designation) may have different functions associated with it. For example, in a divisionalized organization, each divisional manager may have a different set of functions to perform depending on the nature of the division they handle—its size, its location, and its history in the organization. Similarly, in a marketing organization with different branches or zones, the branch/zonal managers located in different geographic regions may have different functions to perform (although their designations are the same). In such cases, it may be useful to constitute separate groups for each role. If it is not feasible to have

such groups for any reason, the role incumbent and or her supervising officer may jointly work and identify the performance areas. The same pair can also identify the KPAs using the procedure described below.

3. The group should then draw up an exhaustive list of all the tasks the role incumbent is expected to undertake. While preparing such a list of tasks, it may be useful to raise the following questions:

- What are the main activities in which the role incumbent is involved?
- What exactly does he/she do in these activities?
- How much of his/her time is spent on each activity?
- What is his/her unique contribution by virtue of occupying this position?
- If his/her performance is to be rated as excellent in the next six months to one year, what would he/she have done as this role incumbent?

The answers to these questions will provide a set of tasks/activities to be undertaken by the role incumbent. In the next step, all these activities may be grouped into meaningful categories of functions. If any activity/task is considered critical and deserves special attention, it could be separately listed as a performance area without grouping it under any category. While there is no hard and fast rule about the number of performance areas for any role, normally these will be less than 10 (ideally 5 or 6).

4. After the performance areas (PAs) are identified they could give weightages for their relation importance to that role. Thus, a weightage of 3 could indicate that the particular PA is very central and important to that role. A rating of 2 may indicate that the PA is quite important but is not central. A weightage of 1 may indicate that the performance area is important. There may be few performance areas which may not be considered as important contributions of the role incumbent. These are the ones on which the employee

need not be appraised separately as they do not need that much attention. Thus, the group could make their sugges-tions on the weightages to be assigned to the performance areas. These weightages are only suggestive and may change from time to time or from one role incumbent to another. The group only gives its suggestions.

5. After such an exercise is done, the KPAs for different roles could be listed and made available to employees in the form of a directory of performance areas. This directory helps as a basic guideline to help every employee plan his/her work for any given period.

6. For performance management purposes, every employee should identify the performance areas in consultation with his/her boss at the start of the year (the exact period to be decided by each organization). This should be done after considering the plans of the organization or his/her department and the nature of demands that he is expected to meet for the coming year. The areas selected or identi-fied should be the areas that the performer and the report-ing manager consider as significant dimensions on which the performer's contributions should be assessed for that year. The reporting manager and the performer may also determine the weightages of each of these areas. (Discussion on weightages may be useful irrespective of whether these weightages are used or not for final assessment.)

In the approach outlined above, steps 2, 3, and 4 should be done by groups wherever feasible. Step 5 could be undertaken by the personnel/HRD/industrial engineering departments. Step 6 is very important as it is the process by which the reporting manager–performer pairs discuss and come to an understanding about the KPAs which is very critical for achieving the objectives of the performance management outlined in Chapter 1. Steps 2, 3, and 4 are a non-time task. Once the basic performance areas for each role are worked out, they only need marginal changes once in a while. In organizations where it is not feasible to have separate groups to carry out this task, the reporting manager–performer pairs can sit together and complete steps 2, 3, and 4 before they come to step 6. Thus, it is a matter of one or two sittings and may involve only about two to three hours of time. This time, however, is worth investing. In the process of agreeing on the KPAs for the assessment period (that is, in step 6), both the reporting manager and the performer should aim at:

1. A clear and common understanding of the various activities to be performed under each KPA by the performer.
2. A clear understanding of the importance of each of these activities and what exactly is expected to be done by the performer, that is, the nature of effort we should put in, the possible outcome expected as a result of his/her efforts, and so forth.
3. An understanding of the expected problems and support required by the performer from the reporting manager as well as others in the organization and the support that the reporting manager can give to the performer.
4. Understandings of the level of performance expected in relation to each of the KPAs and the possible ratings associated with different performance levels. (Quite often it is difficult to be specific. However, some discussions may establish a common understanding.)

This requires a thorough discussion between the reporting manager and the performer. A climate of openness, mutuality and trust facilitates this process. The reporting manager and the performer should be concerned more about increasing their understanding of each other in relation to their roles and strengthening their relationships as well as facilitating the development of the performer in relation to his/her role. Both should keep the purpose in mind. KPAs prepare the ground for employees to understand in a systematic way the capabilities they have and those they lack. This understanding may take place as the employee is performing various tasks and undergoing experiences, success, and failure. It gets organized through a process of review and reflection at the end of the year when the employee realizes the consistency in his/her successes and failures. This is the beginning of development. Thus, KPAs serve as anchors with the help of which the individual employee may gain insights into his/her own capabilities and development needs. In addition, they offer opportunities to decide on his/her own work patterns, experiment with them, and learn wherever such possibilities exist. When a manager feels that he/she has not done a good job in his/her role and is unable to identify where he/she has failed, it is difficult for him/her to do better next time. But when a manager knows that he has failed only in one critical function (KPA) and realizes that this was because he did not properly schedule certain activities that the function involved, he may recognize the need to develop his/her scheduling capabilities. The second manager is in a better position to improve his/her performance because he/she knows what he/she lacks and he/she may make efforts to develop these. KPAs thus help in this process and clarify the thinking of managers.

The understanding between the boss and the subordinate will enable the performer to concentrate his/her efforts on the right kind of things. Due to the clarity of understanding of the various areas of performance, the appraisal is likely to be less subjective.

## PERFORMANCE TARGETS: ADDING OBJECTIVITY

To add more objectivity to the exercise, it is possible to identify performance targets under each KPA. These performance targets may be qualitative or quantitative, but should be time bound and should specify the level of acceptable performance to obtain high performance ratings. The targets should focus more on the nature of efforts to be made by the performer in relation to each of the KPAs. Here is an example.

1. *Role*: Marketing Manager
   *KPA*: Introducing a new product X in the region assigned to him/her.
   *Performance Targets*

- Complete training program for all district representatives to ensure readiness for distribution of product X within the next three months.
- To personally contact a random group of 10 major customers from each district and get their feedback on the products.
- Evolve a marketing strategy by the end of the year to increase sales of the product in consultation with district representatives.

2. *Role*: Manager (Finance)
   *KPA*: Cost reduction (weightage-3)
   *Performance Targets*

   - Complete write-up and acceptance of the company's cost reduction manual and distribute it to all managers by the year end.
   - Collect 10 suggested cost reduction ideas per month from each of six operating managers.

3. *Role*: Manager (Research and Development)
   *KPA*: Development of new production (weightage-2)
   *Performance Targets*

   - Complete the literature and patent search by the end of the year for five patentable ideas useful in entering new markets.
   - Complete design and development of a new prototype in 12 months within the cost of ₹140,000 without farming out work to vendors.

4. *Role*: Junior Manager (Production)
   *KPA*: Work-simplification in machine shop (weightage-1)
   *Performance Targets*

   - Master 10 techniques in work simplification as related to machine shop operations through monthly cost reduction meetings for machine shop supervisors.

5. *Role*: Manager (HRD)
   *KPA*: Introducing a new system of development-oriented performance management (weightage-3)
   *Performance Targets*

   • Collect information about the development-oriented appraisal systems in use from 10 different organizations in the city and suggest a system for use in our organization on the basis of these experiences.

6. *Role*: Branch Manager (State Bank of....)
   *KPA*: Deposit mobilization
   *Performance Targets*

   • Institute a system of deposit mobilization through collective efforts of all officers in the branch by holding monthly meetings and reviewing progress.
   • Personally contact at least 10 potential clients in the town every month and try to get them to open accounts.

*It may be noted that these objectives emphasize the effort that the performer needs to make rather than the results.* For example, in the case of Branch Manager (No. 6) above, the target could be stated as: "To mobilize deposits worth ₹5,000,000 in the next one year."

Similarly, in the case of Manager (Finance) (Role No. 2 above), the target could be "to bring about cost reduction by 10 percent in the next one year."

In both cases the focus is on results rather than on effort. Results of this kind depend on a number of factors. In appraising performance, the focus should be on efforts rather than results. This is because it encapsulates the performance of an entire group or department or an entire function in any organization.

Of course, in this process it is hoped that the results will also be obtained. If results are not achieved even after every employee puts in high effort, it will indicate that there is something wrong somewhere in the organization. If efforts do not lead to results, the organizational processes need to be examined. If efforts do not lead to results in any individual case, the nature of efforts may need to be changed, or other constraints may need to be identified and dealt with. This again may involve joint responsibility of the performer and the reporting manager. Performance management could thus become an instrument to enhance the collaborative capabilities of boss–subordinate to make things happen in the organization and thus contribute to its growth.

---

### SOME EXAMPLES OF KEY PERFORMANCE AREAS

#### Example 1

*Branch Manager of a Bank:* The performance areas are presented below. A list of activities to be performed by the branch managers are presented under each KPA.

*KPA 1: Deposit Mobilization*

*Activities:* Ensuring prompt service to customers, periodic meetings with the staff, contacting prospective depositors, developing strategies collectively, maintaining liaison with government authorities, etc.

*Possible Objectives:* The objective is to increase deposits by at least 10 percent. Effort goals could be:

1. To contact at least about 200 potential customers; and
2. To hold discussions with staff and involve them in improving customer service.

*KPA 2: Advances to Clients*

*Activities:* Checking proposals for advances, periodic inspection of advances, identifying priority sectors for advances, lodging of claims with Deposit Insurance and Credit Guarantee Corporation (DICGC), attending to audit irregularities and steps for recovery of advances, and actions for disposing willful default cases.

*(Box contd.)*

*(Box contd.)*

**Objectives: Effort goals**

1. To establish a system of processing all loan requests within 15 days of receiving the request.
2. To initiate action against all non-receivables by the end of the year.
3. To contact major clients for outstandings and recover at least 50 percent.

### KPA 3: House Keeping

*Activities:* Periodic checking of records and stationery, ensuring stocks of stationery, spot-checking for balancing of books, follow-up action on audit reports and prompt rectification, and monitoring timely submission of returns and statements.

*Objective:* Result goal—To ensure balancing of all books.

*Effort goals:*

1. To check all important records once a month.
2. To develop a system of monitoring returns and statements and implement the same.

### KPA 4: Customer Services

*Activities:* Attending to customer complaints, giving advice to customers, correspondence with customers, contacting customers, and finding out their difficulties.

*Objectives:* Result goal—To ensure a high level of customer satisfaction.

*Effort goals:*

1. To personally attend to customer complaints.
2. To install a suggestion box and act on the suggestions.
3. To reply to all letters/enquiries from customers within a week of receiving them.

*(Box contd.)*

---

*KPA 5: Staff Management*

*Activities:* Sanctioning leave, work allotment, attending to staff grievances, ensuring facilities and work conditions for staff, counseling, identifying development needs and providing opportunities, job rotation, and planning for staff requirements.

*Objectives:*

1. To have a meeting with every staff member once a month and ensure their satisfaction.
2. To initiate a system of informal get-togethers every quarter.
3. To experiment with a system of job rotation given by the HRD unit.

## Example 2

In this example, the performance areas and their weightages for a number of roles, taken from large engineering company manufacturing heavy equipment, are presented. The roles are selected from different departments to give an idea of KPAs. This organization is a multi-product, multi-unit company employing about 15,000 employees. Targets are also given in some cases:

| KPAs | Weightage |
|---|---|
| **Role 1: Assistant Accounts Officer (reports to Accounts Officer)** | |
| 1. To get people from other units/sections to work in place of absentees to pull up areas of attendance work so as to feed the input to EDP as per schedule for computation of wages/salaries. | 3 |
| 2. To compare the wage bill of each month with that of the previous month to check violent variations, if any, arising from possible computer errors. | 2 |
| 3. To verify whether all early payments, court attachments, and other recoveries to be effected subsequent to the receipt of computer statements have been reduced from the net amount payable to the concerned employees before preparation of the Teller Statement for withdrawal of cash for disbursement of wages/salaries. | 3 |
| 4. To ascertain whether the work of statutory remittances such as, ESI contribution, professional tax, CTD, and so forth., are progressing as per program and to facilitate such remittances to be made before due dates so as to avoid penalty and other consequences, if necessary, by drafting people from other units. | 2 |
| 5. To take stock of pending claims in respect of leave travel concession (LTC), Expense Reports & Termination settlements at monthly intervals and to get them cleared wherever such claims are more than a fortnight old. | 2 |

*(Box contd.)*

*(Box contd.)*

| KPAs | Weightage |
|------|-----------|
| 6. To attend to enquiries of employees and ex-employees in respect of their personal matters connected with payroll, which cannot be solved at the staff-level. | 1 |

**Role 2: Assistant Accounts Manager (reports to Accounts Manager)**

| KPAs | Weightage |
|------|-----------|
| 1. To review the system of audit, the procedure followed and the extent of audit checks exercised to ensure adequacy of audit. (Target: To complete one unit per quarter.) | 3 |
| 2. To review adequacy of various other internal controls in operation for effectiveness in the department. (Target: To complete one unit per quarter.) | 2 |
| 3. Coordinate and ensure completion of monthly audit and issue of report and take up follow-up action. (Target: Audit up to June 1982 to be completed by September 1982; report for the first quarter to be issued.) | 3 |
| 4. General review of procedure and system followed in the internal audit, its policy and suggest improvements wherever there is scope. (Target: Complete this item at least in respect of two areas. One regarding selection of vouchers in accordance with drill and another regarding follow-up action on observation made.) | 2 |

**Role 3: Assistant Manager, Stores (reports to Materials Manager)**

| KPAs | Weightage |
|------|-----------|
| 1. Seeing all incoming *daks* (mails) pertaining to stores, department, and attending to important papers. (Target: To ensure that delay in correspondence is avoided.) | 3 |
| 2. To keep a watch over critical items (production and non-production including standard stock items) for receipt with regular follow-up till finalization. (Target: To avoid hold-up of production.) | 3 |
| 3. Clearance of materials received in receiving. (Target: To avoid demurrage/inconvenience to carriers). | 2 |
| 4. Departmental verification of stores. (Target: To ensure no loss of material warranting write-off action.) | 3 |
| 5. Review of: (a) Report finalization (b) Rejected stores items (c) Repairable items (d) Critical standard stock items having stocks less than two months (e) Shop rejection; and (f) Claims on carriers/insurance. (Target: To ensure that functions detailed to officers are carried out promptly.) | 3 |
| 6. To ensure that all the stores and tool cribs function without disruption. (Target: To avoid dislocation in the stores function.) | 3 |
| 7. To inspect all stores to ensure maintenance of proper storage. (Target: To avoid spoilage and deterioration of materials.) | 3 |

| KPAs | Weightage |
|---|---|

8. To ensure that appropriate action is taken for disposal of scrap arising.    3
   (Target: To ensure that periodical clearance is done without accumulation.)

9. To exercise proper control on inventory holdings.    3
   Target:

    (a) To coordinate with Departments for review of excess inventory.
    (b) To identify non-moving stocks and take appropriate action for
        disposal thereof.

10. General Administration    3
    (Target: To ensure smooth functioning of stores.)

**Role 4: Design Manager (reports to General Manager)**

1. Coordination with Research Designs and Standards Organization with regard    3
   to the development of new designs.

2. Guide in the development of new designs for export of the products.    3

3. Coordination with shops and other departments with regard to the prototype    2
   building and productionizing the drawings.

4. Guide in the preparation of specifications, testing procedures, and so forth.    2

5. To provide modern and latest facilities for the design and drawing office,    2
   laboratory, library, and blue printing sections.

6. Guide in the development of different types of product variations.    3

7. Overall supervision of the department, viz., laboratory, library, and blue    1
   printing sections.

8. Guide in the preparation of quotation for quoting against vendors. Scrutiny of    2
   offers received and offering technical comments.

**Role 5: Assistant Manager—Progress (reports to Manager, Planning)**

1. Ensuring availability of right number of cylinders in all the shops when    3
   required economically.
   Targets:

    (a) Assessment of shop-wise requirement before end July.
    (b) Update the loading report every day.
    (c) Stock-outs not more than twice a month
    (d) Ensure collection of empty cylinders within three days of completion.

2. Initiating and monitoring the progress of spares work orders.    2
   Targets:

    (a) Coordinate with shops and keep the Planning Manager posted on all
        relevant information.
    (b) Develop a good record-keeping system for monitoring the progress of
        spares by mid-August.
    (c) Ensure loading of spares JC's, material to meet the committed delivery
        dates and subsequent follow-up with shop verbal/Inter-office Memos
        (IOMs)
    (d) Monthly status of spares work orders to be prepared.

*(Box contd.)*

*(Box contd.)*

| KPAs | Weightage |
|------|-----------|
| 3. Initiating and monitoring the progress of various stockwork orders. | 3 |

Targets:

   (a) Develop a good record-keeping system by mid-August.
   (b) Maintain reliable records on stock work orders.
   (c) Initiate closure of stock work orders promptly.
   (d) Prepare monthly status report.

| | |
|------|-----------|
| 4. Making heat-treated items available to assembly shops: | 3 |

   (a) Weekly review of the progress at various points and makes a report.
   (b) Arrange to send fortnightly/status report to concerned departments within two days of the succeeding fortnight.
   (c) Efficient follow-up with various departments in connection with heat-treatment and keep Manager Planning posted of relevant information.
   (d) Record of work orders of heat-treatment opening/closure.

| | |
|------|-----------|
| 5. Arrange to dispatch/store credit excess, rejected items, loaned items, and sub-contracted items. | 1 |

Targets:

   (a) Action to be taken within six days of receipt of communication in the normal course.
   (b) Efficient follow-up with parties concerned.

| | |
|------|-----------|
| 6. Attending to administrative, personal problems of employees in the department. | 1 |

Targets:

   (a) Sanctioning leave letters within one day
   (b) To bring to the notice of the manager, grievances, problems of employees in time to take suitable action.

**Role 6: Superintendent-Maintenance (reports to Factory Manager)**

| | |
|------|-----------|
| 1. Ensure uninterrupted major plant facilities like sanitation, water supply, and power in the plant. | 3 |
| 2. Ensure transport services for progress department, senior officers, purchase and medical section, and so forth. | 3 |
| 3. Ensure minimum breakdown on shot blast machines, sheet metal machinery, machine shop, and furnaces. | 3 |
| 4. Housekeeping of the plant in general and positive improvement in illumination level. | 3 |
| 5. Timely erection of new machines and progress on old machinery breakdown and developments, including preventive maintenance procedure. | 2 |
| 6. To bring down reportable accident rate insisting on suitable safety measures and bringing about inter-departmental safety competitions. | 3 |
| 7. Maintaining cordial relations with outside agencies to achieve the above. | 2 |

| KPAs | Weightage |
|---|---|
| **Role 7: Engineer-Manufacturing (reports to Superintendent, Production)** | |
| 1.  Entering the shop in time to mark attendance; confirm full shop attendance. | 2 |
| 2.  Checking breakdowns of machinery, taking immediate action when needed. | 2 |
| 3.  Going through the log for safeguarding the priority of jobs. | 2 |
| 4.  Coordination with other departments to solve daily problems. | 2 |
| 5.  Planning targets in advance and ensuring the availability of necessary tools for projects. | 3 |
| 6.  Supervision and regular contact with subordinates for identifying their work requirements. | 2 |
| 7.  Attending meetings and ensuring implementation of decisions. | 3 |
| 8.  Leaving the necessary reports for the follow-up shifts and confirming the same. | 2 |
| 9.  Discussion with reporting officer about advance plan and priority jobs and other information. | 2 |
| 10. Attending to all inter-office memos. | 2 |

# 3

# Defining and Building Competencies

We have mentioned earlier in Chapters 1 and 2 that the performance of any given individual or performer depends on the individual's competence to efficiently execute the various tasks assigned to him/her. The person's commitment or motivation to do this is reflected in the effort he/she puts in and the organizational support available to help him/her successfully carry out various functions. The competencies required include knowledge, attitudes, skills, and so forth, which are needed for the person to effectively perform various tasks or activities, or KPAs and KRAs. Normally, technological competencies are ensured by corporations because they are aware of their employees' previous work experience, degrees, diplomas, and so forth. There are easy methods of ensuring technological competencies. For example, heart surgeries can only be performed by trained surgeons and software programs can only be written by trained software engineers. However, most jobs at the supervisory and managerial levels require different categories of competencies, including managerial (planning, organizing, mobilizing of resources, systems management, and so forth), behavioral (initiative, creativity, sociability, teamwork, self-control, and so forth), and conceptual (for example, the ability to forecast changes in the economy and their impact on a product a company is planning to make) skills. Competency requirements vary from job to job and from KPA to KPA, and in the same job from time to time. Therefore, to perform a given job well, an individual needs to first be aware of the required competencies and should possess them. Most performance management systems give weightage to such competencies in individual performers and assess the individuals annually. There are organizations that give a higher weightage to competencies and values than to accomplishment of results. It is very essential for every role-holder to be aware of the competencies required in an organization from the beginning of the year and to try to cultivate those that he/she may lack so that he/she emerges as a good performer. Identification and definition of competency is an equally important task like identification of KPA or KRA. Most organizations are impatient to let the employees identify competencies for each KPA or KRA and demonstrate those. They assume that once KRAs or KPAs are identified their job is done. However, several organizations take pains to identify and list the common and critical competencies that their employees need to have. The following are some competencies required by various organizations engaged in PM systems:

## Core or Generic Competencies

1. Technical/functional competencies.
2. Commercial acumen.
3. Interpersonal skills and teamwork.
4. Proactive problem-solving and initiative.
5. Communication skills (listening, clarity of thought and expression, and written and verbal competency).
6. Positive attitude (viewing things positively, being optimistic, not being critical or cynical of everything, having the ability to look at the brighter side of change and various other decisions, policies, innovations, and so forth, and not being over-critical or critical all the time of people, events, and so forth).

## Potential Factors or Competencies

The following are qualities that have become increasingly critical for higher level jobs and are meant to prepare executives to effectively fill such roles as they grow in an organization:

1. Ability to handle higher responsibilities including the following or more:
2. Vision and leadership.

3. Ability to assume responsibility and take decisions.
4. Execution.
5. Change management (openness to change, initiating and managing change).
6. Creativity.

# Values

These include beliefs, behaviors, and actions that need to be exhibited by every employee:

1. Integrity and character, defined as coherence between thought, word, and deed.
2. Ability to speak fearlessly about what one feels (not having one thing in mind and speaking different things to please people or gain advantage of some kind or the other).
3. Ability to keep up promises or verbal commitments (doing what one says).
4. Customer focus.
5. Consistent quality.
6. Commitment to excellence.
7. Concern for people.

Some organizations change their requirements for executives from level to level. Others also change the weightages for KPAs and KRAs versus the competencies or attributes.

A good PMS helps individuals understand the competencies required for them to be successful performers from the beginning of the year and enables them to constantly review their performance, identify their competency gaps, and acquire the required competencies. Unless an employee has all the competencies needed to perform a given set of tasks he/she cannot be successful in accomplishing them, which frequently results in poor achievement of results. Therefore, continuous competency development is a critical requirement of the PM process. However, most employees do not realize this and sometimes unconsciously oppose their organizations' competency identification and development interventions. They seem to assume that competency-building is the exploitation of talent and challenge, sometimes by resisting the efforts of their seniors when they point out competency gaps and provide development opportunities to them. Competency development is a self-initiated effort and it is in the interest of every employee to develop themselves. In the following section, some inputs are provided for such self-management. I hope the reader will appreciate the scope of PMS for self-development and self-management through competency-building and future career growth.

# The Effective Personality

An effective person is one who has a high degree of self-awareness. Such awareness is characterized by a good insight into one's strengths and weaknesses. In addition, effective individuals are constantly searching for opportunities to test themselves in new situations, gain more insights into their own personality, improve their strengths, and overcome their weaknesses.

One simple *model for self-awareness*, which is used widely, is the Johari Window (Luft and Ingham, 1973). Individuals' personalities and psychological worlds (attitudes, values, habits, knowledge, abilities, etc.) can be considered to comprise four parts in terms of their self-awareness and awareness of others. These include the following:

An *open* or *public self*, which consists of those aspects that are known to a person's self and also to others, for example, some of our strengths and peculiarities are known to us as well as to those around us (who keep observing and interacting with us). An individual may be an IT expert and everyone around him/her may know this. A good dancer knows his/her competencies as do those around him/her. A talkative person, an introvert, or a sociable person are all examples of how some of our qualities cannot be hidden and constitute our public self.

Only an individual is aware of his/her *closed* or a *private self* of which others are not aware. For example, one may have several strengths, weaknesses, and habits, which are not known to others because they may not like to talk about those. For instance, most people with rigid religious attitudes and prejudices are not likely to go around sharing their views. Interestingly, modesty also prevents people from sharing their strong points with others. As a result, talents exhibited in the early years go unnoticed in later ones, unless a situation is created where their existence is shared with others and opportunities are created to use them. An HRD manager in a company may have worked in an earlier company as a materials manager and may have done a great job in vendor development. However, since the person has been recruited to head HRD, he/she may never get an opportunity to apply his/her talent in the area of vendor development in the organization.

A *blind spot* refers to the part of individuals of which they are not aware, but of which others are. Some or much of what is perceived as our strengths and inadequacies may not be known to us. In relationship-valuing societies and cultures, such as in Asia, people normally tell you things that they know will please you and refrain from giving negative feedback. In such societies, people may have a sizeable chunk of blind spots. Individuals may take pride in considering themselves as flexible, whereas their behavior may be interpreted or experienced by their subordinates as inconsistent and unreliable (because of such people's constantly changing stands and views due to their creativity, which others may be adversely affected by and may perceive the changing ideas as their inconsistency).

People may have a *dark* or *hidden* part, which neither they nor others are aware of. This is because they have never gotten the opportunity to put themselves to the test and discover what they are capable of. During their entire lifetime, they may get the opportunity to discover only a small part of their potential.

1. Having a large area of blind spots impedes effectiveness.
2. Discovering more of the dark arena helps to bring out latent talent.

3. A high degree of awareness of one's strengths, weaknesses, and qualities helps in making conscious choices and enhances effectiveness.

4. Blind spots can be reduced by seeking feedback from others, accepting it, reflecting on it, and using it to improve oneself.

5. The talents of people who are in their private world to a large extent may not be available to others, since they may not be aware of the former's strengths. Such people may need to enhance their communication skills and let others know their competencies.

6. The dark arena can be reduced by people undertaking new tasks, activities, exploring new methods of working, experimenting, job rotation, and so forth. A high degree of action orientation and experimental and risk-taking attitudes need to be inculcated by such people. Pro-action and initiative are the most important prerequisites for this.

7. Leaders and effective managers and people constantly explore their dark arenas and attempt to reduce their blind spots.

8. 360-degree feedback is an effective tool for reducing blind spots, putting to use hidden talents and capabilities, and initiating actions to discover new areas or competencies.

## OTHER DIMENSIONS OF PERSONAL EFFECTIVENESS

It matters very little whether you are an extrovert or an introvert, whether you are a reserved or socializing type, or whether you are a feeling or intuitive type of person. It is important to be aware of what your qualities are and how they affect you and contribute to the outcome of your actions. In other words, self-awareness is an important component of effectiveness. In addition to a high degree of self-awareness and continuous striving to enhance self-awareness, certain qualities contribute immensely to personal and managerial effectiveness. These include:

1. Action orientation—exploratory orientation.
2. Self-disclosure.

3. Receptivity to feedback.
4. Interpersonal sensitivity.
5. Self-confidence.
6. Internality and inner directedness.
7. Trustworthiness.
8. Inner core values such as honesty, sincerity, and truthfulness.
9. Goal orientation.
10. Drive and passion (for results, innovations, achievement, etc.).

### Exploratory Orientation

People who take the initiative to keep experimenting with new situations are action-oriented and not afraid to make mistakes. They can take risks, are restless in their work, have high activity levels, like variety and change, and are likely to discover more and more of their potential. They keep applying themselves to many situations and actively make things happen. Such people can be called action-oriented explorers. Such explorers can discover more and more of their talents and benefit themselves and their organizations.

### Self-disclosure

People who easily communicate with others about themselves; are frank and open; express their views, opinions, knowledge, and feelings freely, and share their knowledge and personal experiences with others (including subordinates, colleagues, and bosses) can be considered as the self-disclosing type. Such people constantly communicate with others and make an impact on them. This helps in generating data. Such individuals have more of an open and public self than a private one. Without an optimal amount of self-disclosure, we deny others the opportunity to know us and ourselves to get appropriate feedback. Low scorers are private individuals and may have difficulty in discovering themselves fully. At least it may be difficult for them to see themselves fully from the eyes of others. Such people make a limited impact on others.

## Receptivity to Feedback

Those who seek feedback constantly or periodically, and try to find out about the impact they and their behavior has on others; those who take criticism sportingly, examine themselves and their behavior and try to learn from feedback, and those who value what others say about them, their actions, and behavior learn from feedback. They are likely to develop themselves and become more effective in the process. Those who are not willing to listen to the views, opinions and feedback from others and those who become defensive and are closed to feedback are likely to develop less. Receptivity to feedback is therefore an essential element of managerial effectiveness and growth.

## Perceptiveness

Those who are sensitive to the cues and nonverbal communication of others, those who are perceptive of the impact of their behavior on others and are therefore sensitive about not saying and doing things that may not be appropriate, those who are sensitive to the needs and feelings of others, and those who make effort to understand other people or groups before saying anything are perceptive individuals. Such people are likely to utilize their time properly and make an impact on others. This makes them effective in most managerial settings.

## Self-confidence

This refers to the self-concept or self-worth that individuals carry with themselves all the time. Confident people are able to accomplish many things. Self-confidence enables them to make use of their strengths, and to be open to feedback and experimentation. Self-confidence puts a glow on people's personalities and makes them attempt to do things and take risks. This is known as "approach orientation" by confident people and "avoidance orientation" by less confident ones.

## Internality and Inner Directedness

This relates to people's tendency to do things on their own initiative and direction rather than merely doing them to comply with others' instructions or role expectations. Inner directed people are dictated by their inner selves and are likely to put more of their talents to use.

## Trustworthiness

Trustworthiness or reliability and sincerity are hallmarks of effective people. They honor their promises and make statements they always mean and honor. Trustworthiness enhances the reliability of a person and creates a healthy society. It enhances confidence and both the inner and outer image of the individual.

## Inner Core Values such as Honesty, Sincerity, and Truthfulness

These are values that give direction to life and also a sense of joy. They are essential for creating a healthy society, which is essential for healthy living.

### Goal-orientation

Goal-oriented people are clear about what they want to do, where they want to put in their efforts, and consequently, reduce wastage of time. Goal-oriented individuals are likely to remain focused. If one knows what one wants to achieve, one has already come half way in achieving one's goal. Most people do not know what they want to achieve and, as a result, remain unfocused and waste a large part of their life.

### Drive and Passion

These include a passion for results, innovation, achievement, and so forth. Goal-directedness gives direction and drive gives intensity. It reduces time and enhances the value of life. People with drive and passion can achieve the same things in less time than those with less of these attributes who have more time to do other things.

These are just a few qualities and attitudes that make an effective person. They are by no means exhaustive. There may be many more such as qualities including emotional intelligence and maturity, and psychosocial maturity which also contribute to effectiveness.

## PMS: A Help for Management and Enhancement of Personal Effectiveness

Arising out of our educational system is the belief that personality development is a one-time effort; that it can be achieved through something like a crash course. However, there are no quick fixes in personal growth. The first step is to know oneself. The key is self-awareness—being alive to one's self, and to one's thoughts, behavior, and motivation through constant introspection, which is a lifelong commitment.

In Daniel Goleman's *Working with Emotional Intelligence*, emotional intelligence does not merely mean "being nice," but at times means bluntly confronting someone with the uncomfortable but consequential truth they have been avoiding. It means managing feelings so that they are expressed appropriately and effectively, and enabling people to work together smoothly toward their common goals.

The conditions for "personal effectiveness" in any given setting, therefore point toward an increasing need for the following:

1. *Self-awareness:* A basic emotional skills involves being able to recognize different feelings and giving a name to them. Equally important is to be aware of the relationship between thoughts, feelings and actions.

   *Specifically, it relates to:*

   • Emotional awareness: recognizing one's emotions and their effect.
   • Accurate self-assessment: knowing one's strengths and limits.
   • Self-confidence: a strong sense of one's self-worth and capabilities (Goleman, 1998).

2. *Empathy:* Getting the measure of a situation and being able to act appropriately requires an understanding of the feelings of others. Sensitivity/empathy helps us share each other's concerns and goals, and walk together toward a common goal of well-being instead of confronting and colliding all the time (Goleman, 1998).

3. *Ability to express emotions:* The ability to identify emotions in one's physical stages, feelings, and thought; the ability to identify emotions of others, in designs and works of art, etc. through language, sound, appearance, and behavior; the ability to express emotions and needs related to those feelings, the ability to discriminate between accurate and inaccurate or honest and dishonest expressions of feeling. (Singh, 2001)

4. *Ability to regulate emotions:* This refers to the ability to be open to feelings, both pleasant and unpleasant; to engage or detect from an emotion, depending upon its judged utility; to monitor emotions in relation to himself/herself and others, such as recognizing how clear, typical, influential, or reasonable they are; to manage his/her own emotions as well as those of others by moderating negative emotions and enhancing positive ones; to build rapport with various segments of society and create a network of people (Singh, 2001).

A precondition for personal effectiveness is increased self-awareness. But only understanding one's self does not make a person effective.

## SELF-MANAGEMENT THROUGH PMS

In his article "Managing Self" (Harvard Business Review, 1999) Peter Drucker recommends that while building a life of excellence one should ask oneself the following questions:

1. What are my strengths? Know what you are good at. A person can only perform from strengths. One cannot build performance on weaknesses, let alone on something one cannot do at all. Analyzing feedback is the only way

in which you can identify your strengths. Write down the expected outcomes for your key decisions and actions and, 9 to 12 months later, compare them with the results. Place yourself where your strengths can produce results. Work to improve your strengths. Avoid intellectual arrogance— acquire skills as required. Remedy bad habits and be careful of your manners. Know what *not* to do—identify your areas of incompetence and avoid them.

2. How do I perform? As any personality trait, *how* a person performs is a given, just as *what* a person is good at or not good at. A reader prefers reading reports before meetings and discussions (for example, late US President Kennedy). A listener likes facing it and talking about the matter instead of reading and writing (for example, late US President Roosevelt). A reader cannot become fully a listener and vice versa.

3. How do I learn? A person may learn by reading, writing, doing, talking, listening to, or with a combination of these. One must always use methods that work. Do not try to change yourself too much. Instead, work harder to improve the way you perform.

4. What are my values? Ethics require that you ask yourself *what kind of person you want to see in the mirror in the morning.* Your personal value system should be compatible with that of the organization in which you work. Typical conflicts to avoid include an organization's commitment to new versus old employees, incremental improvements or risky "break-throughs," emphasis on short-term results versus long-term goals, quality versus quantity, and growth versus sustenance. In other words, *values* are, and should be, the *ultimate test* of your compatibility with an organization.

5. Where do I belong? Mathematicians, musicians, and cooks are usually mathematicians, musicians, and cooks by the time they are four or five years old. Highly gifted people must realize early where they belong, or rather, where they do *not* belong. Successful careers are *not* planned. They develop when people are prepared for opportunities because

they know their strengths, their method of work, and their values. Knowing where one belongs can transform an ordinary person—hardworking and competent but otherwise mediocre—into an outstanding performer.

6. What should I contribute? Given my strengths, methods, and values, what is a great contribution to what needs to be done? What results need to be achieved to make a difference? It is rarely possible to look too far ahead—*18 months* is ideal for achieving meaningful results and making a difference. Set stretched and difficult goals that are reachable. Gain visible and measurable outcomes. Define your course of action— what is to be done, where and how to start, and what are the goals, objectives and deadlines that need to be set

7. Responsibility of relationships: Bosses are neither the "title" on the Organization chart nor the "function." To adapt to what makes the boss more *effective* is the secret of "managing the boss." Working relationships are as much based on people as on work —co-workers are human and individuals like you. Taking the responsibility for communicating how you perform reduces personality conflicts. Organizations are built on trust between people who *understand* one another, which does not necessarily mean that they like each other.

Development requires acquisition of competencies. These competencies may be in terms of knowledge, attitudes, values, and skills. They may be in technical, management or human relation areas, or in conceptual and visionary thinking. As technologies, environments, and the profiles of organizations and people keep changing, enterprises are continuously faced with new challenges. Employees in supervisory and managerial positions need to face these challenges much more than those at lower levels. To face the challenge of the changing nature of jobs, to contribute one's best to an organization, and to pave the way for their career growth, supervisors and managers need to keep acquiring and sharpening their competencies. Therefore, continuous "competency development" is a "necessity." Most employees do not recognize this fact and take their development for granted. Every job provides learning opportunities for an interested individual. However, these opportunities may go unnoticed or unutilized if the individual does not learn. Organizations can be viewed as excellent learning communities for those interested in development.

## CONDITIONS FOR DEVELOPMENT

For individuals to grow, the following conditions should be met or ensured:

1. They should be interested in developing themselves.
2. The organization should value employees' development and learning.
3. Employees should be clear about the direction in which they can develop.
4. They should make clear choices about the direction in which they would like to grow and develop.
5. They should make an attempt to become aware of the strengths and weaknesses that will help them move toward that direction.
6. Employees should be able to identify opportunities within and outside the organization for their development, including opportunities for overcoming their weaknesses and increasing their strengths.
7. They should identify mechanisms for using these opportunities and the support they need from their superiors and others for their development.
8. They should make focused efforts to develop.
9. They should review their progress periodically with the help of other people.
10. Reporting officers should enable an appropriate emotional and professional climate for the development of their juniors. While it is difficult to definitely identify conditions that will enable such a climate, openness, frankness and free exchange of opinions, mutuality, support and trust are likely to help.

Thus, promoting employee development is a function of employees and their reporting managers. Interpersonal feedback, communication, and periodic reviews are mechanisms that help employees to develop. However, these mechanisms may be dysfunctional if they are not used properly or if used in a ritualistic manner. A genuine concern for employees' development and a desire to help them are required. Reporting managers who believe that they are helping themselves by assisting their juniors to develop can facilitate development of a sense of independence and mutuality in their units.

Periodic reviews and counseling sessions are useful instruments for establishing mutuality—a condition essential for employees' development. Some of the skills required for development and counseling are outlined in the following section.

A high degree of initiative and activity makes people explorers. They apply themselves in new situations, do their work in different ways, experiment, take risks, and in the process *discover more and more of their own potential. Such individuals tend to reduce the* dark *of the* unknown *part of their personalities.*

A high degree of self-disclosure enables people to generate data about themselves for others to observe, recognize, react to, and evaluate and provide opportunities for themselves to make an impact on others. A managerial role requires individuals to make an impact on others, and without self-disclosure at an optimal level they may not be able to make this impact.

To assess the nature of the impact they have made and discover more of their strengths and weaknesses, individuals need to be receptive to feedback from others.

To be effective, they also need to have interpersonal sensitivity and tact and to understand the moods and feelings of others to increase the effectiveness of their own interpersonal and communication.

Proactively, self-disclosure, being receptive to feedback, and perceptiveness constitute the four important components of personal effectiveness. A high degree of personal effectiveness enhances managerial effectiveness.

## PMS AND SELF-MANAGEMENT

When taken seriously, PMS can be an effective tool to enhance one's personal and managerial effectiveness. Organizations are platforms for people to apply, test, and develop their talent. KPAs and KRAs or any tasks or activities we perform require continuous application of our competencies. Organizations that give scope to employees to have some KPAs or KRAs on their own and the freedom to try out new methods are providing significant opportunities for their employees to apply and develop talent.

Performance planning is the time when managers or a performers can plan for self-discovery by taking initiatives and trying out tasks they have not performed so a far, or in using methods they have not used. Most organizations give scope to their employees to take risks within certain limits and discover themselves. Initiative and exploration are of use to organizations. In such circumstances, employees can discover a great deal about themselves.

Performance analysis, conducted periodically and discussed with seniors, colleagues, or juniors, provides people the opportunity to discover hitherto unnoticed strengths or areas of improvement.

Performance-related conversations and review discussions help in the receiving and giving of feedback and contribute to individuals' development.

Self-appraisal used in most PMS formats, if taken seriously, provides food for thought and helps to enhance self-discovery and self-awareness.

Discussions on competencies listed by organizations and performance-related conversations help to enhance employees' awareness and facilitate their plans to cultivate competencies.

## SELF-APPRAISAL IN SELF-MANAGEMENT

Self-appraisal has an important role to play in employees' development. As we have seen in the previous chapters, development needs to be self-directed. Individuals are not likely to learn and develop themselves unless they make a conscious effort to identify possible directions of growth and continuously monitor this growth. For employees to develop their capabilities to perform particular functions associated with their roles, they must realize the importance of these functions in their roles as well as the links between learning to perform the functions and their future growth in (or outside) their organization. They must also know how they are performing these functions, their own capabilities and those they lack. They can discover this by performing these functions and receiving feedback from others about their performance levels and capability indicators. They can use this feedback and reflect on their experience to finally identify their capabilities and those they lack. They can then make plans to develop these capabilities with the assistance of their supervisors and others in the organization. Thus, individuals are always the focal point in determining their own development and improving their performance. Organizations provide a supporting environment and other facilities required for this development. It is in this context, that self-appraisal becomes an important step in the development and improvement of performance.

Self-appraisal should be a continuous process. More than their reporting officers, employees should take steps to continuously assess their performance, identify their strengths and weaknesses, keep a record of the efforts they make as well as their success and failure while performing different functions. They should also analyze the causes for their success and failures. While this process should go on continuously, individuals also should devote some time to reviewing their efforts, to assimilate and identify consistencies in their successes or failures, and prepare their development plans. The performance management period provides a formal opportunity for individuals to review their performance and growth over the entire year.

The following can be considered as the purpose for self-appraisal:

1. To provide an opportunity for employees to recapitulate:

   • The various activities they have undertaken in relation to different functions associated with their roles.

- Their achievements and failures with regard to these.
- The capabilities they demonstrated and those they felt they lacked in carrying out activities and the various managerial and behavioral dimensions they demonstrated over the year.

2. To identify their own development needs and plan their development in the organization by identifying the support they require from their reporting officers and others in the organization.
3. To communicate to their reporting officers their contribution, accomplishments, and reflections to enable them to view their appraisees' performance in the right perspective and assess it objectively. (This is a necessary preparation for performance review discussions and performance improvement plans.)
4. To initiate an organization-wide process of annual review and reflection to strengthen self-initiated development of managerial effectiveness.

Self-appraisal should start at the end of the performance period just before the performance review discussion takes place. It should start with the appraisees taking up their KPAs and objectives for the period and reflecting on their achievements and failures. They should have with them the notes they have maintained about events, critical incidents, and reflections during the period and use these to recapitulate their contributions as well as successes and failures. They can analyze their performance by using the guidelines suggested in the next chapter, "Performance Analysis." They can also assess themselves by using the organization's rating scales, if any. In addition, they should make brief notes of their reflections in their appraisal forms to communicate these to their appraisers.

The appraisees should also follow this process on behavioral and managerial dimensions. In addition, they should make suggestions about their identified developmental needs. The self-appraisal forms completed in this process should then be passed on to their reporting officers for their assessment and planning for performance review and counseling discussions. Appraisers should treat such self-appraisal reports received from their appraisees seriously. Appraisers normally do not get enough time to observe each of their subordinates closely. More often, they tend to form impressions about their subordinates on the basis of one or two of their striking failures. Sometimes, one or two successes may also leave a highly positive impression. It is necessary for appraisers to review every aspect of their appraisees' performance as well as behavioral and managerial qualities if they want to understand them and contribute to their development. The only way appraisers can get relevant information about their appraisees and their performance is by asking them about it. Data provided by appraisees through self-appraisal serves this purpose. Some appraisers are worried that their subordinates will only highlight their accomplishments and strengths, but not their failures and weaknesses. This perception is often wrong. However, even when it is true, appraisers do not need to worry because their appraisees have every right to highlight their accomplishments. Appraisers have the obligation to take cognizance of these in their appraisal. If there are failures and weaknesses the appraiser perceives, these can be pointed out during appraisal discussions. It should also be remembered that when appraisees only highlight their strengths and accomplishments, they are raising the expectations of their bosses of them for the subsequent period when more challenging goals can be set for them.

Therefore, self-appraisal can be a useful component of a development-oriented performance appraisal system if viewed seriously by appraisees and appraisers and used appropriately to generate a greater understanding of the former.

## Self-Appraisal for Managerial Effectiveness

There are organizations where "self-appraisal" does not find place in the performance appraisal system. Often a small space is provided for the performer to write down his accomplishments or tasks assigned and results achieved. This cannot be called self-appraisal. In such cases executives often ask what should be done.

*The author would like to assert that self-appraisal can be done independent of the performance management systems. Every manager should develop a discipline of reviewing his/her own performance as a manager at least once a year.* Such reviews should be systematic and truthful. As no one else is involved in this process, the manager can say to himself/herself things that he/she may not like to share with others. Such a self-appraisal process may focus on the following questions:

1. What have I accomplished in the last one year?
2. How do I rate my accomplishments or contributions as against last year, and as against all that was possible this year?
3. What contributed to my performance? What factors helped me and what factors prevented me from doing better?
4. What are my own competencies and attitudes that helped me perform better and that prevented me from giving my best?
5. How are my attitudes affecting my growth and development as a competent manager?
6. What opportunities have I missed during the last year and how do I propose to use them this year if I face similar situations?
7. What support do I need from my seniors and from the organization to be able to make a better contribution?
8. What support do I need to develop my own potential and capabilities for the future?
9. What are my action plans for next year to become a more effective manager?
10. What do I want to communicate to my superiors to help them understand me better and also to help them to empower me for better performance?

# Appendix

Self-Appraisal: A Format

Name:

Period: From　　　　　To

| KPA for the period | Activities and targets | Accomplish-ments | Facilitating factors | Inhibiting factors | Action plans (Development actions, support requirements) |
|---|---|---|---|---|---|
|  |  |  |  |  |  |
|  |  |  |  |  |  |
|  |  |  |  |  |  |

# 4

# Performance Analysis for Individual and Organization Development

Let us go back to Raman's case. He had the following KPAs:

1. Learning from class teachers
2. Working hard at home
3. Learning at coaching classes
4. Doing extra studies

Let us assume that during the year, a few things happened. There was a change in the teachers' department. The new math teacher was not very competent, and the students understood very little from her and considered attending classes a waste of time. Raman tried hard to ask questions and seek clarifications, but the teacher considered him as a troublemaker for the questions he asked. The question paper for the final exam was leaked and the examination center where he was appearing had to re-conduct the examination because the examiners were very strict for that particular set of centers due to what appeared in newspapers. While studying at home, Raman targeted five hours on week days and eight hours on holidays. He could not do this because there were power cuts most of the time due to which he got very distracted. He took some time to find alternative places where he could go and study for his examinations. In addition, at the end of the year, there was a death in his family and he had to visit the place where the death had happened with his parents. However, he carried his books with him and solved question papers, and also took the help of his father while traveling. The question papers in science were considered very tough that year. Raman had prepared well and whenever his new teacher was not cooperative he called up his old teacher who was in another city and took her guidance. He took also the help of his coaching teacher whenever he had difficulty in understanding anything in class. The mathematics paper was easy and he had got 100 percent marks, while the science examination was tough and many students complained that they had been asked out-of-syllabus questions. Raman fared very low in the science subjects, which pulled down his final percentage. With all his efforts, he was only able to get 85 percent and was not able to get admission in any of his dream colleges.

If we have to manage performance, we need to understand what this constitutes. Comprehending the constituents of performance by breaking it into various elements and then understanding the factors that cause performance is called performance analysis. Just as we analyze various compounds and chemicals by subjecting them to tests in laboratory conditions, performance analysis is also a process of analyzing various constituents of performance as it occurs in natural settings. The performance of individuals, dyads, teams, and organizations can be isolated and analyzed. Just as organizations conduct a strengths, weaknesses, opportunities, and threats (SWOT) analysis of their performance and plan strategies to improve it, we need to do a SWOT analysis of every individual's performance and plan strategies to improve it. Such an analysis should be done with total transparency and sincerity if this performance analysis has to be of use. Performance analysis is an important component of appraisal. Any rating given to performers should only be after a thorough analysis of his/her performance. To analyze performance, it is necessary to follow the performance equation mentioned earlier.

## The Performance Equation

Individual performance = Ability × Motivation × Organizational Support + or − Chance Factors

This equation implies that any given individual's performance in a given period and a given role or job (or set of tasks that constitute the role) is a function of his/her competence to do that job or role or set of tasks associated with that role, multiplied by his interest or motivation to do that job and the support he/she gets to do that job during that period. It is moderated by chance or environmental factors.

Performance management involves defining performance, understanding the competencies required to do the job or various tasks associated with the job, developing the competencies, creating the motivation needed, or putting hard work or effort to do the job and getting all the support needed to do that job or series of tasks associated with that job or role.

Performance analysis involves analyzing or understanding the various factors contributing to performance (positively or negatively) for a given period and managing them to enhance performance in the subsequent period.

It involves understanding, at first, the tasks associated with the role, setting standards, and measuring the achievements against these standards. This deals with the right side of the performance equation.

It also involves identifying the competencies needed to perform each of the tasks, ascertaining the level to which each of the tasks have been performed, understanding the reasons for good or poor performance of each of the tasks, and analyzing them into ability factors or competence factors, motivational factors, and organizational support factors.

Performance analysis also involves identification of factors within the control of the individual, his/her seniors, and the organization.

A good performance analysis lays the foundation for making good performance improvement plans and ensuring improvements in performance.

If subjectivity in appraisals has to be reduced, the reporting manager should not only assess the level of performance achieved by the performer, but also understand and assess the conditions under which the performer has accomplished his/her tasks. The reporting manager should know if the performer could have done better with more effort or with some more control over certain things he/she has done. The reporting manager should also know the nature and extent of effort put in by the performer. He/she should know the difficulties faced by the performer and also the extent to which the performer is aware of his/her own strengths and weaknesses in relation to his/her performance in different tasks. The reporting manager should then use this understanding and knowledge to reinforce the strengths of the performer, help him/her recognize his/her weak points, determine the support to be given, and identify developmental needs as well as help the performer in identifying KPAs and targets for the next period. Thus, performance analysis can be considered as the heart of the appraisal system. This becomes clear when we see how it forms the basis for appraisal ratings, counseling discussions, identification of developmental needs, and action plans.

## OBJECTIVES

Performance analysis should lead to the following:

1. Identification of the factors that have helped the performer reach the level of performance he/she has achieved in relation to various KPAs and targets and various other functions associated with his/her job. These may be called "facilitating factors."
2. Identification of the factors that have prevented the performer from doing better or those that have hindered his/her performance may be called "hindering factors."
3. Identification of factors (from those given earlier) that the performer can do something about (to retain if they are facilitators or reduce and eliminate if they hinder), about which the reviewing officer or somebody else in the organization can do something about, and about which not much can be done would suggest action plans for the performer as well as for the reporting manager.
4. Identification of developmental needs for better performance on critical functions associated with the present role can be done.

5. A better understanding of the performer, his/her role requirements, and the situation in which he/she is working and also sharing with him the expectations and understanding of the reporting manager can increase communication between them.

## METHODOLOGY

The following steps should be followed to conduct performance analysis:

1. After discussions on KPAs, objectives, and other dimensions with the reporting officer, the performer should periodically keep reflecting about how well he/she is progressing in his/her work and in relation to KPAs and other dimensions.

2. During the performance period, whenever the employee experiences success or feels helped in his/her performance, he/she should note this down on paper (or a diary). In noting this, the focus should be on the factors that are helping him/her do well and how these are facilitating his/her performance. A brief mention is enough as reminders for him/her in the final performance analysis.

3. Similarly, whenever he/she experiences failure, runs into difficulties, or feels that he/she is prevented from doing better, he/she should note the factors that are causing this. (It is a part of the managerial role to continuously keep communicating such factors to one's reporting officer and take his/her help to overcome these.) However, this should be noted somewhere for the annual review.

4. At the end of the performance period, the performer should consider his/her performance on each of the KPAs and other dimensions. Taking into consideration the effort he/she has put in, the difficulties he/she experienced, the results he/she achieved and the context in which these were achieved, he/she should rate himself/herself on a rating scale (or at least categorize his/her performance as excellent, good, average, poor, and so forth.)

5. After assigning himself/herself of the rating, he/she should start listing all the factors that have helped him/her in accomplishing whatever he/she did, in detail. Similarly, he/she should list all the factors that have prevented him/her from doing better or were constraints on his/her performance. In listing these factors, he/she should take the help of the notes he/she had maintained during the year (steps 2 and 3). He/she should go through each item in his/her KPAs to make the list exhaustive. (While KPAs are helpful for performance analysis, the performer should go beyond KPAs and look at every aspect of his/her work and list the facilitating and inhibiting factors.)

6. After listing the facilitating and hindering factors exhaustively, the performer should then classify these factors into the following categories:

• *Facilitating Factors*

(a) Personal or individual facilitating factors (FIS): All the factors that are attributable to the performer, his/her abilities, efforts, etc. (for example, knowledge of job, interpersonal competence, previous experience, initiative, hard work, and so forth).

(b) Facilitating factors attributable to the reporting officer (FROs): All the factors that are attributable to the reporting officer (for example, fast decision-making, staff support, delegation, guidance, approachability, and so forth).

(c) Facilitating factors attributable to the organization and its systems (FOS): All the factors that are a part of the organization, its structure, policies, procedures, systems, and so forth (for example, flexible policies, good work conditions and control systems, open climate, accountability, collaboration from other departments, support from reviewing officers, and so forth).

(d) Facilitating factors attributable to the subordinate (FS): Factors attributable to the performer's subordinates (for example, hard work by them, motivation, cooperation, not taking leave, punctuality, high ability, and so forth).

(e) Facilitating factors attributable to the external environment (FE): Those that are not a part of these four categories and that are attributable to the larger socio-economic, political, and other conditions of the environment external to the organization, for example, liberalization of policies by the government, support provided by newspapers, co-operative government officials, improved economic situation, poor image of competitors, and so forth).

- *Inhibiting Factors*
The same categorization as given earlier:

(a) Inhibiting factors attributable to the individual (II): Poor memory, family problems, need to devote attention to children's education, poor health, problems of expression and language, and so forth.

(b) Inhibiting factors attributable to the reporting officer: Delays in decision-making, lack of guidance and direction, busy boss, ambiguous goals, allotment of tasks on an ad hoc basis, and adequate facilities not being provided.

(c) Inhibiting factors attributable to subordinate staff: Lack of cooperation, union problems, absenteeism, slow work, poor capabilities, close supervision required by them, and so forth.

(d) Inhibiting factors attributable to the environment (IEs): Sudden changes in the economic, social or political climate, delays in supplies, unexpected events affecting work, strikes, and so forth.

(e) Inhibiting factors attributable to the organization and its system (IOs): Policies like unplanned transfers, changes in top management, introduction of new technologies that demand time, and so forth.

7. After such an analysis, individuals (performers) should reflect about individual facilitating factors they would like to maintain or further strengthen and the inhibiting factors that they would like to overcome in the future. They should think about the mechanisms they would like to adopt to improve their strengths and overcome their weaknesses. They may also think about the support required from their reporting officers to implement their plans.

8. The individual should also reflect on the support that could be extended by his/her reporting officer to maintain external facilitating factors and reduce or weaken inhibiting ones.

9. He/she should then give his/her performance analysis to his/her reporting officer for his/her comments, additions to the factors identified, and performance review and counseling discussions. The performance analysis projects the achievements/contributions of the performer, his/her failures, and factors contributing to both of these. This analysis also communicates to the reporting officer the difficulties experienced by the person while engaged in various activities (PAs) during the year.

## USING PERFORMANCE ANALYSIS FOR COUNSELING AND IDENTIFICATION OF DEVELOPMENT NEEDS

Performance analysis done in the manner outlined earlier helps in counseling and identifying development needs as well as in planning action for improving performance by removing blocks being experienced by a performer. By adding to the factors identified by the performer, the reporting manager communicates the attention he/she has been paying to the performer and his/her role. By adding to the individual facilitators and inhibitors, the reporting manager is contributing to an increase in the self-awareness of the performer through a process of feedback. Recognition of strengths not identified by the performer gives positive strokes when the reporting manager communicates these.

Agreeing to the strengths already identified by the performer also increases the awareness of his/her strong points. Disagreements should lead to discussion during counseling sessions in which the reporting manager is likely to change his/her perception of the performer or the performer may get new insights. Adding to the weak points through a process of feedback may help the performer explore areas he/she needs to improve. Disagreements about some personal inhibiting factors may also help the employee develop self-awareness.

The reporting manager need not write everything on the form, just as the performer does not need to do so. Only brief points should be written as guides for discussion. These forms should remain with the performer and the reporting manager. They need not go to the reviewing office and should not go to the personnel department.

While counseling, the reporting manager and the performer should try to understand each other's expectations, difficulties and perceptions, and grow close in the process of planning to improve their performance. In this process, they may also identify development needs in the performer in areas where he/she needs to acquire capabilities. Some of these development needs may have to be attended to by the training division or the HRD department through training programs, job rotation, etc. Other development needs may require proactive action on the part of the reporting manager in the form of additional guidance, on the job training and discussions with the performer. Some of these required actions may require self-study and development by the individual.

Performance analysis should provide the basis for all of these. An example of how performance analysis data provides information about facilitating and inhibiting factors for a variety of actions at the performer, reporting manager and organizational levels is provided later in the chapter.

# PMS for Organization Development

PMS as an HRD tool, if designed and implemented properly, results in multiple advantages. This chapter focuses on PMS as a talent management tool. It explains the multiple dimensions of PMS in promoting a performance culture, a discipline of planning, talent utilization, upward learning, human capital building, on-boarding, integration and assimilation, and organization development (OD). This chapter presentation outlines the essential elements a PMS should have to serve as an OD and change management tool. It draws from various contemporary experiences of Indian corporations in different sectors. Some metrics for scoring and enhancing the value of PMS are also highlighted.

Most performance management systems across the world seem to have one or more of the following components:

1. Performance planning through KPAs or KRAs
2. Competencies and competency definitions
3. Rating scales for assessment
4. Performance review discussion (PRD) or performance coaching
5. Identification of developmental needs
6. Performance analysis
7. Self-appraisal
8. Appraisal or assessment by seniors or Supervising managers
9. Potential assessment
10. Recommendations for recognition and rewards

One of the reasons for the failure of performance appraisal systems across the world is an overemphasis on them as objective performance measurement tools. A deep look into the theory of numbers and of scaling indicates that measuring the performance of managers and supervisors by using numbers and treating them as the properties of an interval scale (additive, multiplicative, subtractive, and divisive) has a serious flaw. When two departmental managers are assessing their juniors, each one of them is using his/her own frame of reference and the circumstances under which each manager or employee functions are not often comparable by virtue of the function and other factors associated with the work. For example, the circumstances under which a development R&D manager performs in pharmaceutical organizations are entirely different than those under which a personnel manager or marketing manager functions. Yet we try to compare ratings in distributing incentives, attempt to apply a normal probability curve, etc.

No two numbers are comparable in appraisals. The numbers in performance appraisals do not follow any rules except those of the nominal scales. However much a company may try to promote objectivity, it should be recognized that at best the numbers assigned by each reporting manager follow "ordinal scales." We cannot say with confidence that a rating of 4 assigned on a 5-point scale by a production chief is indicative of the same performance level as a rating of 4 assigned by a marketing chief, or for that matter two marketing chiefs operating in two regions, for their juniors. The ratings depend on many factors—the supervisor or rater, his/her previous background, personality, expectations, the performer (assessee) and his/her background, the way the goals are set, the level of the goals, the expectations of the assessor from the performer, the chemistry with which they started setting goals, the culture of the organization, etc. No two numbers are comparable. We cannot say the a person who gets a 68 rating on a 100-point system is definitely superior to another who gets a rating of 64, especially if the 64 is in a setting where the performer faced significant odds (including perhaps those of his supervisor). Yet we treat these as sacred and use them to fit into normal probability, add, subtract, multiply, and calculate incentives, etc. I think it is fundamentally wrong to fit qualities in quantities and use these for anything beyond a discussion or analysis.

By reflecting on this and various other experiences in my work on performance appraisals, I would like to suggest the following:

1. Ratings in appraisals are notional and at best should be used for discussion to integrate performance on a number of non-additive parameters (such as adding their achievement of sales targets for regional sales executives, the percentage increase in their customer base, how well they have developed their juniors, and how much they have followed their organizations' various systems). *These cannot and should not be used to force fit ratings into a normal curve blindly or determine incentives mathematically.* At best, they can be used for discussion and review of performance. Ratings are poison, but they may be inevitable side-products of the performance process. However, they should not become the primary preoccupation of appraisals.

2. Performance should be assessed against expectations, which can be changed during the course of employees' performance with the availability of new information, data, and challenges. Expectation sharing and reviews are the most important part of performance management.

3. It is high time we drop the term appraisal and use the term "management." Management is broader and encompasses many factors in a system. It includes planning, development, improvement, recognition, and so forth. Those who prefer to be even more focused can use terms such as PMS, PDS, Performance Improvement Program (PIP), and so forth (see comparison between PAS and PMS; Rao, 2003).

4. Merely changing the title does not help—the spirit needs to be enhanced. This can be done by taking a new look at the potential of PMS and by using it for objectives other than appraisals, generation of numbers in percentages, and so forth.

5. Good performance should be rewarded. But what is good performance should be understood from the beginning by each individual and there should be a shared understanding of what rewardable performance is and what is not by performers and their superiors. This understanding should take place at the beginning of the performance period and not at the time rewards are decided on.

6. Small rewards and recognitions should be encouraged and supervisors should have autonomy to recognize and reward the performance of their performing employees. This may constitute a significant part of the compensation (5–10 percent) of juniors. Recognition should take place all through the performance period and not be limited to annual stock-taking or performance reviews.

7. Annual review of performance should be conducted by using innovative methods and not become a part of life. Such reviews need not necessarily result in numbers being assigned to individuals.

## MULTIPLE OBJECTIVES OF PMS

PMS can have multiple objectives. These include the following:

1. Enabling continuous improvement in employees' performance.
2. Developing the discipline of planning work and managing time and talent.
3. Ensuring role clarity.
4. Recognizing strengths and areas needing improvement in relations to performance by identifying development needs to enhance performance.
5. Building competence among individuals, teams and organization as a whole.
6. Establishing a data base for rewards, promotions, recognition and motivation.
7. Having an insight into self because a high self-awareness is essential for better leadership and managerial effectiveness.
8. Seniors-juniors or bosses-subordinates developing mutuality and respect for each other.
9. Developing problem-solving capabilities in employees.
10. Inculcating a learning culture.
11. Enabling seniors to learn from juniors, and vice versa.
12. Providing mentoring and coaching support to employees and effecting improvement in their performance.
13. Preparing employees for competition and continuous change.
14. Conducting objective assessment of the employees' performance and generating data about them for various HR decisions such as rewards, rotation, recognition, higher responsibilities, and so forth.
15. Integrating and aligning the work of individuals and their teams with organizational goals and tasks.

However, these are not mutually exclusive and can overlap. Organizations understandably often tend to emphasize non-essentials and stress on the short term to long term. Often, there is an undue stress on objectivity and rewards as though employees work all the year round for annual rewards and recognition only. By linking PMS with rewards and recognition, most organizations undervalue individuals' interest in work and create politics in organizations. In fact, PMS sometimes seems to create politics and de-motivation or the reverse of what it is intended for. This takes place by organizations selectively rewarding a few and ignoring many, awarding rewards once an year rather than continuously, and taking away power and authority from supervising line managers and concentrating it in the hands of a few HR managers and the top management. This does the greatest damage to the cause of good PMS.

I have come to the conclusion that the most important objectives of the PMS should be the following:

*To enable each individual employee to plan his/her work for the entire year (or a part of it as is possible in an organization), to ensure that he/she undertakes productive activities, utilizing his/her competencies in the best possible manner and contributing to the achievement of departmental or organizational goals and results, while at the same time constantly learning and developing one's own capabilities and enjoying work.*

The most important parts of this objective include the following:

1. Work planning and accountability: If you plan your work you will be more accountable in your work. You are also likely to enjoy it out of a sense of accomplishment. Work planning also ensures alignment with organizational goals as individuals plan their work in the context of organizational priorities.
2. Competency utilization: You are able to undertake work or at least give adequate opportunities to yourself to utilize your competencies.
3. Workplace learning as a tool of continuous learning and development: This is the greatest reward you can get from your work. When you learn and grow, your competencies are built and you enhance your own brand value. If you grow

beyond your role and if the organization cannot accommodate, you can always find other opportunities.
4. Build mutuality and teamwork for work satisfaction, motivation, and self-respect.

The process of implementing PMS may also ensure additional objectives to be met. The processes should include the following:

1. Participative planning.
2. Periodic planning and review.
3. Periodic analysis of performance blocks and opportunities.
4. Collective planning.
5. Collective ownership where required.
6. Promotion of competencies, values and desired culture by making these a part of planning.
7. Participative review and learning from each other.
8. Mechanism of monitoring performance and implementation plans and ensuring organizational support.

Therefore, PMS can be great tool if designed comprehensively and implemented in all earnestness. It should have little place for politics and manipulation.

# Performance Planning

## INVEST TWENTY AND DIRECT 2,000 TO 20,000 PROGRAM

Recently, I was working on the PMS for a company outside India. I was asked to help them implement a new system they had just designed. It is an infrastructure company with many general managers and senior general managers at the helm. I asked 25 of those attending the workshop to answer the following four questions:

1. To what extent did you have a clearly set work plan for the last six months?

2. To what extent did the seniors with whom you work share the same understanding of your work plan and priorities in the last six months?
3. To what extent are you able to put to use most of your capabilities in the last six months?
4. To what extent are you clear about the work plan and priorities for the next six months?

They were asked to use the following scale: 100 percent = fully, 75 percent = mostly, 50 percent = somewhat, 25 percent = a little, 0 percent = not at all. Their responses are presented in Table 4.1.

Responses to question 1 in the Table 4.1 reveals that the average percentage of the extent to which there is clearly a set work plan for the top management of this company is 74 percent. If we consider unplanned work a waste, it is about 26 percent in this company. If the CTC of all 25 top level managers is about US $2 million, there is a waste of half a million dollars in the year due to unplanned work, and the opportunity cost may be much more. Such unplanned work is passed down the hierarchy and multiplies. Therefore, the solution is to reduce this wastage by planning work.

**TABLE 4.1**

Responses of 25 General Managers (Top Management Team) on Performance-related Questions

| Question | Number of participating responding (N = 25) | | | | |
|---|---|---|---|---|---|
| | 100% | 75% | 50% | 25% | 0% |
| 1. To what extent did you clearly set your work plan for the last six months? | 3 | 18 | 4 | 0 | 0 |
| 2. To what extent did you share the same understanding of your work plan and priorities with your seniors in the last six months? | 7 | 10 | 5 | 3 | 0 |
| 3. To what extent were you able to put to use most of your capabilities in the last six months? | 2 | 15 | 7 | 1 | 0 |
| 4. To what extent are you clear about the work plan and priorities for the next six months? | 9 | 13 | 3 | 0 | 0 |

*Source:* Unpublished Data from TVRLS Reports.

*PMS can therefore be a good tool to reduce wastage through proper performance planning.*

Responses to "To what extent did you share the same understanding of your work plan and priorities with your seniors in the last six months?" reveals that shared understanding is 71 percent. If PMS is effective, this shared understanding can be improved. Shared understanding between the performers and their seniors is indicative of interpersonal competence, role clarity, focused work, and good interpersonal competence and mutual support, as well as a number of other positive outcomes.

Answers to question 3 indicate that the average of the capabilities that were used in the last six months is 68 percent. This indicates that there is 32 percent wastage of talent.

The next question indicates that the average of the extent to which there is clarity about work plans and priorities is 80 percent. There is 20 percent potential wastage of time used by top management.

Simple questions and analysis such as this indicate that there should be a focus on the need for better utilization of talent by planning work and encouraging a shared understanding of the work. A good PMS can reduce wastage of time and talent, and ensure better utilization of human resources.

The scope for all of this is indicated by the answers provided by a number of managers from multinational corporations, family-owned businesses and professionally managed companies in India and around the world (see for details Rao, 2008).

It is these insights that have given rise to a program we have designed at TVRLS called the "Invest Twenty and Direct 2,000 to 20,000.™" I have been propagating it by communicating to line managers and top management that their managers can learn to direct 2000 hours of their performance time to 20,000 hours of their juniors' time by merely investing 20 hours of their own time for planning their and their juniors' work. So Invest 20 and Direct 2,000 to 20,000. We have helped many senior managers cost the value of their time and demonstrated the benefits of such planning. Executives can be shown to affect savings in their own time and get a better ROI on their time investment. In other words, organizational performance, utilization of resources as well as of talent (which is becoming more and more expensive day by day) and cost reduction can be achieved with better planning.

## TALENT UTILIZATION

When Steel Authority of India Limited (SAIL), a public sector giant in India, decided to change its PMS in 2007, it made leadership development as one of the objectives that the new system would facilitate. It adopted the following as objectives of the system:

1. To enable employees to plan their work, utilize their capabilities and maximize their contributions.
2. To create a performance culture through continuous performance improvement of individual employees, teams, and the organization.
3. To identify and develop leadership talent for the future.

Accordingly the components envisaged included:

1. Goal alignment cascade workshops for performance and development planning.
2. An online system for performance management.
3. Assessment and development of competencies for the future.
4. Performance review and assessment.
5. Final performance categorization of ratings by Performance Management Committee (PMC).
6. Separate grading for performance and potential.
7. Transparency through communication of performance rating to executives.
8. Assessment of assessors.
9. Audit of PMS.
10. Leadership development and competency building through 360-degree evaluation and Assessment and Development Centers (ADCs).

The following list of competencies, potential factors and values were also to be developed:

1. Technical/functional competencies.
2. Commercial acumen.
3. Interpersonal skills and teamwork.
4. Proactive problem solving and initiatives.
5. Communication skills (listening, clarity of thought and expression—written and oral).
6. Positive attitude (viewing things positively with optimism and not being critical or cynical about everything; ability to look at the brighter side of change and various other decisions, policies and innovations, and not being over-critical or critical all the time of people and events, and so forth).

These competencies are assumed to be important for performing well on any job in the organization.

Potential factors are the qualities that have become increasingly critical for senior management positions and are meant to prepare executives for handling higher roles as they grow in organizations. The following include abilities that will enable these executives to handle higher responsibilities:

1. Vision and leadership.
2. Ability to assume responsibility and take decisions.
3. Execution ability.
4. Change management (openness to change, and initiation and management of change).
5. Creativity.
6. Values including beliefs, behavior, and actions that are to be exhibited by every executive:

   - Customer focus
   - Consistent quality
   - Commitment to excellence
   - Concern for people
   - Integrity and character

Most importantly, SAIL decided to put in place special projects that would be undertaken as part of the organization's performance planning to demonstrate and utilize the talents of its managers. It has been able to ensure a significant degree of human capital utilization through this approach.

## UPWARD LEARNING

Most pharmaceutical organizations employ medical representatives (MRs) to sell their drugs to doctors and to make sure that adequate supplies are available to drug stores. Normally, MRs are required to introduce the medical products of their companies and explain their merits to physicians and others. They are required to follow up their visits to seek feedback regarding their companies' products and encourage medical practitioners and drug stores to prescribe their companies' products to their patients and customers, respectively. MRs are required to maintain proper records of receipts and distribution of samples. (This is open for inspection by their area managers.) They offer credit facilities, commissions, and so forth, to their customers, as authorized by their companies. They books orders and forward these to their controlling offices.

Imagine a pharmaceutical company with over a thousand MRs who report to area sales managers. Cedilla, a pharma company, has 60 MRs on its rolls. Cedilla has recently decided to introduce a PMS according to which each area manager is required to meet his/her MRs in a team and get feedback on their experiences from the doctors and pharmacists they have met in the previous quarter. Thereafter they will have short, one-on-one discussions with their area managers once every six months. In the performance review discussion, the area managers will actively listen and ask questions to learn about the circumstances under which the MRs are working, the kind of comments made by their clients on the company's products and the products of competitor companies, the experiences shared by the pharmacists, and any other information the MRs gather that will have implications for its Drug Development and R&D departments, supply chain department, and others. The area managers in turn are expected to consolidate their learning and share it with their seniors in the head office during their quarterly or half yearly performance review discussions.

This is aimed at enabling significant upward learning. After a series of programs on its PMS, Cedilla Pharma realized its significance in facilitating upward learning. The company will assess its performance as well as achievement of its targets, based on the useful information gathered by the MRs and shared with their seniors.

In a pyramid structure, the field staff is constantly in touch with customers and ground realities. Normally, seniors at the top level believe and behave as though they are direction- and information-givers. The information they normally give deals with an organizational vision, mission, goals, targets, work practices, and so on, and rarely provide customer-related information, since they are not in touch with customers. Yet the success of an organization depends on how well it has understood customers' needs and requirements, and serviced them. In the past, PMS did little to encourage upward learning.

A well-designed PMS that facilitates upward learning can be a useful tool to develop a customer- and employee-sensitive learning organization. Utilizing the quantum of knowledge that will be available to Cadilla Pharma will give direction to its R&D, supply chain, pricing, marketing, and other activities.

## ON-BOARDING, INTEGRATION, AND ASSIMILATION

Ketan Mehta, Vice President of a mobile handset manufacturing company (MHMC), had resigned. He was instrumental in doubling the company's samples and increasing its market share in the last few years. He is considered a very high performer. The company was planning to expand to other countries and found a good scope for this expansion, especially to South Africa. After a few weeks of Ketan leaving it, MHMC recruited Harry Selvaratnam, a Harvard MBA with experience in working in African countries. Being an expatriate, he was offered double the salary Ketan was getting at the time he left the company. Eight weeks after Harry had joined, MHMC's management consultant met him to enquire how he was liking the company and his job. Harry remarked that he was trying to understand various departments and also the way his own functioned, their interrelationships, and so forth. Four months later, the consultant met him and got the same answer. It was only at their third encounter that Harry said that he had achieved a good understanding of the situation, his colleagues, the way the company worked and what was expected of him, and was ready to perform.

This clearly indicates that the MHMC has not given adequate thought when it inducts its senior employees. It should not take six months for a top level manager to understand his/her colleagues, juniors, seniors, and the company's expectations from its working styles. What if a new Vice-president decides that he is a misfit in the company after six months and decides to leave? The company suffers for another six months.

If only the MHMC had thought of the detailed performance plan made by Ketan Mehta for the year of his work and had taken care to put in place a performance plan (based on his plan) for the newcomer, and even put Harry in touch with Ketan Mehta and his juniors, seniors, and internal and external customers in the first week? The induction and integration process for new recruits at senior levels can be made more efficient and faster by the implementation of a well-managed PMS. I have been promoting a system of passing on performance plans to new recruits and encouraging them to have dialogues with their juniors, seniors, and internal and external customers as part of their socialization and induction process. It has been found that assimilation and integration processes become faster and more effective through the use of a well-designed PMS.

## ORGANIZATION DEVELOPMENT

Performance analysis consists of analyzing the performance of performers at the end of a year or a six-month period to identify the factors that helped them in their achievements and those that hindered them. These factors can be further classified into competencies that relate to their ability, motivation, and the organizational support given to them. Sometimes, these can be further classified as competencies that need to be addressed by the performers and those that need to be addressed by their bosses, seniors, departments, or organization.

Consider the following tabulation of factors arising out of an analysis of the performance of 30 branch managers of a bank. Its HR department collected relevant details from the performance analysis conducted on the branch managers. The analysis was a useful starting point for initiating organization development (OD) activities to improve the branch's performance. This can be effective as an organization development intervention. The OD facilitators (internal or external) can enhance the competency base of branch managers or help them work with the regional office to improve manpower planning, management of the branch's premises, decision-making improvements, etc.

---

## Illustrative list of facilitating and hindering factors identified by a group of branch managers as a part of their PMS

### FACILITATING FACTORS ATTRIBUTABLE TO THE PERFORMER (NUMBER GIVEN IN BRACKETS)

1. Patience and willingness to listen to the problems of the staff and customers first, and then work out a solution to the problem (7)
2. Perseverance (5)
3. Soberness and tact (5)
4. Goodwill and fellow-feeling toward others (4)
5. Keen desire to help customers by giving them personal attention (5)
6. Interest in bank's work (5)
7. Ability to motivate staff (8)
8. Specialization in advances at training programs attended and in their careers till date (7)

*(Box contd.)*

*(Box contd.)*

9. Quick decision-making (6)
10. Adequate delegation (4)

## FACILITATING FACTORS ATTRIBUTABLE TO OTHERS (ORGANIZATIONAL SUPPORT)

1. Full and timely support of controlling authority and his/her office (11)
2. Sincere and hard-working branch staff (14)
3. Good work conditions premises (6)
4. A regional manager who is appreciative of good work done (5)
5. Good potential for business in the area of operation (2)

## HINDERING FACTORS ATTRIBUTABLE TO THE PERFORMER

1. Softness or lack of aggressive selling (6)
2. Over-sensitive/Over-emotional and gets upset easily (4)
3. Poor health (3)
4. Inadequate knowledge of job, particularly relating to small-scale business (6)
5. Lack of confidence while dealing with aggressive staff (5)
6. Difficulty in motivating staff (5)

## HINDERING FACTOR ATTRIBUTABLE TO OTHERS (ORGANIZATIONAL SUPPORT)

1. Shortage of staff (9)
2. Branch premises with inadequate infrastructure(4)
3. Branch located very far from most residential areas (3)
4. Competitors' (companies, cooperative banks, and so forth) tactics (4)
5. Inadequate potential for business in area of operation (3)
6. Delay in decision-making at local head office (10)
7. Competency gaps in staff (4)

# Performance Analysis of a Pharma Company

As a part of implementation of a PMS in this company, the managers were asked to list factors that had facilitated their work in the last six months and those that had prevented them from doing better. The following is an analysis of the most frequently mentioned factors by the company's senior and top management group. Only those that were most frequently mentioned are listed for the half-year period.

## FACTORS THAT HINDERED EFFECTIVE PERFORMANCE

1. Interdepartmental coordination and bureaucratic approach. Some team-building may help. Cross-functional collaboration needs to be strengthened.)
2. Delays in decision-making.
3. Dearth of competent staff.
4. Lack of infrastructural support.
5. Role clarity lacking in some cases.
6. Dearth of professionalism with ad hoc decisions being taken.
7. Financial constraints and inadequate funds.
8. Lack of authority and operational freedom for some senior managers.
9. Past baggage is still an issue that affects the motivation of some managers.
10. Support from HR, Administration, Purchase, and Finance departments.
11. Autonomy, encouragement, and motivation for performing staff.
12. Need for boss–subordinate relations to be strengthened in a few cases.
13. Lack of support from HR—policies laid/recruitment of professionals.
14. Delays in introduction of new products.
15. Lack of clarity of vision.

16. Unnecessary competition of price war.
17. Policies—HR, travel, appraisal, and so forth, hindrances to good work.
18. Frequent meetings and presentations leaving no time for actual implementation or execution.
19. Delays in purchases.
20. No delegation of power to second line management.
21. Dearth of support for infrastructure (IT and others).
22. Lack of understanding/coordination between bosses and staff.

## MOST FREQUENTLY MENTIONED FACILITATING FACTORS OR STRONG POINTS

1. Freedom to work independently.
2. Good campus and infrastructure.
3. Strong brand image and motivated field staff.
4. Good teamwork in departments and teams.
5. Clarity of objectives and performance plans including role clarity.
6. Competent and motivated staff.
7. Application of democratic methods in dealings with staff and consumers.
8. Good incentives.
9. Sound brand equity of products.
10. Continuous and regular monitoring to ensure corrective action in time.
11. Good facilities and infrastructure including canteen facilities.
12. Freedom to act and take decisions.
13. Identification of individuals' capability and assignment of tasks based on this.
14. Knowledge of the market/products.
15. Least interference with total delegation.
16. Very few clashes by exercise of control/ego.
17. Open policy of discussing problems and finding mutually acceptable solutions.
18. Work opportunities provided to staff to work in different areas.

19. Punctual and hard-working.
20. Quick decision-making on issues in some parts of the organization.
21. Strong intellectual capital due to long experience in the organization.
22. Positive environment enabled by seniors to enhance performance.

The same factors are sometimes mentioned by some people as "facilitating" and others as "inhibiting." This means that areas of strength and weakness are not uniformly distributed. In other words, some departments and seniors get freedom and autonomy while others do not. However, decision-making-related delays seem to be widely shared.

On the basis of this exercise, the top management team established task forces to go into details to reduce inhibiting factors and enhance facilitating nes. Initially they appointed four groups to delve deep into issues deeper. The groups focused the following:

1. Decision-making and delegation: To enhance the speed and quality and at the same time empower and delegate wherever needed, retaining current empowerment levels.
2. To find areas needing interdepartmental collaboration and cross-functional communication, develop a mechanism to strengthen inter-departmental and intradepartmental teamwork, and create a culture of collaboration and teamwork.
3. To examine all the infrastructural facilitating factors and factors that affect good work and come up with solutions to improve infrastructural support in various areas—travel, canteen, HR support, IT support, and other facilities.
4. To examine HR and other polices that affect the morale and motivation of employees and suggest changes.
5. Group to focus particularly on clarity of roles and competence-development issues, and examine HR systems and their implementation to facilitate them.

Thereafter, the senior management team met and diagnosed the issues. Some of them co-opted their juniors to collect data. Various meetings were held, and in the next six months, significant improvements were made in boosting the credibility of the PMS system as a tool to enhance performance. Some of the issues identified were taken up in appropriate forums, for example, the board committees got involved in enhancing and delegating more purchase powers to the purchase committees.

# Human Capital Building

In conclusion, it can be said that the implementation of a well-designed PMS is a good way of building human capital in an organization. It can enhance the competencies and organizational capabilities of employees, and help them deal with various issues. It can also provide them with opportunities for growth and enable them to enhance their impact on customers by studying them and operationalizing appropriate strategies.

A well-designed and well-executed PMS can be an effective tool to enhance a company's human and intellectual capital.

# 5

# Reducing Biases in Ratings and Managing Forced Distribution

Performance appraisals are often perceived as failures, as the greatest expectation from them seems to be objectivity. They are seen as unsuccessful essentially because of the issues associated with the ratings. The author has always been of the view that ratings are the poison generated in the process of extracting nectar. *If performance management is the nectar-generation process (development and performance improvements), the ratings generated from the process are like poison. They could kill the entire spirit of performance management unless understood properly, and the over-obsession with them is rectified.* However, they have become inevitable as most organizations insist and behave as though performance management is essentially a rating-generation process. A lot is talked about and discussed as to how to control liberal ratings, how to normalize them, how to ensure objectivity etc. These are the primary concerns in most organizations, and they ignore the most important parts of performance management, which are performance improvement and individual, dyadic, and team development.

*Attempting to attain perfect objectivity in ratings is a futile exercise.* It must be recognized that performance appraisal ratings are essentially subjective. You cannot compare an individual's performance in one department such as production, with another individual's in another department such as marketing, and equate them just because both are designated as assistant managers. Their task structure, qualifications, the nature of work, and their bosses are all different. We waste a lot of time trying to compare the incomparable. We forget that reducing the entire year's work of an individual to a number and equating that number is antihuman and antidevelopment.

The measurement of human behavior and performance, therefore, have serious limitations. It is important to understand the nature of measurement. There are four types of scales that can be used as measures—nominal, ordinal, interval, and ratio scales. These have interesting properties. These are briefly described as follows:

*Nominal scales:* Everything exists in a certain quantity. The moment you say something exists and assign a name to it, and associate some property with it by the virtue of the name assigned, you have scaled it. This is the most primitive form of scaling. It is a nominal scale. It involves naming of an individual, quality, process, or phenomena. It is the most primitive form of measurement. Examples of the nominal scales include license plates, house numbers, security numbers, castes, groups 1, 2, 3, and so forth.

*Ordinal scales:* Ordinal scales indicate the order or position of an object or variable in relation to other objects or variables. For example, the first born, second born, and third born from an ordinal scale. The same thing goes for ranking scales. They indicate positioning, but do not indicate the distance between the positions. The age difference between the first born and the second born may be three years, and the difference between the second and the third born may be 10 years. The first ranker may score 97 percent, the second ranker 87 percent, and the third ranker 86 percent. These are ordinal positions and are slightly better developed scales than the nominal scales.

*Interval scales:* In interval scales, the difference between any two consecutive numbers is equal to the difference between any other two numbers. The numbers are additive and subtractive, but not divisive and multiplicative. The difference between 70 kg weight and 69 kg weight is equal to the difference between 14 kg and 13 kg. Whenever you take two consecutive numbers, the difference is the same. This is the property of interval scales. If this scaling is applied to performance appraisals, the difference between the performance levels of a performer getting 78 points on his/her appraisal and the one getting 77 points should be equal to the difference between the one getting 45 marks and the one getting 44 marks. We know that our performance appraisals are not so accurate as to enable us to add and subtract. However, we pretend that performance appraisals are subject to addition and subtraction. *Some companies even multiply them by multiplying the weightage of KPAs with the score on the KPA. This is absurd, given the nature of measurement.* Performance appraisals are not even amenable to ordinal scales. We cannot say with confidence that X amount of performance of a production manager is equal to Y amount of performance of the marketing manager. You cannot arrange marketing, production, IT, and finance managerial performance on the same comparable scales. Yet, we pretend that our appraisals can be objective and ratings follow interval scales. If we understand scaling principles, we will not waste our time trying to improve objectivity in appraisals, which are essentially subjective phenomena. It is futile to compare the performance of one individual from one department or the same department working in another set of conditions to another person, and try to arrange them on a normal probability curve.

*Ratio scales:* These are highly sophisticated scales with an absolute zero, and are amenable for addition, subtraction, multiplication, and division. These are the scales used in space and physics; we are not even concerned with these as we are nowhere near them.

Unfortunately, these arguments have not cut much ice in the past. Organizations continue to pursue some form of ratings or the other. This is because good performance has to be recognized and even rewarded. Improvements have to be measured and ensured. Performance needs to be benchmarked. Due to these practical considerations, measurement has become the inevitable evil of performance management. Hence, this chapter is intended to help the reader understand the dynamics of ratings and the problem areas, in order to bring about greater sanity in appraisals.

An important component of any performance appraisal system is performance assessment through ratings. An assessment may be made using categories such as "excellent," "outstanding," "good," "above average," "average," "below average," "poor," etc. A five-point, seven-point, or a nine-point scale can be used to assess performance. If categories are used, they need to be defined and points might be assigned to them (for example, outstanding = 7, very good performance = 6, above average or fairly good = 5, average = 4, below average = 3, poor performance = 2, and very poor = 1).

In the PMS described here, the performer completes a self-appraisal and gives his appraisal and analysis report to his/her reporting officer at the end of the year. The reporting manager is expected to study the report, and make his/her own observations on each of the KPAs, objectives, managerial dimensions, behavioral dimensions, and facilitating and inhibiting factors identified in performance analysis. He/she then has a performance review and counseling discussion with the performer on a day planned for this purpose. Prior to such discussion, the reporting manager may make a provisional assessment and rate the performance of the performer on each of the KPAs/objectives and managerial and behavioral dimensions. If the performer rates his/her performance on different dimensions, it is useful for the reporting manager to also give provisional ratings. Whether the self-ratings of the performer differ from those assigned by the reporting manager or not, they should have a discussion on how each of them arrived at the ratings they gave for each dimension. In this process, they are likely to exchange views and communicate with each other on a number of issues. The performer may share more information. The reporting manager may give feedback or share his/her expectations with the performer. The processes that should take place and the purposes of this discussion are explained in the chapter on performance counseling.

If the process requires both the performer and the reporting manager to assign ratings, this could become the starting point for the appraisal discussion process. However, to be effective, this process requires the reporting managers to share his/her ratings (even if they are provisional) with the performer. It requires complete openness and trust between the two. It also demands an emotional climate of acceptance between them, so that they are not carried away by the ratings, which is not more important than sharing experiences and giving and receiving feedback. If such an open and healthy atmosphere does not exist in an organization, it is better to start with a system in which the ratings assigned or to be assigned by the reporting manager are not shared with the employee, but the review discussion and counseling takes place (as described in the next chapter). The reporting manager may finally assign his/her ratings confidentially, although he/she should give some indication about the assessment during the review discussions. This should only be done till such time as more openness and trust is built up. The continuous practice of confidentiality may hinder the development of relationships based on trust.

Self-appraisal may include analysis only, or analysis and ratings both. This means that the reporting manager may carry out only an analysis and assign no ratings, or may assign ratings after the analysis. The possible eight combinations of self-assessment, reporting officer's assessment, and confidentiality or openness of the final assessment are as follows:

| Model no. | Nature of self-appraisal | Reporting officer's appraisal | Openness |
|---|---|---|---|
| 1 | Only analysis, no ratings | Only analysis, no ratings | Confidential |
| 2 | Only analysis, no ratings | Only analysis, no ratings | Open |
| 3 | Only analysis, no ratings | Analysis and ratings | Confidential |
| 4 | Only analysis, no ratings | Analysis and ratings | Open |
| 5 | Analysis and ratings | Only analysis, no ratings | Confidential |
| 6 | Analysis and ratings | Only analysis, no ratings | Open |
| 7 | Analysis and ratings | Analysis and ratings | Confidential |
| 8 | Analysis and ratings | Analysis and ratings | Open |

The most desirable model is number 8, where both assign ratings and share them (provisional and final) with each other. This is what should be aimed at. Equally effective is model number 4, in which only the reporting manager gives ratings and shares them (provisional and final). The next best are model numbers 6 and 2, where reporting managers do not give ratings, but analyze performers' performance and share with them their perception of the performers' accomplishments, contributions, strengths, and weaknesses. The reporting managers may give their final ratings confidentially, but share their analysis prior to that and look at the performers' performance. The other models (1, 3, 5, and 7) are not suitable for development-oriented appraisal systems.

# The Need for Performance Ratings

Whatever may be the model used for, the final assessment (in the form of ratings or assignment of points) is very useful for developmental and administrative decisions. If appraisals do not result in such ratings or points being assigned to performers on different KPAs (or objectives), and behavioral and managerial dimensions, it becomes difficult to know subsequently how well an individual is progressing. It also becomes difficult to maintain and process information about the capabilities of employees to handle different functions. The qualitative analysis done by each performer and the reporting manager is difficult to use for training rotation, placements, transfers, promotions, decisions, etc. Once the ratings are available, it is easy to identify individuals who can perform certain functions well, or those who have demonstrated certain managerial and human capabilities. In view of this, appraisals should result in performance ratings on different functions as well as on the different dimensions of behavior. It is for this reason that there has been a great deal of research in the West on improving the quality of ratings (more objectivity and lesser errors and biases). In the subsequent sections of this chapter, we will examine the factors that contribute to the poor quality of ratings, and then see how it can be improved.

# Factors Affecting Ratings in Performance Appraisals

The most commonly expressed dissatisfaction about performance appraisals is in relation to the subjectivity in performance ratings. Employees are concerned about this because performance ratings entered in personnel records are likely to have a huge impact on subsequent promotions, placements, transfers, and development decisions taken by an organization that affect their careers. Performance ratings have attracted a lot of attention of psychologists and other behavioral scientists who have been making efforts to discover the various factors affecting rating and behavior, and decreasing the quality of appraisals. A variety of rating scales have been developed and experimental studies conducted to control various biases and errors in performance ratings. Various hypotheses have also been proposed on the basis of theories and findings available from a person's perception, interpersonal attraction, attribution, information processing, and other such areas of social psychology. Most of this work has been done in western settings, often with varying results obtained by different researchers on the same issue. Experimental research with implications for appraisal ratings on Indian subjects is fairly recent, and is being actively pursued at one or two places only. However, there has been significant research on this topic in the West. Journals such as the *Journal of Applied Psychology, Personnel Psychology, Organisational Behaviour and Human Performance, Public Personnel Management,* and the *Journal of Personality and Social Psychology,* and *Academy of Management Review* carry such research articles frequently. However, such research is largely unsystematic and is subject to fads and fashions. It focuses too much on formats rather than processes (Decotiis and Petit, 1978). The following are some of the recent studies and theoretical propositions. They relate to the relevance of some of this research to our understanding of the dynamics of appraisal ratings. It is hoped that the reader will appreciate the complexity of the issue of appraisal ratings and continue to strive to improve their quality.

## Subjectivity and Errors in Ratings

As long as human beings are involved in assessing other human beings, there is bound to be a certain amount of subjectivity. Subjectivity or biases occur when the ratings assigned by any reporting manager are determined by factors rather than performance or behavior of the performer on the dimension under assessment. The following are some commonly observed phenomena that contribute to errors and biases in appraisals increasing subjectivity:

1. Sometimes reporting managers like or dislike one or two actions or qualities of the performers immensely, and therefore tend to rate them positively or negatively on all other dimensions (called the "halo effect").

2. Some reporting managers tend to believe that they should be "nice" to their subordinates, and therefore assign them lenient ratings ("leniency effect"). Other reporting managers have the opposite philosophy and view of their subordinates, and they tend to rate them too strictly ("severity effect").

3. Some raters do not want to give too high or too low ratings to their subordinates. Due to their over-consciousness, they tend to rate most of their performers around the average ("central tendency" or "averaging tendency").

4. Some raters tend to like the subordinates who are like them, and therefore assign them higher ratings than to those who they perceive as different from them. Some other raters tend to like those who have characteristics they do not have, but would like to have ("assimilation" or "differential effect").

5. Quite a few raters make judgments about others on the basis of their first contact with them, and carry these impressions over a long time ("first impression errors").

6. Sometimes raters assign ratings on the basis of their subordinates' recent behavior, forgetting their past behavior over a period (the "recency effect").

7. Some reporting managers tend to assess performers on the basis of their expectations and perceptions about how their own bosses are going to appraise them.

## BEHAVIORALLY ANCHORED RATING SCALES

Smith and Kendall (1963) have evolved a procedure for developing evaluative rating scales anchored by examples of expected behavior. The format proposed for these rating scales is a series of continuous graphic rating scales, arranged vertically. Behavioral descriptions, exemplifying various degrees of each dimension, are printed beside the line at different heights according to their scale positions, determined by the judgment of those who are expected to use the scales. The examples (or behavior descriptions) are intended as anchors to define the levels of the characteristic as well as the operational definitions of the dimension being rated. Ratings should be assigned by checking at any position along the line. The anchors are defined in terms of behavior expected to be shown by the rate relating to that dimension. For example, while assessing the behavior of nurses, the anchor can be stated in the form of an expectation such as "If this nurse were admitting a patient who talks rapidly and continuously of her symptoms and past medical history, could she be expected to look interested and listen?" instead of statements such as "Shows an interest in patients' description of symptoms."

Use of expected behavior is intended to encourage conscientiousness by making predictions such as (a) so concrete that in view of the previous agreement reached by the peer group, the central tendency or hedging effects will be minimized, and (b) so verifiable that the insight, judgment, values etc. of the rater are potentially challenged if the later behavior of the ratee fails to confirm the prediction.

Based on the procedure used by Smith and Kendall (1963), any organization interested in developing such scales (known as Behaviorally Anchored Rating Scales or BARS) may follow these steps:

1. Identify the roles or categories of roles for which a rating system has to be developed. A category of roles should have some common capabilities (managerial and behavioral) for their effective performance. These categories could be broad. For example, all the secretaries in one category, or the branch managers, middle-level managers, senior managers, marketing managers, etc. in different categories.

2. Constitute peer groups of reporting managers with these roles—as many as possible. These groups may be called for a short workshop or they could work through periodic meetings. There may be several groups for one category of roles.

3. Ask each group to first identify and list the qualities or characteristics that are important for the role category.
4. Select the most frequently mentioned dimensions. If necessary, representatives of the groups can get together and finalize the list for each category of roles. Critical incidents can be discussed for more clarity.
5. Ask each group to formulate general statements representing definitions of the high, low and acceptable performance of each quality.
6. Ask groups to prepare examples of behavior in each quality and edit them in the form of expectations (for example, when faced with staff shortage, examine work and reallocate staff to handle the critical functions).
7. Ask some of the groups to act as judges. They should attempt to independently reclassify each of the behavior descriptions into one of the dimensions measured.
8. Eliminate either the dimension or the behavior example, where there is no agreement with the original classification.
9. Use some of the groups to describe outstanding and poor performers in each role category. Use these descriptions to check whether the dimensions identified in steps 2 and 3 are critical to the role category.
10. Present the finally selected behaviors in vertical scale formats. Since the time BARS was developed, a large number of research studies have been conducted to examine its effectiveness in reducing errors and increasing the quality of ratings.

In the Smith and Kendall (1963) format of BARS, raters were to be given a set of vertical graphic scales and instructed to record the behavior observed on each applicable scale throughout the appraisal period. They were instructed to observe behavior, decide to which dimension it belonged, and then indicate on the scale the date and details of the incident. The notation of the incident was to be made at the effectiveness level on the scale that was considered the most appropriate for the incident on that behavioral dimension. Scaling of the effectiveness level of the observation, that is the place on the page at which the observer recorded the incident, was to be aided by comparing it with a series of illustrative behavioral "anchors" and "genetic descriptions" (Bernardin and Smith, 1981, p. 159).

After observing and recording such incidents over a period, the reporting manager can arrive at a summary rating. Thus, in this format, the sequence includes observation-inference-scaling-recording and summary rating.

Rosinger et al. (1982) described the development of a Mixed Standard Scale to assess performance. The following steps are involved:

Step 1. Task analysis that results in behavioral descriptions of major activity areas and tasks.

Step 2. Assignment of importance scores to each task through systematic collection of data on frequency of performance and criticality of the task.

Step 3. Development and refinement of behavioral statements regarding different proficiency levels.

Step 4. Establishment of validity and reliability.

The appraisal format they suggest is criterion-referenced rather than norm-referenced, and it includes three anchors (average, excellent, and poor) for a number of dimensions.

The Mixed Standard Scales are somewhat similar to BARS. There have been a number of research studies, modifications, and developments in new scales. Comparisons between BARS and other rating formats have not shown BARS to be psychometrically superior or to offer more accurate performance ratings (Bernardin, 1977; Dunnette and Borman, 1979; Borman, 1979; Jacobs et al., 1980; Kingstrom and Bass, 1981; and Landy and Farr, 1980). It is, however, acknowledged that numerous methodological weaknesses exist in these searches when comparing BARS with other scales.

Although BARS may not produce error-free or accurate ratings, there is some research-based evidence (though largely inconclusive) available to indicate its potential use for more effective feedback (Hom et al., 1982). The accuracy of a recipient's perception of performance feedback should be enhanced because BARS define scale dimensions and anchors in concrete, behavioral terms, making them more interpretable to the recipient than those found in traditional formats. Although BARS are designed to maximize the interpretability of raters (to facilitate valid ratings), the same may also be true for ratees receiving feedback from this instrument. Feedback from BARS may also be more accurately perceived if the numerical ratings are documented by specific behavioral examples, preventing distortion or denial of feedback (Hom et al., 1982, p. 569).

Research with formats of much greater sophistication than the traditional graphic, trait approach shows fancy scales such as BARS, which do no better at inhibiting rating inflation (Landy and Farr, 1980). Numerous other studies have compared different types of rating formats such as Mixed Standard Scales, BARS, or Simple Graphic Scales. In general, these studies have revealed relatively little differences in the extent of rating errors as a function of the format (Bernardin and Cardy, 1982). In fact, there is a strong indication that ratings are as much or more a function of the idiosyncrasies of the rater who made them than that of the actual behavior of the ratees.

## ASSESSMENT BY PEERS

Some literature is available on performance assessments made by peers (colleagues at the same level in the organizational hierarchy with working relations with the performer). Peer assessments are made through nominations, ratings, or rankings. Love (1981) compared reliability, validity, friendship bias and user reaction using nominations, and rating and ranking formats. His study was conducted on 145 police officers using a 9-point BARS for ratings. Criterion rankings and ratings were provided by their squad supervisors. In this study, all peer-based methods showed significant reliability and validity, and the validity coefficients were not significantly biased by friendship between peer assessors and assessees. Rankings and nominations displayed significantly greater reliability and validity than ratings. However, users' reactions were negative to all the methods. They indicated that peer assessment was not fair or accurate, were not liked by them, and did not propose their names for promotion.

## SOME THEORETICAL CONSIDERATIONS ON FACTORS AFFECTING APPRAISALS

Some of the most important conclusions to be drawn from research on human information processing are that our processing capabilities are limited, and that perception and recall frequently do not match reality. The limitation on our processing capacity is handled nicely by cognitive representations called "schemata" (Neisser, 1976). A schema directs our attention and aids in categorization and recall of information. However, it can also lead to systematic inaccuracies. Biased ratings may result when a rater relies on an irrelevant, over-simplistic, or otherwise faulty schema. For instance, the gender of a ratee may be irrelevant to job performance, but may set up a schema (in this case, a sex stereotype) that may bias perception and recall of the ratee's performance. A ratee's sex, race, age, and even a single instance of behavior may elicit a schema, which the rater uses to process and recall his/her performance. Research indicates that once a ratee is categorized, further perception and recall of his/her performance is biased toward that category (or schema) (Cantor and Mischel, 1977). There will be a bias to attend to information that is consistent with the schema (Snyder and Swann, 1978). When recalling information concerning a ratee's performance, the rater will be biased toward recalling information that is made available by the schema, that is, the ratings will be biased toward those dimension values which best fit with (most closely resemble) the schema for the ratee (Tversky and Kahneman, 1974). It also appears that humans are typically unaware of these biasing processes and will deny the operation of such a bias even when it is clearly present (Nisbett and Wilson, 1977, p. 353). Bernardin and Cardy (1982) proposed that accuracy in the performance of the rater is a function of the rater's ability and motivation to rate accurately. The level of trust the rater has in the appraisal system affects his/her motivation to rate accurately. Bernardin and Cardy (1982) also suggest that a rater's motivation and ability to rate accurately are dynamically interrelated. For example, when there is low trust in the appraisal system, the rater may rely heavily on the information provided by his/her stereotypic schemata rather than to search for information. When there is high trust, the rater may actively search for information on the ratee's performance rather than to rely on his/her schemata.

There are numerous parameters that can affect the accuracy of appraisals. The greater the number of these considered, the better-off the practitioner will be. On the basis of a review of several researches on performance appraisal, Decotiis and Petit (1978) have developed a model of a performance appraisal process. The model is based on the premise that the accuracy of performance appraisals can be viewed as a function of (a) a rater's motivation to appraise accurately, (b) job relevance of the rating standards used by the rater, and (c) the rater's ability to evaluate the ratee's job behavior. On the basis of their model and their survey of several researches relating to this, they proposed the following:

### Rater's Motivation

1. Rater's motivation to assign accurate performance ratings is higher when the purpose of appraisal is personnel research than when the purpose is either employee development or administration of organizational rewards.
2. Rater's motivation to assign accurate performance ratings is higher when the purpose of appraisal is employee development than when the purpose is administration of organizational rewards.
3. Regardless of purpose, rater's motivation to assign accurate performance ratings is higher when the results of the appraisal are confidential from the ratee.
4. When the purpose of appraisal is either employees' development or administration of organizational rewards, and the rater is required to discuss the result of the appraisal with the ratee, the rater's motivation to assign accurate performance ratings is higher when he/she perceives feedback as a legitimate aspect of his/her role.
5. When feedback of the results of an appraisal is required, the rater's motivation to assign accurate performance ratings is higher if the rater perceives that he/she has the necessary insight into the ratee's job behavior.

6. The easier a performance appraisal instrument is to understand, the more likely raters are to perceive it as being adequate for the purpose at hand.
7. A performance appraisal instrument that is based on systematically gathered job information will be perceived by a rater as more adequate for the purpose of appraisal than an instrument developed on an ad hoc basis.
8. A performance appraisal instrument that is based on job information, easy to understand and is perceived as adequate for the purpose of appraisal will lead to an increase in the rater's motivation to assign accurate performance ratings.

## Rater's Ability

1. The more opportunities the rater takes advantage of to observe a ratee's job behavior, the higher his/her ability is to assign accurate performance ratings.
2. The more correct the behavior observed by the rater, the higher his/her ability to assign accurate performance ratings.
3. All else being equal, the closer the rater's organizational level is to the ratee's, the higher the rater's ability to assign accurate performance ratings.
4. Raters from different organizational levels sample different aspects of a ratee's behavior. Therefore, the higher the correspondence between the content of the rating instrument used and the rater's sample of the ratee's behavior, the higher the rater's ability to assign accurate performance ratings.
5. A rater's ability is higher when he/she understands the linkage between the ratee's job behavior and organizational outcomes, than when he/she does not understand these.
6. A rater's ability is higher when his/her personal style stresses goal attainment for ratees rather than consideration of them as individuals.
7. Raters trained in the principles and problems of performance appraisal have a higher ability to assign accurate performance ratings than untrained ones.
8. Rater's training methods that stress on active learning result in their higher ability to rate performance accurately than training ones that stress on passive learning.

## Availability of Appropriate Rating Standards

1. The higher the correspondence between the job context and the rating standard used by a rater, the more accurate is the performance rating obtained.
2. The more the differences in the patterns of ratees' job behavior are incorporated into rating standards used by raters, the more accurate the performance ratings assigned by them.
3. Regardless of the rater's sex, women tend to be rated lower than males performing similar tasks.
4. When a rater and a ratee are of the same race, the ratee will be assigned higher ratings than when the rater and the ratee are from different races.
5. The higher the correspondence between the content of appraisal and job content, the higher the likelihood that accurate performance rating will result.
6. The higher the correspondence between performance appraisal procedures and the dominant organizational philosophy, the more likely it is that performance will be appraised accurately.
7. The more likely it is that raters will be held accountable for the ratings they assign, the more accurate will be their appraisal ratings.

Feldman (1981) has described in detail the various cognitive processes that influence appraisal. Person perception, the basis of performance evaluation, is conceptualized as a dual-process system. People assign individuals to categories. These categories are fuzzy sets, defined by family resemblances among their members and exemplified by category prototypes or images. Stimulus persons may be assigned to categories automatically by the virtue of their being in possession of obvious or salient attributes. The specific categories to which they are assigned constitute a function of perceiver and situational factors (for example, personal constructs and contextual salience) (p. 134). This automatic process may be superseded by a controlled or consciously monitored one when no salient category provides a satisfactory fit or information discrepant with initial categorization is obtained. Categorization affects the performance evaluation by limiting and selecting information about employees when memory-based judgments are made, by influencing stimulus-based judgments through the operation of attributional biases (p. 135). When employees are evaluated, information has to be retrieved from memory. Recent research has shown that memories about people (except on their very recent behavior) are biased toward the prototypes representing the categories to which they have been assigned. Dispositional factors in the perceiver and situational influences render certain categories more salient than others and certain memories (and prototype-generated false memories) more available than others. These further bias prediction of future behavior via the operation of representativeness and availability heuristics in judgment. Seeking further information to improve evaluation is an inherently biased process because people's information-gathering strategies selectively attend to supportive information and elicit hypothesis-confirming behavior (p. 138).

On the basis of his analysis of cognitive processes and information processing effects on performance assessment, Feldman (1981) suggests the following implications for the users of appraisals.

1. BARS and behavior observation scales may be seen as an attempt to define a more valid prototype of the successful or unsuccessful employee. Training in the use of such scales is an attempt to teach common prototypes to a set of raters to improve validity of these.
2. Multiple evaluations of performers may help overcome the idiosyncratic biases of any one person's category system, though common prototypes may still retain some.
3. The use of hard criteria should be encouraged in performance assessment (absenteeism, punctuality, job samples, and so forth, wherever appropriate).
4. Evaluators should be trained to make behavior sampling a routine part of their jobs to circumvent memory biases.
5. The use of trait ratings should be discouraged.

Cognitive complexity is another variable that has been thought to affect the accuracy of appraisal ratings. Cognitive complexity was defined by Schneier (1977) as "the degree to which a person possesses the ability to perceive behavior in a multidimensional manner" (p. 541). Cognitively complex people have a highly differentiated system of dimensions for perceiving the behavior of others as compared to cognitively simple ones. Schneier's (1977) study supported a cognitive compatibility theory of performance appraisal that the compatibility of raters' cognitive structure with the cognitive demands made by the rating format is crucial for quality ratings. Schneier found that cognitively complex raters were more confident in their ratings with BARS, were less lenient and restrictive of range errors, and showed less of the halo effect as compared to cognitively simple ones. Subsequently, five empirical investigations were carried out and no support has been found to this cognitively appealing theory of cognitive compatibility (Bernardin et al. 1982). Four experiments conducted recently by Bernardin et al., (1982) also failed to support this theory. There are some interesting research findings from attribution research that seem to have implications for performance analysis, and through it, for rating behavior.

When supervisors attribute the poor performance of their subordinates to individual factors (internal) rather than to environmental or task-related factors (external), they are likely to give poor ratings or show a higher punitive response to their subordinates. Supervisors are more likely to blame their subordinates for their poor performance than the environment, because an environmental attribution might suggest that poor supervision was involved. Kipnis (1972) demonstrated that supervisors gave more internal attributions for their subordinates' failures than for their success. Studies show that external attributions are more likely when the environment is made more salient than when the environment is not salient (McArthur and Post, 1977). Mitchell and Kalb (1982) in an experimental survey supported subsequently a field study, which demonstrated that experience in a task may make supervisors more aware of the external causes of poor performance such as a disruptive environment. The implication is that inexperienced supervisors should pay more attention and check their tendency to only attribute the failure of their subordinates to internal factors, and thereby improve the quality of their ratings.

Another factor that influences raters' biases is their inability to differentiate the performance inputs (efforts) of performers from their performance outcomes (results). While effort and ability are attributable to performers' results or outcomes, they are a consequence of interactions between the individuals and environmental factors. Most often, reporting managers tend to assess their subordinates on the basis of outcomes, and particularly when the outcomes are poor, they tend to rate the inputs as also being poor. In an experimental study by Mitchell and Kalb (1982), supervisors with and without knowledge of outcomes of their subordinates' behavior were studied for their attribution tendencies. Those with outcome knowledge tended to attribute negative outcomes more to their subordinates. Reporting managers therefore should be aware of these tendencies and focus more on the behavior of their subordinates than on the outcomes of their actions.

## REDUCING RATERS' BIASES

The theoretical considerations mentioned earlier bring out the complexity of the appraisal process. As stated earlier, as long as humans are going to assess other individuals, there is bound to be a certain amount of subjectivity. One way of reducing this is by making assessors more aware of the dynamic factors affecting their perception and evaluation of their subordinates. This can be done through raters' training, their participation in the construction of rating scales, and the use of certain statistical methods. Some research-based evidence is available on these aspects:

### Raters' Training

Raters' training has generally been shown to be effective in reducing errors, especially if the training is extensive and allows practice (Landy and Farr, 1980; Kearney, 1978; and Decotiis and Petit, 1978).

Hyde and Smith (1982) have pointed out what training can or cannot do to remedy the various problems associated with performance appraisal. They hypothesize that training can have a minimal impact on motivation among raters and ratees, as this is a behavioral problem and not a skill deficiency. Training of reporting managers also has very little impact on time delays in feedback as this is essentially a system problem. Training also has very little impact on solving of appraisal problems arising due to interdependence of tasks as well as their observability or performance, structure of authority system, power differentials, and nature of communicated appraisals, as these are all complex interrelated organizational problems that must be confronted before any appraisal system can be developed. Training has a certain impact on helping reporting managers comprehend the conflicting objectives of appraisals (for example, development and control at the same time) and meet their requirements. It has the highest potential for enabling effective change in reducing subjective errors in evaluation, such as the halo effect, polarity, central tendency, etc. Hyde and Smith (1982) have suggested a four-phase-training for effective introduction of the appraisal system.

Phase 1: Knowledge presentation.
Phase 2: Analysis and evaluation of methods and errors.
Phase 3: Practice evaluating performance.
Phase 4: Evaluation of training.

## Raters' Participation in Scale Construction

Another method used in reducing rating errors is by the participation of the raters in scale construction. Empirical studies indicate that when raters participate totally in constructing the scales they use, it is likely to reduce rating errors (Friedman and Cornelius, 1976; and Warmke and Billings, 1979). Friedman and Cornelius (1976) found that full participation in scale construction significantly reduced the halo effect and increased convergent validity among Reserve Officer Training Corps Cadet's ratings of instructors. This study showed that the effect held across scale formats (BARS and graphic scales) and construction of one scale also reduced errors on another unfamiliar scale. Warmke and Billings (1979) indicate from their study that even a short two-hour time investment required for scale development can increase scale acceptance and reduce rating errors.

## Statistical Control of Rating Errors

With inconsistencies in research findings on the effectiveness of BARS in reducing rating errors, attempts have been made by some researchers to statistically control the "halo effect" and such other errors. Holzbach (1978) presented a logical basis for using partial correlations as methods for reducing the halo effect errors. His suggestion is based on the assumption that raters are unable to arrive at ratings on individual performance dimensions that are independent of their overall evaluation of the ratees. Therefore, it is possible to remove the halo component from dimension ratings by statistically eliminating the variance in common between the dimensions and overall ratings. Holzbach (1978) reported striking reductions in mean dimensional inter-correlations after removing the effect of overall rating. Landy et al. (1980) found support for the effectiveness of partialing. Harvey (1982) examined this practice by questioning the lack of an empirical base for the causal assumptions made on the halo effect as well by empirically demonstrating that re-analysis of data used by Landy et al. (1980) indicates that effectiveness partialing out may be an artifact.

Researchers in this area do not seem to have tried out statistical feedback for raters as a mechanism to reduce raters' biases. If biases take place in the minds of raters, it is futile to look for corrections through statistical controls, which can at the most enable temporary reductions, and that too to a questionable degree, as indicated earlier. Statistical feedback given to raters can be a potential way of reducing errors and bringing about a common frame of reference among different raters. Such raters' feedback requires the following analysis to be done by personnel and HRD departments and fed back to the raters:

1. Trends of the appraisal ratings of every reporting manager should be studied over a period of time. Data such as the following need to be compiled, analyzed, and fed back.

   • Number of ratees rated by the reporting manager in the last few years (a three-year period at the minimum).

- Dimension-wise analysis of performance rating assigned by the reporting manager to all the performers rated by him/her (for example, the frequency and percentage of times a rating of 5 was assigned on "initiative" or the frequency and percentage of times a rating of 3 was assigned on initiative, and so forth.). These can be further analyzed for each category of ratees (secretarial staff, supervisors, assistant managers, and so forth) if the rater is the reporting officer for a number of them. Since KPAs may not be common to all the performers, all KPAs should be treated as equal and combined for such calculations.
- A dimension-wise average (or per KPA average) and standard deviation of the ratings should be assigned to all the performers rated by a reporting manager.

2. Trends of appraisal ratings given by peer reporting managers (of similar rank, position, role incumbency, etc.) should be given to their subordinates (with or without mentioning their names). Analysis, such as in Step 1, should be provided to enable raters to compare whether they have been lenient or strict.

3. Company-wise trends (frequencies, percentages, means, and standard deviations) of appraisal ratings should be calculated for the last few years on each dimension.

This data helps reporting managers to view their rating behavior vis-à-vis those of others in the company, and accordingly modify it if needed. Discussions can be held between the raters and the ratees on this data so that they can benefit from these.

## Performance Ratings for Development versus Administrative Decisions

A performance appraisal system should assess managerial and behavioral capabilities as an integral part of its functions. In a development-oriented appraisal system, performance ratings are not ends in themselves. They are one of the instruments that aid the process of development. Hence, these dimensions should be identified and incorporated in the appraisal form with a view to generate data for developmental purposes.

Subjectivity is a part of development and executives should not be over concerned about generating objective data. Their concern should be more on generating and including the most appropriate dimensions that are important for existing jobs to be performed well as well as for developing their potential for future roles. Rating scales, such as BARS, are useful to the extent that they provide clarity on behavior associated with different dimensions. If such scales can be developed and can complement the objectives of development, it should be encouraged. Involving the executives in developing such scales, reporting managers sharing their expectations with performers at the start of the year, training them, and giving periodic statistical feedback about their rating behavior may take care of some biases.

It is necessary to separate appraisal ratings for developmental purposes from those for reward purposes. In a development-oriented appraisal, performance standards are decided between the reporting manager and the performer in the beginning of the year, and may differ from performer to performer. For reward administration, promotions, and other administrative purposes, appraisal ratings based on common performance standards (common at least to performers at the same level in the managerial hierarchy) are required. Here, reporting managers compare (and even unconsciously rank) the subordinates they are appraising, and then rate them. Objectivity is important for such purposes, and given our culture, we may not be able to do away with confidentiality for some more time. Even if employees are confidentially rated on some dimensions for administrative decisions, biases are likely to be less if such ratings are given after assessment for development purposes. Making development-oriented appraisal systems available to reporting managers is likely to significantly increase their performance-related information and reduce their biases. Participation in a development-oriented appraisal system may improve the cognitive complexity of reporting managers as well as performers and may help reduce their biases. It may also help executives develop cognitive flexibility in categorizing employees by making available a large number of schemata on the basis of information available to reporting managers. Since the counseling process (discussed in the next chapter) strengthens the dyadic relationship between reporting managers and performers, and generates trust, biases may be further reduced. However, when two different appraisal formats are used separately for development and administrative purposes, there is a possibility of reporting managers assigning different ratings for the same individual in the two forms. Performers should be helped to comprehend this difference due to varying performance standards being used for the two appraisals.

# Forced Distribution or Bell Curve and Its Management

In India, most organizations use the bell curve or the forced distribution method. This is a measure of the inability of a corporation to get managers to assess employees realistically and faithfully without leniency or other biases. The author is associated with many organizations, particularly in the public sector, where most employees are rated above 90 percent across the board, making it difficult for the top management to distinguish good performers from weak, average, or poor ones. As a result, the top management has started insisting that managers distribute their ratings into a forced distribution using a normal curve (see Figure 5.1).

The concept of forced ranking or normalization is based on the principle of relative comparison. It involves normalization of performance ratings and plotting it on a bell curve. It is also known as normalization of appraisal rating or the vitality curve.

Managers are asked to rate employees in a department with the predetermined distribution of high, average, and low performers. Categories vary (outstanding, excellent, very good, good, average, and below average) as well as percentages—normally 20 percent, 60 percent, 20 percent, or their variations. Forced distribution is achieved by one or more of the following:

FIGURE 5.1

The Normal Probability Curve

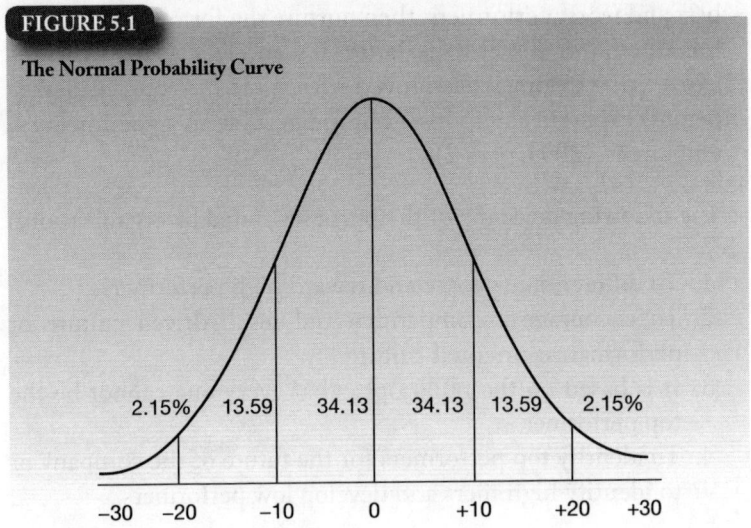

2.15%  13.59  34.13  34.13  13.59  2.15%

−30  −20  −10  0  +10  +20  +30

*Source:* Author's personal database.

1. First assessor
2. Reviewing officer
3. Departmental review committees
4. HR department
5. Top management
6. Statistical techniques

The practice of forced ranking (FR) gained popularity when Jack Welch applied it rigorously in GE during his tenure. According to Cooper and Argyris (1998), FR is a performance intervention which can be defined as an evaluation method of forced distribution, where managers are required to distribute ratings for those being evaluated into pre-specified performance distribution rankings.

Meisler defines it as follows:

It's a workforce-management tool based on the premise that in order to develop and thrive, a corporation must identify its

best and worst performers, then nurture the former and reha-
bilitate and/or discard the latter. It's an elixir that in these
slow—growth times has proved irresistible to scores of des-
perate corporate chieftains—but indigestible to a good many
employees. (2003, para 2)

The following are some of the purposes stated by organizations:

1. To differentiate people and reward high performers.
2. To encourage a competitive and result-driven culture or
   performance-oriented culture.
3. It is based on the philosophy that every one cannot be the
   top performer.
4. To identify top performers for the future of the company or
   to identify high fliers and develop low performers.

Although individuals' supervisors conduct the formal performance
review discussions, management members assign their rankings.
This is followed by debates on the performance of comparable individuals from across the organization. Often, these management
members are not knowledgeable about individuals' performance.
Therefore, individuals' rankings depend on their supervisors' willingness to fight on their behalf. The other advantages and disadvantages of following the bell curve or normalization of rating
method are given below:

1. It forces appraisers and managers to think.
2. It can create a competitive environment.
3. It helps benchmarking.
4. It brings down inflationary ratings.
5. It makes people focus on their performance.
6. Low performers can be identified and developed.
7. Benchmarks for high performance can be created.

However, the forced distribution can have many negative effects or
disadvantages. Some of them include the following:

1. Genuine high performers may get pushed down due to the forced curve. Aggressive bosses can push some of their juniors down. In some companies, weak managers have been found to give high ratings and push their teams.
2. Assertive departmental heads and managers can push large number of high performers.
3. It can create unhealthy competition instead of healthy collaboration.
4. It has a very high potential for introducing organizational politics, especially if the forced ratings are linked to promotions and high incentives. Negative effects are intensified with differential incentives and rewards.
5. It can give rise to rumors and mutual blame games.
6. It makes people suspicious and lose trust in their seniors, colleagues, and juniors.
7. This is further intensified if rewards are built into future salaries and benefits.
8. Visible people get higher ranks and sincere low key performers are pushed out.

## MANAGING FORCED DISTRIBUTION

The best way to manage forced distribution is not to have it at all, and let the process take place naturally. If it cannot be helped, it should be practiced for a certain period of time, until employees start differentiating to the desired extent. The following methods can be used to manage forced distribution and its negative effects:

1. Train raters to become more objective.
2. Delink from rewards and incentives but use information for various talent management practices.
3. Do not do this automatically based on numbers. Understand the nature and limitations of various scales explained in the beginning of this chapter.
4. Encourage debate and discussion before finally categorizing people into groups and labeling them.

5. Realize the flaws in using numbers generated by ratings as the main source of distribution.
6. Most ratings are based on approximations of interval scales and are not equalized between raters, and even with the same rater, for differing categories of employees (newcomers, difficulty levels of KPAs, diversity, background differences, and so forth).
7. Accept subjectivity as a part of life.
8. Differentiate when you are sure that measures adopted are certain and accepted largely.
9. Educate employees and committees continuously to accept the dynamics of differentiation and benefits.
10. Give adequate weightage to team assessment and rewards to nullify unhealthy competition and differentiation created by forced distribution.
11. Listen to grievances patiently.
12. Focus the attention of employees on performance-related improvements rather than on categorization.
13. Demonstrate and share information on how people have moved from one category to another in the past.

Tips for Avoiding Problems of Using Forced Ranking System

1. Have open and clear communication stating the purpose of the forced ranking system and explaining that the criteria to be used in the process of normalization will help to remove fear and resistant among employees.
2. Ensure that criteria used to rank employees is clear, objective, measurable, and most importantly, not vulnerable to assumptions or stereotypes relating to protected classes.
3. Carry out intensive training for every employee (appraiser) who will conduct performance appraisals.
4. It is important to assess the potential adverse impact on protected groups prior to finalizing decisions related to forced rankings. If there are statistical discrepancies, there needs to be a study on whether these are legitimate or the result of biased decision-making.

The intent behind the concept of forced ranking is to promote good performance and reward those who are hardworking and deserving. It also encourages productivity, so that employees become more committed toward achieving their goals. However, it is important that the HR department communicates the purpose of the process and maintains transparency to the largest possible extent. Thorough training needs to be conducted for appraisers to understand the concept and methodology to make the process successful. Another step that the HR department and the management need to take is to promote implementation of a thoughtful performance appraisal and a logical ranking system to avoid biases as much as possible.

However, steps should be taken to proactively arrest the negative impact of forced rankings on teamwork as well as on employees' morale and engagement.

# 6

# Performance Conversations and Performance Review Discussions

Performance conversations (PCs) pertain to performance-related issues. They can either be initiated by performers, or their superiors, or reporting officers, or seniors. In fact, they can be initiated by anyone who is interested in improving his/her performance, competencies, commitment, or organizational support. We have discussed earlier that improvements in performance can be achieved by managing various parts of the performance equation simultaneously, or step by step.

Performance is normally planned by performers with the approval of their seniors or reporting managers. Once performance is planned, along with competencies and support, the next step is to perform. During the performance process, many issues may arise, which relate to one or more of the following:

1. Dealing with performance plan, including clarity of KRAs, KPAs, key performance indicators, targets, time taken, weightage, or any other issues.
2. Dealing with clarity of roles, and also with competencies or support requirements from own department, or internal or external customers.
3. Dealing with changed circumstances requiring re-planning of work or changes.
4. Changes that may arise due to transfers, new appointments, technological changes, and so forth.
5. Changes that may occur due to the changed preference of seniors or organizational priorities.
6. Clarification on the style of doing work, speed, quality, cooperation expected from others, not anticipated competency gaps, competency utilization possibilities, method changes, and so on.

Whenever such changes occur, it is useful to have short performance conversations and ensure that performers and their reporting managers are on the same wave length and share an understanding.

A performance conversation may last anywhere from five to 30 minutes. While there is no hard and fast rule about when a conversation can be called a performance conversation, normally a prolonged conversation may not be warranted for short and periodic discussions, sharing of information, reworking of priorities, and seeking or giving guidance.

PCs are short discussions on performance-related issues, and are aimed at enhancing an understanding of performance parameters that improve the performance of the performers, the team, the reporting manager, or all of them. PCs are short. They constitute point-by-point focused discussions and can be formal or informal. The process is always informal. They can be made formal by making them mandatory for five minutes every day between the team members or one-on-one discussions between performers and their reporting managers. They can be informal as and when required: once a week, or fortnight, or any time anywhere.

They may be relating to performance plans, clarifications, information, guidance on queries, and may include idea-generating or idea-giving exercises, or even a problem-solving exercise.

The objective of PC is performance improvement through an enhanced understanding of the situation, plan, or the problem at hand. They include enhancement of communication and trust-building mechanisms. Performers, who have frequent PCs with their reporting managers, learn from them, communicate with them, and also influence them by providing information. Similarly, reporting managers learn from their juniors, communicate with them, influence them, and help them. All the following processes in relation to performance review discussion (PRD) are equally applicable in PCs.

A PC is a two-way communication performance issue relating to the self, the dyad, the team or the organization between performers and their seniors, or reporting managers, or the team for a short time to lift up the level of understanding of factors causing or hindering performance. It should result in performance improvements, directly or indirectly, immediately or in the long run. They also help to build mutuality, trust, communication and problem-solving abilities.

PRD is a substitute name for what used to be referred to earlier as performance counseling or coaching. The term performance counseling is quite often misunderstood and wrongly interpreted as the process of the boss *correcting* or *controlling* employee's behavior by giving him/her negative feedback in an assertive manner. When employees make mistakes or become unmanageable or non-cooperative, executives often say that they need counseling. Some managers are also known to make statements such as "I called him for counseling and gave him a piece of my mind," "in counseling, I told him clearly that I am not going to tolerate his behavior any-more," "I called him for counseling and finished him off," and so on. Unfortunately, due to the misuse of the term "counseling," it has acquired negative connotations in the minds of most managers. They confuse counseling as being equivalent to "verbal threats," "criticism," and "negative feedback." Actually, such behavior prevents counseling.

The second reason why counseling has acquired a negative image in the minds of employees is because it is often equated with clinical counseling and psychotherapy, which are often associated with problem cases. In fact, the major difference between clinical counseling and performance counseling is precisely that performance counseling is normally done in the regular course of performance and not only if there are problems.

PRD is preferred in place of performance counseling in view of these difficulties.

It is a neutral term and refers to a formal discussion between the reporting manager and the performer on the latter's dyadic performance for a given period of time to identify the factors that have positively or negatively affected his/her performance, and to prepare action plans to improve this by using the performance equation. It is a systematic review of the performance of the performer and reporting manager. However, its focus is on the performer. It only focuses on the reporting manager to the extent that his/her own performance (style, support given, guidance, etc.) has affected the performer.

When there are day-to-day performance-related problems, executives should resort to appropriate methods of solving them rather than to discuss it in PRD. This is because an exclusive focus on a particular problem or issue may hamper it. While specific problems may be discussed as a part of analyzing and understanding performance patterns, the main focus is on the entire performance (tasks and behavior) during a particular period. In clinical counseling, people facing problems go to a therapist for help on their own initiative, and therefore have a high motivation to solve their problems and improve their capabilities to deal with their environment. In PRD, reporting managers initiate the discussion as a part of an appraisal system or a process that takes place in the organization.

The onus of making the PRD successful rests jointly on the reporting manager and the performer, although the reporting manager has a major responsibility by virtue of his/her position in the organizational hierarchy. It is this that makes PRD complex. Reporting managers, who are at a higher status level, have to carry on the task of helping their subordinates by creating an atmosphere of acceptance. Thus, unlike clinical counseling, in PRD, reporting managers have the additional task of motivating performers to participate effectively in the process. In addition, while continuing to exercise their authority as bosses outside the PRD session, they should generate a climate of acceptance, mutuality, trust, and openness. Recognition of this complexity is essential for the successful implementation of PRDs. Failure to recognize this often leads managers to point out inconsistencies in their bosses by making statements such as "He was nice during PRD but once out of it, he had been very strict with me." However, while PRD should lead to enhanced mutual understanding, they need not result in leniency or softness in dealing with people.

While PRD should take place at least once a year as an integral part of PMS as has been outlined in this book, it can be carried out more frequently by managers. It is advisable to have them frequently, depending on the needs of performers and availability of their bosses or senior reporting managers. In fact, the more attention managers pay to PRDs, the more time they are likely to gain in the long run because of the improved capabilities of their subordinates.

Any organization that is interested in using a good PMS which is aimed at developing employees, needs to practice and pay enough attention to PRDs. Performance appraisal does not serve the purpose of developing employees unless an effective system of PRD is introduced and practiced in an organization. Such discussions can be defined as the help provided by managers to their juniors in analyzing their performance and other job behavior in order to increase their job effectiveness. They essentially focus on an analysis of individuals' performance on the job and identification of their training needs for further improvement.

A PRD is a dyadic process. It is based on the relation between two persons: a manager providing help or having a PRD and an employee to whom such help is being given or who is a performer. It differs from training mainly in the intensity of the dyadic relationship and its focus on establishing mutuality and confidentiality. Managers provide such help or hold PRDs at various stages, when the employees are facing difficulties or problems. The focus of PRD is on employees' performance in the tasks assigned to them. PRD is also sometimes called "coaching," mainly because its purpose is to improve the performance of employees. However, although the word "coaching" is widely used for this purpose, the term PRD is more neutral and is a much wider and appropriate term for such a process.

## Objectives of PRDs

PRD aims at developing performers as well as reporting managers. However, it focuses more on performers. It involves the following:

1. Helps them realize their potential as managers, leaders, etc.
2. Helps them understand themselves, their strengths and weaknesses.
3. Provides them an opportunity to acquire more insights into their behavior and analyze the dynamics of such behavior.
4. Helps them have a better understanding of the environment.
5. Increases their personal and inter-personal effectiveness by giving them feedback on their behavior and helps them analyze their inter-personal competencies.

6. Encourages them to set goals for their further improvement.
7. Encourages them to generate alternatives to deal with various problems.
8. Creates an empathic atmosphere to share and discuss their tensions, conflicts, concerns, and problems.
9. Helps them develop various action plans for their further improvement.
10. Helps them review their progress in achieving various objectives in a non-threatening manner.

It also helps reporting managers know more about performers, the conditions (task clarity, ability, motivation, organizational support etc.), affecting their performance, competencies and limitations. It also enables them to influence performers in terms of opportunities to make an impact and prove themselves.

## Conditions for Effective PRDs

PRD is a means and not an end in itself. Performance improvements and development do not occur just because of it, which could be an effective instrument in helping people integrate with their organization and have a sense of involvement and satisfaction. The following conditions are necessary for PRD to be effective:

1. *General climate of openness and mutuality:* If the organization or department in which the employee is working is full of tension, and people do not trust each other, PRD cannot be effective. A climate of trust and openness is essential for effective PRD.
2. *General helpful and empathic attitude of management:* PRD involves providing effective help to an employee, which is not possible unless the reporting manager has a helping attitude and empathy for the performer.
3. *Sense of uninhibited participation by subordinates in the performance review process:* Unless subordinates in a department or organization feel free to participate (without inhibition) in the process of review and feedback, PRD cannot be effective.

It does not constitute a one-way process of communicating to employees what they should or should not do. It is a process of developing dialogue, which eventually contributes to better understanding on the part of the performer.

4. *Dialogic relationship in goal setting and performance review:* PRD focuses on performers' achievement of the performance goals they set in consultation with their managers. Joint participation by employees and their reporting managers are necessary in goal setting as well as in performance reviews. Without such a collaborative effort, PRD does not achieve its purpose.

5. *Focus on work-oriented behavior:* The main purpose of PRD is to help employees improve their performance. Such discussions can be effective if the focus is kept on work-related goals rather than attention being diffused into various other areas. A discussion may include other related and personal issues, but these are used to refocus on improvement in organizational roles rather than on personal or general personality problems.

6. *Focus on work-related problems and difficulties:* PRD is not only related to achievement of goals, but also to contextual problems in achieving or not achieving the goals. Analysis of performance, therefore, is the basis of PRDs. Details of performance review and analysis are discussed in Rao and Pareek (1978).

7. *Avoidance of discussion of salary and other rewards:* PRD may not serve its purpose if it includes discussions about a salary raise and rewards. Its main purpose is to use performance appraisal in improving the performance of employees and on planning, rather than understanding the relationship between performance and rewards. Bringing such a discussion into a PRD may vitiate its main purpose.

## WHAT CONSTITUTES A PERFORMANCE REVIEW DISCUSSION?

A PRD is held by a senior for his/her junior in competence, knowledge, psychological expertise, or in the hierarchical position in an organization. There are three main processes involved in

PRD, communication, influence and help, during which a reporting manager communicates with a performer. Communication involves receiving messages (listening), giving messages (responding), and providing feedback. The person holding a PRD does all the three things. PRD also involves influencing the performer in several ways. Managers cannot escape the fact that they are influencing their juniors in such a way that the latter are able to move in a certain direction. However, this influence is of a special type. It enables the junior to exercise greater autonomy, provides positive reinforcement so that desirable behavior is strengthened, and creates conditions in which the person is able to learn from the behavior of the reporting manager through a process of identification.

The third element in the process—helping—functions in a similar way. It involves three different elements. Helping behavior is based on the concern and empathy the reporting manager has for the performer as well as on the mutuality of the relationship. The performer responds as much to the reporting manager's needs as the former does to the latter's. And finally, helping primarily involves identification of the developmental needs of performer so that he/she can develop and increase his/her effectiveness. This dynamic process of PRD is shown in Figure 6.1. The various elements of the process will be explained in more detail further in the book.

## COMMUNICATION

Interpersonal communication is the basis of a performance review in which both the employee and his/her reporting officer are involved. The general climate of such conversation in a performance review should be congenial, which may help the employee to be in a receptive mood. It is important to keep in mind that communication is greatly influenced by how problems and issues are perceived by the two persons involved in the conversation. Communication may get distorted if people are not empathic to each other and do not try to understand each other's points of view. Nonverbal communication is as important as verbal communication. People speak much more through their gestures than words. The tone and manner of speaking is also important.

**FIGURE 6.1**

**The Process of PRD**

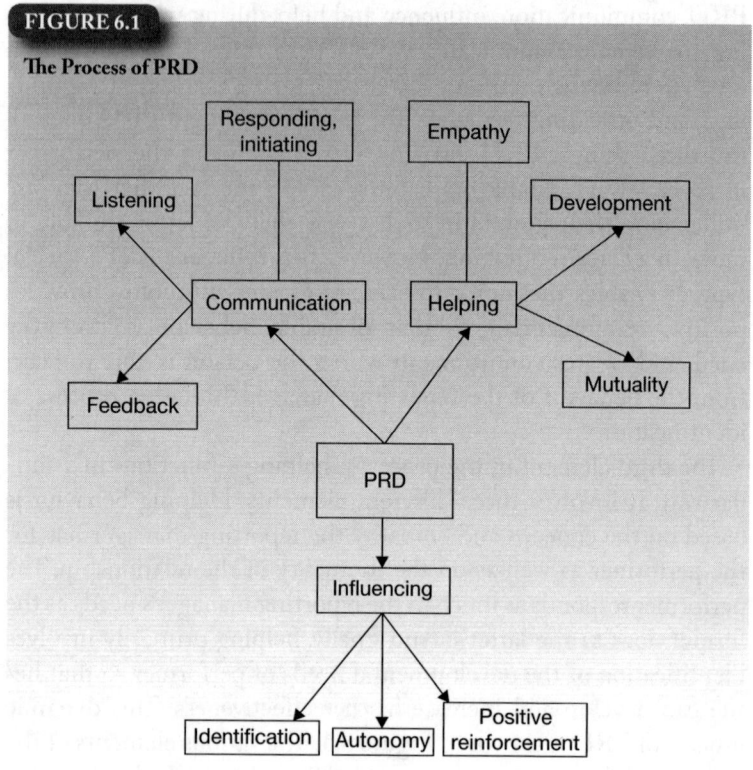

*Source:* Rao and Pareek, 1978.

There are three main elements in communication.

## Listening

Listening is the first effective step in communication. It involves paying attention to the various messages being sent by the other person. The obvious message constitutes the ideas being communicated (cognitive message). But the hidden message may be the feelings and the concerns the other person may not be able to put clearly in words. Listening to feelings and concerns is very important for effective PRD. It involves skills that can be practiced. Some exercises can be used to improve listening to such hidden messages (see Rao and Pareek, 1978).

**Asking Questions and Responding**

Questions can facilitate or hinder the process of communication. They can serve several purposes such as helping in getting more information, establishing mutuality, clarifying matters, and stimulating thinking. In a PRD, questions play a very important role. Some questions can shut off the performer or make him/her dependent on the reporting manager. Another set of questions can build the autonomy of the performer. Obviously, the latter is helpful, not the former.

### *Questions that Do Not Help*

The following types of questions are not only unhelpful, but they also hinder the process of effective PRD.

- *Critical questions:* Questions that are used to criticize, reprimand, or doubt the performer's word create a gap between him/her and the reporting manager. The way the question is asked (tone) may indicate that the question is a critical one. The choice of words may also indicate the critical nature of the question. "Why did you fail to achieve your targets?" communicates criticism, whereas "why could you not attain your targets?" normally communicates an invitation to examine the hindering factors. "How did you again fall short of your target" is a reprimanding question. "How can you achieve this target; you failed last time?" indicates doubts about the ability of the performer. All such critical questions either shut off the performer or make him/her diffident.
- *Testing questions:* Questions that are asked to determine whether a person is right or wrong, or how much he/she knows are evaluating or testing questions. Such questions may tend to make the other person defensive. In a testing question, the person who is asking the question takes a superior attitude, and the other person is put in a kind of witness box. Such questions may also take the form of cross-examination. A reporting manager who proposes to find out why his/her employee was not able to meet his/her

target can easily slip into the cross-examination, testing, or evaluation mode. Again, the tone of the manager may determine whether the question asked is a testing one. These are sometimes similar to critical questions.

- *Resenting questions:* A person may ask questions to indicate his/her resentment over the behavior of the other person. When an employee in a PRD asks, "how should I attain a higher target?" it may indicate his/her resentment, depending on the tone in which such a question is asked.

- *Leading questions:* Quite often, we unwittingly ask questions that indicate the kind of answers we want in return. Such a question may be asked after making a statement. For example, a reporting officer may say to his/her employee, "you could not attain the target because the maintenance department did not cooperate. Is that true?" or it may be put in the question form, "were you not able to attain the target because the maintenance department did not cooperate?" Both are leading questions, which almost seduce the other person to go along the line of thinking of the one who puts the question. It tends to stop further exploration and is not helpful.

### Questions That Are Helpful

The following types of questions may be helpful in developing a more healthy relationship and increasing the effectiveness of the performer.

- *Testing questions:* Questions that are asked to indicate that the questioner is seeking help or suggestions may indicate the trust he/she has in the other person. The question, "How do you think I can deal with the problem I am facing?" seeks help from the other person. Such questions may be asked by the employee as well as the supervisor.

- *Clarifying questions:* Questions may be asked to collect information, or more facts and figures. Such questions are very helpful. If reporting managers ask their employees several questions to obtain more information about various aspects, the latter will help them obtain relevant information to understand their problems. After listening to a person for some time, a reporting manager may paraphrase his/her statement (also called mirroring). He/she may then ask a question to confirm whether his/her understanding is correct. For example, the question "You are worried about your lack of knowledge of the new system. Is that so?" is a clarifying question. Clarifying questions help the manager and the performer remain at the same level throughout the conversation.

- *Open questions:* The most useful questions are those that stimulate reflection and thinking on the part of the performer. "Why do you think we have not achieved the targets this year while the other company has done so?" is an open question inviting the other person to explore the various possible dimensions and to share these with the person asking the question. Open questions encourage creativity and a tendency to explore different options that may have been neglected till then. Such questions are very useful.

### *Responding to Questions*

Reporting managers sometimes use responses. Some of these are useful and others dysfunctional. Some reporting managers may use certain types of responses than others more often. It is necessary to be aware of these. Responses that alienate performers, or criticize him, or order them are likely to be ineffective. Empathetic, supportive, and exploring responses are usually effective.

### Feedback

Interpersonal feedback is an important input for increasing self-awareness. It helps to reduce the blind spots in people, and help them become more aware about their strengths and weaknesses. If properly used, it results in enhanced mutuality between two people. The processes of inter-personal feedback and conditions, which make these effective, have been discussed in detail in the book (Pareek, 1977). The following suggestions are reproduced from that source.

Feedback is effective if the person who provides it (reporting manager) makes sure that it is the following:

1. Descriptive and not evaluative
2. Focused on the behavior of a person and not on him/her
3. Data-based and specific, and not based on impression
4. Reinforcement of positive new behavior
5. Suggestive and not prescriptive
6. Continuous
7. Mainly personal, providing data from one's own experience
8. Need-based and solicited
9. Intended to help
10. Focused on modifiable behavior
11. Satisfactory for the needs of the feedback provider and the one who receives
12. feedback
13. Checked and verified
14. Well timed
15. Contributes to mutuality and building up of a relationship

### Reporting Manager

The person who receives feedback should be encouraged to explore ways to improve his/her behavior rather than be forced to adopt defensive behavior. The following defensive behavior may not help a performer use feedback properly.

1. Disagreeing with feedback as opposed to owning up responsibility for behavior.
2. Rationalization (explaining away feedback by giving reasons) instead of self-analysis to find out the cause of such behavior.
3. Projection (communicating negative feelings to the other person) as opposed to empathy (trying to understand the point of view of the performer).
4. Displacement (expressing negative feelings to a person who may not fight back) instead of exploration (taking the help of the other person in knowing more about the feedback given).

5. Quick acceptance without exploration as opposed to collection of more information and data to understand the behavior.
6. Aggression toward the person providing feedback instead of seeking his/her help in understanding it.
7. Humor and wit as opposed to concern for improvement.
8. Counter-dependence (rejection of authority) instead of listening carefully to the person giving feedback.
9. Cynicism (generally strong skepticism that things cannot improve) as opposed to a positive critical attitude to accept some feedback and question others.
10. Generalization (explaining things in a general way) instead of experimentation.

## INFLUENCING

Influencing another person means making an impact on him/her in a relationship. Such an impact need not necessarily be restrictive. Influencing a performer in an effective PRD has three aspects.

### Increasing the Person's Autonomy

Usually, influencing people is understood as restricting their autonomy and directing them into channels that are pre-determined by the person exerting influence. Positive influence is the opposite. The other person's autonomy is increased and he/she has a larger scope to make his/her own choices. Even this constitutes influencing a person, although of a different kind. Flanders (1970) makes a distinction between two modes of influence: (a) the direct mode of influence (which restricts the freedom of the other person), and (b) the indirect mode of influence (which increases the freedom of the other person). Flanders has developed some categories to indicate the two modes. He classifies criticism and punishment in the first category, and encouraging a person in the second category of influence. The reason is obvious. When a person is criticized or punished, some actions for which he/she is criticized or punished are inhibited and the person avoids those in future. This restricts his/her freedom. On the other hand, if a person is praised or recognized, he/she feels encouraged to take more initiative in exploring new avenues. This increases his/her autonomy. Pareek and Rao (1971) have discussed this in detail, focusing on how teacher education and training strategies can be remodeled, based on research findings about these two kinds of behavior. In a PRD, much more use is made of the indirect mode of influence by recognizing and expressing feelings, acknowledging and praising a performer's good ideas, and raising questions that promote thinking and exploration.

## Positive Reinforcement

Skinner (1971) has established that a change in behavior cannot be brought about in humans through punishment or negative reinforcement, but only through positive reinforcement. Influencing a person positively involves providing encouragement and reinforcing success so that he/she takes more initiative and is able to experiment with new ideas. Change cannot take place without experiment and risk-taking, which are encouraged through positive reinforcement.

## Identification

Levinson (1962) has stressed the importance of the process, whereby employees identify themselves with their managers. One major influence that helps employees develop their capabilities is the opportunity for them to identify with individuals with more experience, skill, and influence than them. According to McClelland (1976), this is the first stage in the development of psychological maturity or power motivation and this legitimate need should be fulfilled. Levinson (1962) talks about several barriers that may come in the way of this legitimate process of identification: lack of time, intolerance of mistakes, complete rejection of dependency needs, repression of rivalry, and unexamined relationships. He suggests that to help development of the process of identification, it is necessary for the managers to also examine their own processes and need of interacting with their subordinates.

## HELPING

A PRD is essentially meant to provide help. This involves several processes, but there are three that are fairly important.

### Concern and Empathy

If managers have no concern for performers, they cannot effectively help them in a PRD session. Such concern is shown when the reporting manager is able to empathize with his/her juniors. These is reflected in the kind of questions he/she asks, and the tone in which the conversation takes place. Managers should constantly ask themselves how much concern and genuine empathy they have for the juniors with whom they have PRD sessions. Without this genuine concern, a PRD may only degenerate into a ritual, and the performer cannot achieve his/her goals.

### Mutuality of Relationship

A PRD should not be regarded as merely giving help. It is also about receiving help in various areas. A PRD cannot be effective unless such a relationship is established, and both the persons involved feel free to ask for and provide help to each other. Mutuality is based on trust and a genuine perception that each person has enough to contribute, and that although reporting managers are in a superior position, they continue to learn and receive help from their juniors.

### Identifying Development Needs

The main purpose of a PRD is to identify the development needs of employees. This can be done in various ways. A PRD should result in clear and systematic identification of such needs and subsequent plans on how they can be fulfilled. Sperry and Hess (1974) have advocated the use of contact PRD, which they defined as the process by which managers effectively help their juniors in the techniques of keying, responding, problem-solving, and development by guiding them. Contact PRD is based on a transactional analysis approach and makes use of several skills that have been discussed earlier. Keying refers to reading people. Managers use an appropriate frame of reference to understand what their juniors mean by their verbal and nonverbal responses. Responding relates to what managers communicate to their juniors. What is learnt from keying is replayed in a manner that adds to, subtracts from, and interchanges with the meaning performers communicate. Guiding is the technique managers use to motivate or help their juniors to change their behavior. As motivators, managers can increase their juniors' drive to more effectively accomplish their objectives.

Morrisay (1972) has suggested some other techniques, such as the you-we technique, the second-hand compliment, advice-request, and the summary. In the you-we technique, one uses "you" to compliment and "we" to criticize (for example, "you are doing a great job, but we have a problem"). A second-hand compliment entails communicating to a junior a compliment received from a third party (for example, "Mr Raman says you have done an excellent job for him"). An advise-request is asking a junior employee for suggestions and advice. Summarizing at the end helps to clarify decisions taken, fix responsibilities, and integrate the whole discussion.

## Sequential Process of PRD

PRDs are meant to help employees grow and develop in an organization. Every manager has a PRD with his/her junior, knowingly or unknowingly, in his/her day-to-day work life. Effective reporting managers are those who help their juniors become more aware of their strengths and weaknesses, and help them grow and improve their strong points and overcome their weaknesses. Through mutuality and support, they help their performers develop by providing the right emotional climate. Mutuality involves managers working together with their juniors and developing future plans of action for the latter's growth and contribution to their organization. Support involves accepting an employee as a total person with his/her strengths and weaknesses, and encouraging him/her with warmth. A PRD requires certain inter-personal skills, which can be acquired easily if managers are genuinely interested in developing their juniors. PRD skills are important for managers, particularly at the time of performance reviews. Good managers counsel their juniors regularly in their jobs whenever the need arises. Annual performance reviews provide formal opportunities for formal PRD. A formal PRD process passes through certain stages that are important for managers to take note of. The PRD process has three phases: rapport-building, exploration, and action planning. At the rapport-building phase, a good reporting manager attempts to establish a climate of acceptance, warmth, support, openness, and mutuality. Managers do this by empathizing with their juniors by listening to their problems and feelings, by communicating their understanding of these to the latter, by expressing empathy, and showing genuine interest in them. At the exploration phase, reporting managers attempt to help their juniors understand themselves and their problems better. They may do this by raising questions to help them scrutinize their problems and diagnose the problem properly. At the action planning phase, reporting managers and their juniors jointly work on or plan specific steps for the development of the juniors. Managers make a commitment to provide specific support to help in their juniors' development. Figure 6.1 presents the three phases (and sub-phases) of the PRD process. Reporting managers' behavior, which is helpful in the PRD process, and those that are likely to hinder the process are listed against each sub-phase.

## Rapport-building

Rapport-building is essential for an effective PRD outcome. The rapport-building phase involves generating confidence in juniors to open up and frankly, share their perceptions, problems, concerns, and feelings. Reporting managers should come down to the level of their juniors and be attuned to their orientation. This can be done by adopting the latter's frame of reference.

### *Attendance*

The opening phase of a PRD is very important in rapport-building. General opening rituals may communicate the message of attendance to a performer and give importance to the PRD transaction. Invitation rituals such as asking juniors to sit down, closing the door to indicate privacy, asking the secretary not to disturb them and not fielding telephonic calls during the conversation indicate that the reporting manager is attending to the performer. However, all such rituals should come out of a genuine concern and managers should attempt to pay complete attention to their juniors during PRD sessions.

## Listening

As already mentioned, it is important for the reporting manager to listen to what his junior is saying as well as to his/her feelings and concerns. His physical posture (for example, leaning forward) and keeping eye contact with the junior are indicators that the manager is listening to him/her.

## Acceptance

Establishing a climate of acceptance is a necessary part of establishing rapport. Performers must feel that they are needed and their reporting managers are interested in understanding them as persons rather than in their roles or positions in the organization. Reporting managers communicate this to their juniors by listening to their problems and communicating to them that they are listening. They can communicate this to their juniors by paraphrasing, mirroring, or reflecting what the latter is saying. For example, when a junior says, "I am really mad. I have tried to do my best in the past year. I have worked twice as hard as anyone else in the office. But I never get a promotion," he/she is expressing his/her anger. The reporting manager may reflect and say, "You feel that your superiors have not shown proper recognition of your hard work." Such reflection or mirroring will help the junior feel that he/she is understood and that his/her reporting manager is interested in him/her. This results in a climate of acceptance and facilitates the process.

## Exploration

Apart from accepting juniors listening to them and establishing a climate of openness, reporting managers should attempt to understand and help them understand their situation, strengths, weaknesses, problems, and needs. Nobody likes to be directly told what his/her weaknesses are. Reporting managers' PRD skills lie in helping their juniors discover their own weaknesses and identify their problems. At the most, they can ask open and exploring questions.

### Exploration

Exploration helps an employee search for various dimensions of a problem, discover unidentified ones, and bring to the surface unnoticed ones. It can be achieved by asking questions and suggesting that employees talk more about problems they are facing. A variety of questions can be asked, as already discussed.

### Identification of Problems

After a general exploration, questions can be asked to help employees focus on their problems. It is necessary for reporting managers to ask questions to obtain information about concerns and problems, and then narrow down the focus to identify more probable ones. For example, if an employee feels that his/her problem is that others do not cooperate with him/her, the reporting manager may ask questions to narrow this down to the former's relationship with some of his/her colleagues. Questions can then be asked to help the employee see what he/she does that prevents possible cooperation. Eventually, the discussion can focus on how the employee can deal with competitive relationships, and yet collaborate. Identification of a problem is necessary in planning for improvement.

### Diagnosis

Diagnosis of a problem is the next step in exploration. Without diagnosis, there is little scope for solving any problem. Open questions such as "why do you think people are put off when you speak with them?" "Can you recall occasions when you got full cooperation?" "What do you attribute this to?" or "What personal limitations bother you?" might help an employee arrive at a better diagnosis of his/her problem. The main attempt should be to generate several alternative causes of problems.

## Action Planning

Managers are expected to guide their juniors and contribute to their development. PRD interviews should end with specific plans of action for the development of the juniors. Identification of a training need, job rotation, sponsorships for further training, increased responsibility, and role clarity are some of the likely outcomes of such action plans. Three sub-phases can be identified in action planning.

### Searching

The main contribution of reporting managers to action planning is the help they provide to their juniors in thinking about alternative ways of dealing with problems. In addition to encouraging them to find such alternatives, reporting managers can add to this list of alternatives for further exploration at a later stage. This should, however, be done after some time. Juniors should take the responsibility for generating alternatives.

### Decision-making

After the alternatives have been generated, reporting managers can help their juniors assess the advantages and disadvantages of each alternative, make suggestions about the feasibility of the various alternatives, and help them finalize their plans for implementation. These should, however, be regarded as contingency plans, to be altered in light of further experience.

### Supporting

The final and the crucial stage of a PRD is to communicate support and decide how it should be provided while implementing an agreed action plan. The psychological contract of providing help should emerge after considerable exploration and discussion. Support also increases employees' autonomy, and does not increase their dependence on their reporting managers. A plan for monitoring action plans and the needed follow-up can also be prepared.

# Making PRD Effective

In developmental PRD formally organized by an organization, an employee may not ask for a PRD, but his/her superior may organize PRD sessions as an organizational requirement. On such occasions, employees may be forced to attend them. If a PRD is organized without being sought, it is likely to be of limited value. It may be frustrating for the reporting manager and the junior. In such a situation, the reporting manager would do well to forget about the PRD and talk to the employee about his/her interest/lack of interest in growth. The employee is likely to express his/her views if the reporting manager establishes an open climate. If the employee has serious emotional blocks in dealing with his/her superior, there is no use of organizing a PRD. They need a problem-solving session before that. Hence, it has to be made sure before a PRD session that the employee is willing to learn from it. Some juniors are so loyal and some superiors so protective that there is the danger of the former becoming totally dependent on the latter. Reporting managers should check from time to time (through reflection) whether they are making their juniors too dependent on them. They should not take the decisions for their juniors, but allow and help them to take their own decisions, as they should be the main actors.

Make sure that your junior understands the purpose of a PRD. If he/she does not understand or has wrong expectations, he/she may not receive whatever you say in the proper perspective. If you feel that he/she is under some misunderstanding, it is better to use the first session to clarify this, and then schedule another session. Minimize arguments. One argument is sufficient to make both of you defensive. Accept everything he/she says and try to build on it. Acceptance is the best way of bringing about self-realization in a person.

Good PRD sessions fail to produce effective results due to lack of follow-up. Follow-ups through informal exchanges go a long way in communicating your interest in your junior. Otherwise, he/she may feel that a PRD session is only a farce, and lose interest in it eventually.

An effective PRD empowers not only the performer but also the reporting manager. It enables reporting managers to be aware of ground level realities, understand factors affecting the performance of their juniors, and enables them to prepare action plans to improve their entire unit or department's performance. It equips them with new information and knowledge about their juniors, and help them plan their strategies.

# 7

# Using Performance Management System Data for HR Decisions and Performance Improvements

The value of data generated in performance management systems is often underestimated and consequently underutilized. This is one of the major pitfalls of calling a performance management system an appraisal system. The nature of the data that is generated in the performance management process is as follows:

1. Detailed performance plans of individuals: This can be used to align individual goals with organizational goals to clarify roles.
2. Support requirements of each employee to achieve or carry out his/her performance plans and meet targets: In some systems, employees are asked in the beginning to estimate the support requirements they need. This helps seniors to plan for support, and where it is not possible, prepare their juniors to perform under constraints or revision of targets. This is also a means of communication to the top expectations of employees.
3. Performance analysis data generated during mid-year or year-end review: These indicate the facilitating and blocking factors. These data can initiate performance improvement activities by head of departments (HODs).
4. Ratings on qualities: These indicate the areas where employees are strong and those where they are weak, and lay the ground for developmental decisions.
5. Knowledge or skill gaps from performance analysis data: This gives insights into the developmental needs of an individual.

6. Information about the performance standards of different departments and groups.
7. Biases in ratings: An analysis of rating patterns gives insights into lenient and conservative assessors, and can help in training.
8. Unique accomplishments of individuals or their outstanding contributions: High ratees can be studied to see how their potential can be utilized.
9. Trends in performance improvements: Data on targets and accomplishments over the last few years can provide interesting comparisons and patterns of changes in performance.
10. Training need-related data stated by individuals or their supervisors.

The effectiveness of performance management systems depends on how well the data generated by the system is utilized, and to what extent employees see this. Appraisal data can be applied for developmental decisions as well as for HR management. The following categories of developmental decisions can be taken on the basis of appraisal data:

1. Organizing company training programs.
2. Sponsoring executives for external training.
3. Job rotation
4. Career development
5. Potential development
6. Delegation

The following HR decisions can also be made on the basis of appraisal data:

1. Performance rewards
2. Placement and transfers
3. Promotions
4. Change of duties

# Developmental Decisions

The path of development on the job is already carved out for employees in key performance areas, behavioral dimensions, self-appraisal, performance analysis, and counseling. At every reporting manager-performer level, role clarity obtained through mutual discussions on PAs and KPAs; increased understanding and insights generated on managerial capabilities and behavioral qualities required for effectiveness in an organization; identification of facilitating and inhibiting factors through performance analysis; recognition of factors that one can influence and change; discovery of one's own strengths and weaknesses; as well as opportunities for development, all contribute directly or indirectly to employees' development. However, insights gained during performance review and counseling discussions as well as developmental plans prepared by reporting managers and performers should be reinforced and strengthened by supportive administrative decisions taken by the Personnel, HRD departments, or by senior line managers who can take such decisions. For example, appraising officers can make recommendations to meet the training needs of their juniors, but unless administrative action is taken on this, the seriousness and effectiveness of the appraisal system may be lost. In this section, we will look at the various ways in which appraisal data can be used for developmental decisions.

## IDENTIFICATION OF TRAINING NEEDS

Performance appraisal should result in better performance and a sense of satisfaction on the part of each performer. Every employee may not have all the capabilities required to perform each and every function associated with his/her role. Performance appraisal should be able to indicate the capabilities an individual has and those he/she lacks in performing each of the functions (or at least the important ones) associated with his role. The capabilities employee lacks, once identified, need to be developed through appropriate mechanisms. Capability gaps can be identified in performance appraisals by looking at the ratings given on various

KPAs, objectives, and managerial and behavioral dimensions. Low ratings in any area or dimension may indicate capability gaps. Low rating is an indicator of poor performance, which in turn, may be a result of low motivation or low capability. It is therefore necessary to ascertain the reasons for poor performance. This should normally be discussed and decided during performance reviews and counseling discussions with reporting managers, who should then indicate this in the "development needs" section of the appraisal form. Most often, reporting managers have a tendency to directly recommend the names of training programs for which their juniors should be sponsored rather than give details of capability requirements. While this may make HR departments' job easy, there is a danger of individuals being sponsored for training programs that have little relevance for their capability requirements.

The following processes can be used by HR departments to identify training needs and create learning opportunities for employees:

1. Collect the appraisal ratings of all the employees.
2. Categorize employees into role or function-related categories (for example, branch managers, zonal managers, sales people dealing with particular sets of products, marketing managers, production supervisors, and so forth).
3. Identify common performance areas for each category of employees. These areas should require, by and large, similar capabilities.
4. Tabulate final appraisal ratings given by reporting managers against each performance area for all employees in that performance area. Where there are ratings assigned to different objectives, it is useful to tabulate these objective-wise.
5. Trends in ratings are indicative of the areas that need attention. Those areas where ratings are poor indicate training needs. These need to be probed further to determine whether poor ratings are a reflection of capability gaps, motivational issues, or biases. HR managers need to use their insight here. They can interview a few reporting managers and their juniors to ascertain their training needs.

6. On the basis of such analysis, areas where a large group of employees needs to be trained can be identified. In-house programs can be organized wherever there are large groups of people who need to be trained. If only a few people need to be trained in selected capability areas, they can be sponsored for outside programs.

Thus, an active pursuit of appraisal ratings to identify trends in capability gaps is required on the part of the Personnel/HR departments of organizations. Exclusive reliance on reporting managers' recommendations of the training needs of their juniors may not give a complete picture of their developmental needs. A thorough analysis of appraisal forms and ratings is required. Similarly, tabulations on managerial and behavioral dimensions may indicate areas where employees may need help. For example, if most people in a unit/department get low ratings on "initiative," "creativity," or "team spirit," this indicates the need for the members of the unit/department to be helped in developing these quality parameters. Training programs can be organized or other forms of developmental processes (such as weekly process meetings for improving team spirit, periodic creativity exercises, discussions on initiative-taking behavior, and so forth) can also be initiated. In large organizations, appraisal data can be fed into a computer, which can be programed to list those that may need different kinds of training on the basis of the consistent low ratings they have received over a period of three to four years. These lists can then be further processed, and the employees should be contacted before taking any developmental decisions for them.

However, developmental decisions are not likely to be effective unless employees accept them and undertake the task of developing themselves by utilizing the opportunities given to them by their organization.

Performance analysis conducted by employees is another useful source for identifying developmental needs. Individual inhibiting factors identified by employees may be indicators of their capability gaps. Inhibiting factors attributable to reporting officers and others in the organization may also indicate the developmental needs of senior officers. HR managers who analyze such data should be sensitive to various cues being offered by employees and reporting managers in their performance analysis.

On the basis of their own analysis, HR managers should get back to departmental heads and give them feedback of the capability gap trends their analysis reveals, and check with the latter the various hypotheses they may have developed about the training needs of individuals. Performance appraisal systems are likely to be taken more seriously when such an effort is made by HR department.

Job rotation is another effective way of developing employees' capabilities. It requires periodical changing of employees from one job to another to provide them with the experience of handling a variety of jobs in the organization. Some companies use jobs rotation as a mechanism for identifying and developing the potential of employees. For example, an organization that manufactures heavy engineering equipment has a rule that all its new entrant engineers recruited at junior managerial levels should be rotated every two years to work in a different department. Thus, after 10 years of joining a company, a person would have gone through at least five different departments. The individual forms a better perspective about the organization and its functioning. After working in different departments, he/she is able to understand their work, difficulties, requirements, etc., and therefore, is better equipped to collaborate with them and work as a team member. In this manner, seeds are sown to prepare every young employee to become a general manager in the company. In addition, by observing his/her performance in different departments, the organization is able to ascertain the individual's suitability for different departments, and help him/her formulate his/her career path.

It may not be possible for all organizations to have these kinds of mechanisms. However, performance appraisals may point out the need for rotation in some cases. At the time of appraisal, employees may ask for a change if they have invested several years in doing the same job or have not been able to perform some of the functions associated with their present one and prefer to try out different assignments. Such job rotation requests and suggestions should be mentioned in the "developmental needs" section of the appraisal form, and every year, after collecting all the forms, the Personnel or HR department should be able to arrange such changes to the extent feasible. Those individuals or reporting managers, whose requests for change cannot be accommodated, should be contacted and informed about the reasons and future possibilities.

Decisions relating to potential development and career development can be taken by individuals during appraisal discussions. If any set of qualities (strengths) unique to a particular individual are observed, which the reporting manager feels may be useful for certain higher level jobs in the organization, he/she can provide informal feedback about this and help the junior develop other qualities required to perform such roles. In this way, reporting managers can help their juniors prepare for their future possible responsibilities through potential development. Career counseling and delegation can also be given to such employees during appraisal. Delegation can be used as a mechanism for developing employees' capabilities in new areas.

Inputs on development needs are given by employees and their reporting managers through performance appraisal forms. Developmental decisions should be taken by the top management. Here, the Personnel/HRD departments play an important role. They should carefully go through all the data supplied in the forms, review each performer's case every year, and help the top management in taking developmental decisions. In some cases, the final authority to take such decisions is also given to the Personnel/HR department. If no action is required or where the organization considers it difficult or inappropriate to meet any needs given in the forms, the Personnel/HR department should get in touch with the employees or their reporting officers to explain to them their point of view. If such action is not taken, employees are likely to feel that they and their needs are not being paid heed to by the organization.

## ADMINISTRATIVE DECISIONS

Administrative decisions such as salary increments and other forms of reward for good performance, transfers, and placements are normally taken by the top management or the HR department. In some organizations, committees comprising HR and line managers at senior levels take such decisions. Largely, these decisions are based on performance, and performance appraisals play a significant role in this. Most of these administrative decisions fall under "performance rewarding." Let us examine some issues relating to performance rewarding, and see how appraisal data can be used to administer this.

## PERFORMANCE REWARDS

Performance rewarding is a controversial issue in organizations, to which many chief executives do not pay enough attention. People are likely to work harder if they feel their efforts will be recognized by their superiors, and they will be rewarded. Particularly in manufacturing and service organizations, productivity depends largely on the efforts put in by employees. This makes rewarding performance crucial.

Performance rewarding is controversial because there are no easy ways of quantifying performance for reward purposes. Moreover, some chief executives may feel that if an employee is rewarded financially or in some other observable way, it may demoralize those who are only marginally inferior to him. An unfortunate outcome of this is that after some time, high performing employees start losing their motivation because high- and low-performing employees are treated alike in such organizations.

Rewarding employees means giving them something more than what is usually given to employees at their level. If they are rewarded as a mark of recognition for some job done well, they feel motivated. This recognition may constitute tangible benefits, such as certificates, or non-tangible benefits.

Employees are generally rewarded for high performance in their jobs over a period of time (usually a year or two), and this should be differentiated from other forms of awards such as those given for bravery, social service, being the best employee, sportsmanship, etc. Performance awards are given to individuals for consistent outstanding work in their jobs, though rewarding group performance is not uncommon.

## PHILOSOPHY BEHIND PERFORMANCE REWARDING

Several research studies in the past have indicated that the need for recognition is very important, and it dictates employees' behavior. They want their efforts to be recognized and them to be treated as an important part of the organization. If the existence of employees is not taken note of, after some time, they may try to draw the attention of top management to themselves. Performance rewarding is an effective way of communicating to employees that every individual employee is considered important and his/her performance is given due recognition.

Another purpose served by rewards is to reinforce desirable behaviors of employees, so that they continue to contribute to the organization by exhibiting such behaviors. Rewards also help to create healthy competition among employees by encouraging less hardworking ones to compete with the more hardworking ones. This is one of the ways of keeping an organization alive and dynamic.

### REWARD MECHANISMS

Several mechanisms for rewarding performance are used by different organizations. These include salary increases, annual performance awards, outstanding performance awards, promotion to higher positions, change of jobs involving higher responsibilities and status, sponsorship for conferences and tours to other countries, appreciation letters and certificates, transfers, advanced training and development opportunities, announcements in newsletters, and so forth.

### SALARY INCREASE

The general pattern of salary administration in most organizations is by associating salary grades with different positions. Annually, the salary of every employee increases by a fixed amount associated with that grade. In many companies, this is a routine matter and there are salary increments as soon as an employee completes a year of service.

In some companies, however, salary increments are not given until the performance appraisal reports of employees are received from their supervisor. In such companies, employees whose performance is rated higher than that of most others are given additional increments in their salaries as a mark of recognition of their contribution. Since such additional increments cannot be given to all the employees, the company generally follows the practice of rewarding the top 10 percent (or so) of employees every year. This may involve certain restrictions being placed on employees receiving these rewards, for example, no employee can receive the reward consecutively for two years. Some other companies have liberal policies and even reward employees by giving more than one additional increment. Some companies stop the normal increment in the salary of an employee whose performance is not satisfactory. This practice is generally avoided, and even in such companies, stopping of increments is a rare phenomenon and is only resorted to in the case of extremely poor performance as a warning measure for improvement.

There are many advantages of using the system of rewards. It is known that people see financial incentives as valuable, irrespective of their status and personal wealth. Salary increments are carried out over years, and once employees are given increments, they continue to get them throughout their tenures in the organization. Hence, this is an incentive valued by most employees.

## ANNUAL PERFORMANCE AWARDS

In this system, a select percentage of employees is given annual awards that are not linked with their salaries. Thus, an organization may decide to give an annual performance award of a certain amount of money, an employee may be presented with a prize, or extra privileges and benefits may be given to him. This is again based on their appraisal reports.

## OUTSTANDING PERFORMANCE AWARDS

These are performance awards given to a select few for their outstanding performance. Normally, these carry a lump sum amount of money, a certificate, and a memento. Companies can award these in addition to annual salary increments and other rewards.

## PROMOTIONS

In some companies, promotion is treated as a reward. Employees are promoted to the next higher grade or position if their performance in their present jobs has been consistently very good. However, this method of rewarding has some limitations because promotions are possible only when higher level jobs exist. If there are no suitable jobs for such employees, they may have to wait until the time they are available. This may be frustrating for employees. Some companies try to create special jobs for such individuals. However, this may result in unnecessary expansion of the company and managerial problems such as role conflicts or lack of coordination. Jobs should be created only when an organization feels the need for them, particularly when it is expanding and growing.

Another problem in using promotions as performance rewards is that there is no guarantee that past performance is an indicator of future potential in a new job. For example, a successful production engineer need not be a successful production manager because the skills required for the two jobs differ. Similarly, an excellent salesman need not be a good sales manager because selling and managing salesmen and the sales operations of an entire region require two different kinds of skills. Thus, only those with an aptitude and capabilities for higher level positions should be promoted. If this is the case, not all high performers will be promoted. However, performance appraisal still provides an input for promotions, though not a critical one. Some companies have the philosophy that good performance in the present job is necessary for promotion, but it need not be the only criterion that entitles an employee to a promotion. When such mechanisms are used, promotion cannot be treated as a reward, and hence, there is a need for other mechanisms for rewarding good performance.

To overcome this problem, some organizations have resorted to upgrading employees' status and salaries as a reward of their good performance. For example, in the Philippines, a teacher in the education department, who has been doing well, can be promoted to be a master teacher. There are several levels of master teacher, and he/she, working in a school, can have the same status and salary as one of his/her superiors. This takes care of the problem of job creation for high performers.

## CHANGE OF RESPONSIBILITIES AND STATUS

Some organizations reward their employees by assigning them higher level responsibilities. The head of a department may delegate more powers and authority to a high-performing employee. A salesperson may get a larger area of coverage or more prestigious areas for his/her operations, or new products that are generally given to a competent salesperson. There are many such mechanisms by which the contributions of employees can be recognized. Such forms of rewarding generally have high motivational value.

However, one pre-condition for this is that such employees and their colleagues in the organization should clearly perceive such additional assignments as increasing the former's status and responsibilities. This is an opportunity given to them to demonstrate their capabilities to reward their performance. It is not sufficient that only the superiors of such employees think so, because the employees may consider it an additional burden.

## SPONSORSHIP FOR CONFERENCES, TOURS, AND VISITS TO OTHER COUNTRIES

This is another frequently used mechanism by some companies. Outstanding performers are given priority for attending training, conferences, etc. in other countries, or they may be sponsored to visit other similar organizations in other countries to learn from their experience. This may be considered a developmental reward, since it provides an opportunity for such employees to develop themselves. Some companies, while following this practice, never make it explicit, so the employee sponsored may not always realize that his/her performance is being recognized.

## ADVANCED TRAINING AND DEVELOPMENTAL OPPORTUNITIES

High-performing employees are sponsored to attend training programs as preparation for their promotion or higher responsibilities. In some cases, the management does not reveal this to the employees and they may get the feeling that there is something lacking in them, and that is why they are being sponsored. Thus, this may have the opposite to the intended effect unless clearly explained.

## TRANSFERS

In organizations with wide geographic coverage, transfer of employees from one place to another is necessary. Employees normally have their own geographical preferences. For example, most of them prefer jobs in well-developed cities and towns, or their own hometowns if they want to be near their families. Such preferences of employees are met when their performance is good. There are some organizations that give priority to the transfer requests of high-performing employees. When such preferences are met, the employees concerned may feel happy and motivated.

A transfer decision may also be taken to ensure the better matching of the person with the job. By giving employees more challenging jobs in different locations through transfers, may motivate them and promote their professional development.

## PLACEMENT DECISIONS

Performance appraisal inputs can be used for placement decisions. Improving employee–job matching is helpful to individuals as well as organizations. An employee who is not performing well because of a mismatched job can be helped by identifying suitable jobs for him/her in the organization. For this, appraisal ratings can be used by the HR department to identify employees needing such help. Those getting consistently low ratings over a period of time (two years or so) can be contacted and discussions can be held with them and their reporting managers. Their strengths should be identified, and jobs requiring such qualities should be assigned to them. If inadequate performance is the result of poor interpersonal relations, and if there are difficulties in improving this, such employees can be transferred to work with different bosses.

Another set of placement decisions may relate to employees who perform a given role well, but have additional capabilities that remain unexploited. If there are challenging jobs that can use their talents, they can be placed in those. In all such decisions, employees should be consulted as far as possible.

## APPRECIATION LETTERS AND CERTIFICATES

This is another mechanism used particularly for employees at lower levels. Such certificates, signed by the chief executive or a top level officer, may mean a lot. These are distributed at annual functions. When there is a large group of people receiving such certificates, they are handed over to heads of departments for distribution. Some employees value the certificates highly and feel proud to receive them.

## ANNOUNCEMENT IN NEWSLETTERS, JOURNALS, AND SO FORTH

This is another way of recognizing and rewarding good performers. It is not an uncommon sight to see the pictures of "Employees of the Month" displayed in the lobbies of some hotels. This form of recognition also has a motivating effect on employees.

The author has surveyed the mechanisms of rewarding good performance that are practiced by 45 different companies (Rao, 1982). From this survey, it was found that about 73 percent of companies give salary increments; 40 percent of them give promotions, 27 percent give cash awards, 24 percent foreign travel, and 16 percent appreciation certificates; 11 percent nominate employees to attend advanced training; 9 percent on study tours; and 7 percent give higher responsibilities as mechanisms of rewarding their good performance. Transfers and announcements in newsletters are also used in at least 2 percent of the companies surveyed, and 7 percent of them reported that they did not have a reward system.

Whatever mechanism is used, to make rewards achieve their purposes, the following points should be kept in mind:

1. Employees should know the aspects of their performance that have been judged or assessed for deserving a reward.
2. They should clearly know the nature of rewards being given to them.

3. The employees as well as their colleagues in the organization should perceive the rewards as a form of recognition and attach the appropriate value to them.

The rewards are likely to be effective when these conditions are met. Reward management, while extremely desirable, is not easy. The following are some of the common problems encountered by the managements of companies:

1. Quantification of performance
2. Comparison of performance with different types of jobs
3. Differentiation between abilities and efforts for high performance, and giving weightage to them
4. Demoralization among employees who are not rewarded, but who consider themselves as high-performing
5. Isolation of individual employees' contribution from group contribution
6. Subjectivity in assessment of performance

There are no complete solutions to these problems. Therefore, every organization should find its own ways of minimizing these. Companies interested in putting in place a reward system may find the following guidelines of some value:

1. *Quantification of performance:* Quantifying performance is easier when each job is defined clearly in terms of its functions. Employees' performance should be assessed annually on each of these functions, using a seven-point, nine-point, or 10-point scale. Employees should have a clear idea of the performance expected of them in relation to the different points. This should be followed if the other qualities of employees are also being assessed. For a sophisticated user, weightage can be assigned to different functions and behavior, and these can be taken into account for final computation of the performance index. Companies may also decide in advance on the weightage they give to behavior dimensions and functions. Several problems associated with quantification have already been discussed in earlier chapters.

2. *Comparison between performances in different jobs:* In every organization, the nature of jobs performed by employees at the same level differs. Some require high technical skills, others more managerial skills, and others routine ones. For example, employees working in the Research and Development (R&D) department of a high-technology industry may feel differently from those working in the HR or Billing departments. There is no way of equating performances in different categories of jobs. As far as possible, while assigning rewards, it is better to award a proportionate number to each category of jobs (or each department). Thus, if the top management decides to reward the top 10 percent in a company with 1,000 employees, the production department may have 25 persons to reward if it has 250 employees, the finance department may have three persons to reward if it has 30 employees, and so on. If some departments, such as sales, need to be pushed more, the top management can always offer them a few additional rewards. Similarly, different criteria may be used to reward senior managers (HODs). If managers at this level are generalists rather than specialists, they can be compared more easily across the departments for their contributions.

3. *Abilities and effort:* Performance is the outcome of both ability and effort. A highly capable individual may need to put in only a marginal effort to give a high performance, whereas another individual with inadequate capabilities may need to put in significant effort to produce even an average level of output. However, if only output is rewarded, highly capable employees may get a considerable leisure time in addition to rewards, whereas those putting in intensive efforts may get consistently low ratings. Reward management becomes difficult if there are such differences in ability. Since this is the case, more often than not, the top management should have a clear philosophy on this. It is necessary to reward a combination of ability and effort. Performance in different functions should generally be assessed in terms of the effort put in by an individual in relation to his/her capability. Thus, if a highly capable employee does not put in an effort, his/

her performance should not be rated high, even if the output is good. Similarly, if a less capable person puts in significant effort and works very hard, even if his output is not excellent, he/she can be given better ratings. This scheme rewards "effort" more than "ability" and "outcome." At the same time, when highly capable people work hard, they should be given adequate weightage. These formulae may be useful.

| Ability | Effort | Suggested performance rating |
|---------|--------|------------------------------|
| High | High | Highest |
| Moderate | High | Higher |
| Low | High | High |
| High | Moderate | Upper average |
| Moderate | Moderate | Average |
| Low | Moderate | Lower average |
| High | Low | Low |
| Moderate | Low | Lower |
| Low | Low | Lower |

4. *Demoralization:* Due to the subjectivity involved in performance assessment, there are always some employees who are disappointed that they have not been rewarded for their performance. The number of such employees can be minimized if there are clear-cut policies of rewarding performance. If the employees are marginal cases, their supervising officers could counsel them and give them relevant feedback. Alternatively, demoralization can be ignored because such feelings only last while rewards are being announced. If this increases their demoralization and poor performance, such people should be counseled.

5. *Individual vs. performance:* No tasks can be accomplished by any one individual in an organization. Tasks are accomplished by team efforts. In rewarding performance, we have talked about individual performance so far. In order to promote more collaboration and teamwork in large organizations, it is useful to reward groups or teams of employees for their joint contributions. When such "group rewarding" is introduced,

it may be done on a selective basis, using criteria including new innovation, discipline, cost-consciousness, and so forth, in addition to the output of the department.

6. *Subjectivity:* As long as human beings assess others, there is bound to be subjectivity, which cannot be eliminated completely. It can be substantially reduced by following some of the procedures suggested in the previous chapters. Top management should be sensitive to criticism and avoid morale-related problems, but it does not need to be unduly concerned about its existence, since it is natural.

Some of these problems discourage top managers to award any kind of rewards. In their eagerness to avoid problems, they throw away the baby with the bath water. As a result, their organizational performance may go down.

Interpersonal comparisons are a part of human nature. If an organization does not have any system for rewarding high performers, sooner or later, they will ask themselves the following:

I work hard but get the same treatment as the ones who do the least amount of work. I also get the same salary increase as the lowest performer. So why should I exert my energies unnecessarily? Why should I not be like him (who is a low performer) and enjoy life?

This is the beginning of a silent deterioration of human productivity in an organization. Over a period of time, the lowest performing employee becomes the standard for comparison for all employees and everyone attempts to be like him/her. In this process, the lowest performing individual starts doing even less than before, and the company is doomed.

Therefore, the choice before chief executives is to reward high performers using some form of reward system, contain or counter the problems associated with it, and move forward, or to have no such system and eventually "kill" human effectiveness and organizational efficiency by moving toward low standards of performance.

Thus, performance appraisal data can serve as relevant input for a variety of decisions that may contribute to an organizational health and productivity by its human resources development.

# 8
# Best Practices in Performance Management*

This chapter is based on a survey conducted on best HR practices by IIMA for Steel Authority of India Limited as a part of the latter's HR awards. The survey was conducted by the author as a consultant to the Administrative Reforms Commission of India and the Ministry of Finance's appointed committee on HR in public sector banks (Khandelwal Committee). In addition, two other surveys were conducted by the author for the Administrative Reforms Commission. In all these reports, current practices were surveyed, and observations or recommendations were made.

Performance management processes deal with all that is done to ensure proper work and performance planning, goal setting, identification, and reduction of blocks hindering performance, measuring and developing performance, enablement of organizational support, and development of opportunities for effective performance.

Performance management practices, whether they are paper-based or online, are oriented toward planning for and gauging employee performance, and ultimately aiding their overall development. The processes generally include some form of target setting, assessment and review, and feedback and final recommendations on development of and rewards for performance.

---

* A large part of this chapter is reproduced with permission from *HR Best Practices: Manufacturing Sector in India* by Nisha Nair, Neharika Vohra, T. V. Rao, and Atul Srivastava, New Delhi: Steel Authority of India, 2010.

# Planning for Performance: Goal Setting

Goal setting is an important part of planning for performance. It generally follows a top-down approach with organizational goals getting cascaded down to the individual level. Some of the processes followed for goals setting across organizations are discussed here.

The performance management process at Jindal Steel & Power Limited (JSPL) is referred to as performance development and review (PDR) process. As part of goal setting, the reporting officer and the employee hold a discussion to establish clear and specific performance expectations for the employee for the year. It is an opportunity for the reporting officer to explain what the PDR process is, define roles, discuss job requirements, answer employees' questions about the process, and work together with them to reach a consensus on and commitment to performance standards. The primary objective is to set the right direction. Discussions relating to goal setting, thus, aim to: (a) introduce and explain the process, (b) clarify the parameters on which an employee will be evaluated, and (c) establish and agree upon performance expectations. However, the process differs at Jindal for employees in the executive and above grade as well as for those who are below the executive grade. The performance management system for people in the below executive grade is not target-oriented and goals are not decided at the start of the year for them. In Moser Baer, direct linkages are made to the business/function scorecards of assistant manager and above while setting targets, but for senior officers and engineers, targets are not directly cascaded from their scorecards, but are based on their role/responsibility, for example, line efficiency, waste reduction, and so forth. According to the balance scorecard approach, business goals are drafted on the four perspectives of financials, customer, internal processes, and learning and development. KRAs are derived from the organizational scorecard, and are aligned with it.

Indian Oil follows a top down approach, where KRAs are cascaded down from the business scorecard with specific KPIs, which are measured against time and given specific weightage. Tata Motors follows a similar practice with individual performance plans being cascaded from the balance scorecard to the smallest work unit. Goal setting, which is done at the beginning of the financial year, starts with a company-level strategic plan that is cascaded and individual plans are prepared. For workmen, based on the factory score card, individuals work out a plan in line with their safety, quality, delivery, cost, morale, and environment (SQDCM) targets. Dabur India uses a mix of the balance scorecard and management, and has objective principles for goal setting.

Very often, goals are set using the specific, measurable, achievable, realistic, and time bound (SMART) framework, which is also used by HPCL and Schneider Electric India. The processes can also be carried out online. At Schneider, there is also a face-to-face objective setting dialogue between reporting managers and their teams/subordinates after HR shares the company's guidelines with employees and managers. It is also mandatory to include behavioral expectations based on Schneider's values: passion, open, straightforward, and effective (POSE). These objectives are prioritized, based on business and departmental requirements, and SMART objectives need to be mutually agreed on. Individual objectives are aligned with functional/business unit objectives. At Honeywell India, the goals of individuals across the organization are aligned to the five Honeywell initiatives: growth, productivity, cash, enablers, and people.

## ASSESSING, MANAGING, AND DEVELOPING PERFORMANCE

The process for assessing and managing performance generally consists of assessment against individual KRAs, a midterm review, and a final review. Based on the assessment, promotions, increments, and bonuses are decided. It is also linked to training and individual development plans. Many companies have a separate process for potential assessment, as will be discussed in the next section in more detail. Some sample processes for assessment and management of performance are discussed in the following portion.

The performance management system at Philips Electronics India is called people performance management (PPM). The appraisal process for managers and above is online, while paper forms are used for employees below managerial level. The forms are first filled by employees (self-evaluation) and then submitted to their superiors who then provide their recommendations and promotability ratings. In cases where there is dual reporting to functional managers, co-assessors also provide their comments in the appraisal process. These are only viewed by managers. The promotability ratings are categorized as fast track, growth path, and well-placed. The final ratings are discussed with the employees, and if there are any differences in opinion, these are recorded in the PPM document and finally signed off. The PPM document also includes assessment of Philips' leadership competencies, SMART objectives, and development activities for the previous and coming period. The HR team also organizes a session before starting the process to communicate the contents and explain the process of PPM to all management staff. At IFFCO, HR functionaries are involved in educating appraising officers at different levels about the need for assessing employees on the performance factor alone and not on any extraneous factors. An attempt is made to minimize areas of subjectivity in the process and officials at managerial levels are provided guidance in writing reports that are free of bias.

At the start of every performance year in Honeywell India, employees are issued files called "growth files" to record their performance. They keep track of their performance on a day to day basis and record their achievements in the file. They are responsible for keeping their growth file safe and updated all the time. Every quarter, employees are required to produce their file for a performance review to their supervisors. They are also assessed on their Honeywell behavior during this time. After the review, comments on their performance are recorded in the growth file, which is then returned to them. The year-end performance assessment considers employees' performance during the year. The rating scale used is "exceed," "at," and "below." "Merit increase" is linked to ratings review and feedback. Assessment criteria at Honeywell are based on: (a) competency level: every employee needs to have competency in one plus two secondary processes, (b) defects produced: defects produced by employees, (c) Kaizens: number of Kaizens

implemented every month, (d) safety incidence: near misses/
first aid incidence, accidents, and so forth, (e) team 5S score, (f)
production target: target vs. actual production and hit rate, (g)
employee attendance, and (h) appreciation: the number of rewards
and appreciation received by employees. Employees are evaluated
against goals, Honeywell behavior, Honeywell initiatives, assessment of their growth potential, risk of retention assessment, and
risk of attrition in their position in the organization.

At Sanghi Industries, employees are rated through their KRAs
and attributes. The KRAs are further divided into the sub-functions
of functional goals, total quality management, endeavors in cost
reduction, team development, and system improvement goals. The
attributes on which employees are assessed include attitude and
behavior, communication skills, job knowledge, organizational
skills, leadership and conceptual depth, and safety-related awareness in the case of plant personnel.

Tamil Nadu Newsprint and Papers Limited (TNPL) follow a
system where there is annual performance appraisal of all levels
of employees and a quarterly performance appraisal of all trainees and probationers. The company adopts a bottom-up approach.
Individual production units furnish data on production plans, raw
material consumption, benchmarks to be adopted, and so forth.
These are then consolidated and placed before the Board, which
gives its approval and further directions.

The performance appraisal process at Schneider Electric India is
conducted online. Performance objectives set up in People Soft is
delivered using the HR IS system. Managers create the performance
document in the system and complete the performance evaluation
online. Employees engage in self-evaluation and comment on their
managers' evaluation. The process includes defining performance
and key performance areas, planning for performance (including
measurable indicators, analyzing performance, monitoring and
reviewing performance, and finally rewarding performance).

A paper-based performance appraisal process is used in Sona
Koyo Steering Systems. Following the distribution of appraisal
sheets and collection of filled-in appraisals, there is a session when
the divisional departmental heads meet to finalize the appraisal

process of employees. Final appraisal targets are frozen in the session. This is followed by a mid-year review on the basis of which competency gaps and training needs are assessed. Promotions and increments are based on the final year-end review, which ends with counseling and collection of feedback from employees. A number of other organizations such as ITW Signode, JSPL, and NTPC also follow the paper-based performance management system.

At the first phase of assessment at TCG Life Sciences, employees assess and rate themselves on various designated attributes, identify their strengths, areas of development and critical incidents, and note down how they feel about the company's policies, environment, culture, and so forth. At the second phase, completed forms are sent to supervisors to evaluate their juniors. This is followed by a review meeting between appraisers and appraisees. The final scores are arrived on mutual consent. If there is any disagreement at this stage, a second reviewer (such as a line supervisor) steps in, and in consultation with the appraisee and appraiser, focuses on resolving the conflict and deriving the final scores and future goals. The filled in form is sent to the HR department, where the performance rating is calculated and the individual's present performance is evaluated. Finally, the master performance score sheet is prepared for moderation (discussed further in the next section). The online performance system at HPCL has a link, "Change/Modify Targets Request", through which appraisees can put in a request for changing their targets any time during a financial year. JSPL has set up a helpdesk to facilitate its mid-year review process. Forms are sent out to appraise and transfer forms between appraisers and reviewers so that the process is over in time.

## Moderation Process

Many companies have a process of moderation or calibration to even out performance ratings and eliminate bias. To ensure parity in scores given by different assessors, a normalization process is followed at NTPC, where similar grades and departments are grouped into clusters and then normalized. HPCL has also introduced the moderation process to check appraisers' biases, if any, and moderate possible wide variations in ratings given by different appraisers within streams/functions. HPCL's top management is involved in the processes of moderation. The Bell Curve method is used and employees are distributed on a normal curve into "excellent," "average," and "below average" categories. Comparison of the performance of employees and subsequent ranking is undertaken to meet predetermined Bell Curve percentages. After submission of the first mapping of ratings and promotability by Philips Electronics India's departments, there is a calibration process organized by its HR department among its management team, to ensure uniformity in the way ratings and promotability are assessed across departments. At TCG Life Sciences, there is a moderation committee (top management) that reviews the master score sheet and takes decisions on the hike percentage for different levels, thereby pre-empting any anomaly by fitting these into the Bell Curve distribution. The moderation process is based on individuals' last two appraisal ratings, skillsets, qualifications, and experience.

## Developing Performance

Based on assessment and review of performance, training and development needs are identified and agreed upon for various participants in order to develop the training calendar for the year (as done in various organizations such as Honeywell India, JSPL, Dabur India, and Tata Motors). For example, in JSPL, the training calendar, formulated on the basis of assessment of performance, is also used to develop the monthly training calendar. At the final review stage of the performance assessment and review process, reporting officers and their juniors look back at the goals and behavior, discuss how well the latter have done on the job, and conclude the evaluation year by completing their personal development forms. The dialogue between a supervisor and functional head is aimed at identifying and finalizing implementation plans and training requirements.

To help improve performance of non-performers, Castrol India engages in a personal improvement plan (PIP) process. A PIP process is initiated when employees fail to meet objectives or targets, have occasional lapses in performance which can impact their overall achievement of objectives, their performance has been continuously deteriorating over time, or they need to improve their performance to meet their set objectives. It is viewed not as a tool to punish employees, but as a process to help to improve their performance. A PIP can end with another PIP, a job change, a change in the individual, or even performance managed separations.

## Assessing for Potential

There is a separate system for potential assessment in some organizations, especially at senior levels. At Tata Motors, potential assessment is carried out, based on the developed Tata Leadership Practices introduced by the Tata Group HR department and the company's development center. HPCL also uses development centers, based on competency mapping. Potential assessment of senior-level executives is done through 360° feedback and assessment centers in NTPC. At JSW Steel, assessment is undertaken by assessment centers. Various methods such as a 360° appraisal, development centers, engagement surveys, 4D surveys, and so forth, are used at Philips Electronics India. Potential assessment is conducted by using Schneider Electric India's Talent Acceleration Program (TAP), whereby people are identified as "talent," and undergo technical assessments, such as Personnel Decision International (PDI) or at a local development center, followed by an interview. Based on the assessment results, further development plans are decided. At SKF India, consistent performers are selected for the company's program INSPIRE, where they are further assessed for their potential at assessment centers. Some are sent to a two-day development center, and are assessed on a set of competencies that are crucial for individual and organizational success. ITW Signode assesses the potential of its employees through a combination of competency-based interviews (face-to-face interviews during which their competencies are assessed) and development/assessment centers (where employees are assessed on the company's behavioral competency framework through role plays, group tasks, cases studies, and personal interviews).

For some employees, potential assessment takes part as part of performance management. Employees at JSPL have to rate themselves first on behavioral competencies featured on their assessment forms, after which a reporting officer rates them. These employees are rated on the basis of this. The performance appraisal format at Sona Koyo Steering Systems has three sections, two for performance factors, and one for potential factors. Individuals are assessed on these two parameters separately and then their overall performance is consolidated. Finally, ratings are arrived at for employees. Its PMS competency chart is used to assess potential at Motherson Automotive Technologies and Engineering.

## Systems for Feedback

At Tata Motors, every appraisal cycle is followed by a PMS survey. The focus of the survey is primarily on process. Based on this feedback, necessary corrective actions are taken to improve it during the next cycle. Feedback is also received through Gallup engagement surveys. Department heads receive feedback for their departments, and engagement action plans are prepared in consultation with the HR department.

Feedback is also given during the review stage of performance assessment. At JSPL, this process takes place twice a year, when individuals receive feedback on their strengths and weaknesses from their superiors. Honeywell India follows an approach where once performance-related discussions are completed with their juniors, managers send a performance discussion summary (PDS) online to them. This summarizes all discussions held on Honeywell behavior, goals for the year, development planning, merit increase awarded to employees, and comments on their overall performance for the year. Employees have to either accept this PDS or reject it with their comments, stating why they do not agree with the review comments. If they accept it, the performance review is closed. Otherwise it is reported back to their managers and HR determines that the status as incomplete. In such cases, sessions are conducted to understand why they did not agree with the comments. On this basis, either a reassessment is done or the employees accept the comments. As part of feedback, Moser Baer has a reflection form included in the PMS, which has a section on competency and assessment of values (this is only used for developmental purposes). Apart from the yearly appraisal process, TCG Life Sciences also has a yearly peer feedback and manager's feedback program to map employees' knowledge, performance and attitudes. At JSW Steel, feedback sessions are organized at locations other than the office to provide a relaxed and facilitating atmosphere for employees.

To strengthen its feedback process further, Dabur India has introduced its "Employee Feedback Card." The card captures the essence of the feedback given to employees by their superiors in a standardized format. It serves to provide employees an insight into their areas of development, while ensuring that their superiors have a stake in their professional development. Based on the feedback received through the individual appraisal forms, corporate HR prepares a card for each appraised employee. This is imparted to employees as structured feedback. The feedback card enables managers to give structured feedback, is useful in cascading training and other employee developmental activities on an objective basis, and provides the HR team a systemic input for employee interventions in the future.

## Ensuring Transparency of PMS

Maintaining transparency during the entire process of performance management is essential for employees to have faith in the system and build credibility. Employees should own their appraisal. A step in this direction practiced by Philips Electronics India is that the details of the appraisal form are known to all employees all the time. These include the full details of the appraisal form, which covers their targets achieved or set for the forthcoming period, performance and promotability ratings, development needs, and how they perform on values, competencies, and so forth. At Schneider Electric India, the employees' comments can be viewed by their reporting managers and managers' managers, and vice versa. Managers cannot modify employees' comments. At

Sanghi Industries, appraisees are able to view their ratings with the comments of their immediate superiors, heads of department, peers, and subordinates, if any. Appraisees also have access to the ratings of their colleagues in the department. To ensure greater transparency, TCG Life Sciences has made it incumbent that while filling up appraisal forms, every detail claimed by appraisers or appraisees are supported with proper documentation or critical incident record (CIR). Employees can access their appraisal forms any time during their tenure in the organization.

## Linkage of PMS with Other Subsystems

The PMS system generally has linkages with most other HR systems. The chief among these include rewards and performance-linked salaries, training and development, promotions, and career and succession planning. In addition, it also has other linkages such as OD interventions (as in NTPC). Career discussions that take place between the assessed and the supervising managers are also used to work out employees' job rotation/project assignment and development plan in Tata Motors. It is also used for leadership competency assessment and mobility decisions, as practiced in Philips Electronics India.

The performance system seems to be a multiple-use system, and a comprehensive tool for people management. It is being used by most organizations to manage their performance through SMART goals, balanced score cards, appropriate performance-related rewards, and development interventions. Many innovative practices seem to emerge from this system, which form the basis for other people management practices.

## HR Committees of Public Sector Banks

The committee consisting of Dr A.K. Khandelwal, T.V. Rao, Deepak Phatak, M.V. Nair, and H.N. Sinor has studied various HR systems in operation in Indian banks and has observed the following in PMS:

Most sub-systems of HRD like performance management system (PMS) are routinely administered and are seldom used for the development of employees. Apart from delay and poor monitoring, the PMS does not bring out the talented people to the fore. There is no system of potential appraisal. Talent management on the whole is a critical issue but found to be generally ignored.

PMS is the back bone of any organization, as it is performance that helps it to grow, develop, and strive for excellence. It is the only system that ensures that human capital is properly utilized, encouraged to achieve business results. It is also the main tool to ensure that individual and organizational goals are aligned. It is the only way to ensure that seniors understand their juniors' needs so as to guide them in their plans and enable them to deliver results.

The current PMS in PSBs is an area of serious concern. With the exception of few, most banks are using the standard appraisal format circulated by the Government. Even the appraisal format used for senior executives including CMD and ED is trait based and is totally out of tune with the strategic role these executives are expected to perform. PMS is usually carried out in an opaque way as no feedback is given to officers about their ratings with the exception of one or two banks. The appraisal is routinely administered and generally not used for developmental interventions. Much of the appraisals and ratings have upward bias. A large percentage—80–90 percent—of the performers gets "excellent" rating and does not distinguish performers from non-performers. While on the one hand this has dampening effect on performers, on the other, it defeats the very purpose of identifying top performers. Further, it has in many cases cascading effect leading to mediocrity. In the emerging competitive scenario, promotion of meritocracy through performance differentiation has to be the key objective of a good HRD system. The Committee is of the opinion that Bell curve shape approach be followed in assessing performance.

The Committee would also like to emphasize the role of appraisers in the entire process. PMS can no more be a routine activity. From the perspective of the banks remaining competitive, PMS has assumed paramount role in the total management of the organization. A credible, transparent, and well-managed PMS is essential for ensuring sustained performance and growth of the banks. In this context, the Committee notes that two major banks have already implemented PMS online.

Appraising authorities will have to devote good amount of quality time and attention to make PMS credible. Towards this, it is essential that accountability is fixed on the appraising authorities.

While visioning, strategic planning, annual business planning, periodic performance review, and other such systems do have their impact on the performance of the banks, banks as vibrant business entities would need to take some critical steps for building a high performance culture on an ongoing basis. All officers should be trained on the PMS. There should be continuous education and re-education programs undertaken by the organization. There should be adequate internal talent trained to train others. PMS should aim at continuous performance improvements and development besides performance assessment. Performance ratings should be shared with the concerned employees.

After studying the current state of PMS and rewards, the Committee recommended the following (only selected recommendations are presented here. For details, see the HR Committee Report on Public Sector Banks, 2010):

1. PMS to be a credible, transparent, and interactive system; online system to be introduced.
2. Workmen staff to be covered by PMS.
3. Appraising authorities to be accountable for proper and timely assessment.

4. Discipline of PMS to be enforced by the management.
5. Thrust to be on change from appraisal to management; PMS to include some form of performance planning; all performance plans to include statement of key activities under each KPA or KRA and the time candidates are expected to spend and for the outcome expected out of each key task and linkage to branch/regional/functional/business unit/organizational goals.
6. Performance plans to be reviewed fully by reviewing officers.
7. PMS to be made online, and performance plans to be available to all officers to promote transparency.
8. Performance review discussion to be made compulsory at least once in six months and online.
9. All officers to be trained in PMS.
10. Self-appraisal and performance analysis indicating factors that have helped or hindered performance as well as suggested actions to be undertaken by individuals and organization to be indicated.
11. Every senior officer starting from the branch manager to act as a "Performance Manager," analyze performance-inhibiting factors and undertake development activities.
12. HR managers to be trained to provide assistance to branch/regional/divisional heads.
13. PMS to aim at continuous improvement, development, and assessment of performance.
14. Senior officers to be encouraged to assess their juniors more objectively; review committees to become active and categorize performers as A, B, C, and D category performers; move away from the number game and use numbers only as input for the PRC to decide on categorization of performance.
15. Move to be made to transparent system if necessary (and as demanded by RTI), but prerogative of categorizing performance to lie with review committee.
16. Review committees to be trained to carry out this task objectively; training to be similar to that conducted for the Circle Credit Committee by the State Bank of India (SBI) in the mid-1990s.

# Recommendation (360 Degree Feedback)

1. PSBs to introduce 360 degree feedback as a leadership development and succession management, and a grooming tool for executives in Scale IV and above.
2. This feedback to be introduced for all branch managers of mid-sized and big branches to begin with as well as for regional and other managers and heads of departments (HODs), and immediately for the large number of managers who have already reached the level of assistant general manager (AGM), deputy general manager (DGM), general manager (GM), and executive director (ED).

Eventually, this should become a part of the leadership development process and be managed by the Leadership Development Institute. The Leadership Development Institute or any other body that facilities this initiative for banks should also help them train mentors to guide, coach, and develop internal talent. Infosys Leadership Development Institute is an example of how seniors such as Mr Naryana Murthy mentor future industry leaders. Mr Murthy is the Chief Mentor, and grooms future leaders using 360 degree feedback as one of the tools to guide and coach them.

# Performance Management in the Civil Services

The author of this book has reviewed practices in management of the performance of civil servants in a number of countries.

## PRINCIPLES OF FAIRNESS IN PERFORMANCE APPRAISALS

An examination of performance appraisal systems across the world indicates that universal satisfaction with appraisals is almost impossible to achieve. At times, no one seems happy with appraisals. Everyone craves for objectivity, but no one seems to put in the time and effort required to bring objectivity into appraisals.

Various countries have come up with different methods to manage performance appraisals. Ultimately, fairness seems to be the only principle that can be applied to appraisals.

1. You have no right to appraise the performance of another person unless you define this performance prior to the performance period.
2. You have no right to appraise the performance of any individual or group unless you have set the parameters and standards of performance and explained them to individuals prior to the performance period.
3. You have no right to draw your conclusions on the category of performance of individuals unless you have given them the opportunity to improve their performance.
4. You have no right to draw your conclusions about the performance levels of individuals or a team unless you understood the circumstances under which they have worked and made an attempt to provide all the tools and resources necessary for them to perform well.
5. All employees, and particularly those who are paid public money, have an obligation to account for the time and services they render to society and the government by discharging their duties and responsibilities to the best of their ability. It is their obligation to get their performance defined, standards set, goals clarified and their time accounted for by serving the right causes and purposes. Just as performers have rights, they also have obligations, and providers of employment have the right to seek and enhance accountability through systems such as performance appraisals.
6. Employers have the right to demand good performance, ensure accountability, and set standards through dialogue, discussions, and so forth.

These principles imply the following:

1. What constitutes "performance" should be defined before measuring it. (Job descriptions, KPAs, KRAs, goal-setting exercises, and so forth, are means to measure performance.)

2. Performance should be planned and communicated to performers prior to the performance period and not at its end. (Participative methods in deciding KPAs and goal-setting are intended to achieve this.)
3. Performance standards should be set. (Most appraisal systems define these standards.)
4. Feedback should be given periodically to individuals prior to the final assessment. (Performance review discussions and other forms of feedback such as 360 degree feedback constitute means to do this.)
5. Support should be ensured to enable individuals to perform well. (Performance analysis and training are other ways of providing support from the beginning and are intended to meet this requirement.)
6. The responsibility for performance rests with performers; role of the employer is to facilitate performance. The primary obligation for performing well lies with the performers. It is their responsibility to get their performance defined and standards set.

## RECOMMENDATIONS: PERFORMANCE APPRAISAL

Many commissions have gone into performance appraisal. Their recommendations are based on previous experience of what works and what does not.

1. Objectives should be changed to focus on performance management and public accountability.
2. Performance management and improvements as well as targeted achievements dominate PMS rather than ratings and reports.
3. The following are the non-negotiable components of performance appraisal:

   • Some form of target-setting and performance planning is inevitable.
   • Identification of competencies and incorporating these is also essential.

- There are two parts of performance appraisal:

    i. Tasks and targets
    ii. Accountabilities including competencies and behavior

- Self-appraisal is an integral part of it.
- Assessments should be shared after remarks given by the reviewing authority.
- Reporting and reviewing authorities should be rationalized.
- Since PMS may be linked to salaries, eventually a system of linking these should be worked out as this is not a direct or automatic linking. Decentralized administration should be done.

4. Development of a balanced score card approach:

    - This is a role effectiveness score card (RESC).
    - Identification of the parameters all government agencies should aim at:

        i. Example: direct revenue generation or revenue targets.
        ii. Benefits to the poor or economic value addition to beneficiaries (BPL, SC, ST, OBC, and other categories).
        iii. HRD: Contributions to self-sufficiency, skill development, and so forth.
        iv. Institution-building and/or good governance.

    - Development of performance indicators for each of these variables.

5. Each ministry and other department should develop its own performance indicators.
6. Development of sample performance indicators for measurement:

    - Take sample jobs and develop performance indicators (PIs) for use in the PMS.

- Widely circulate the concept of PIs and balanced score card.
- Develop a list of competencies on the basis of the competency mapping exercise to be incorporated in the PMS.

7. PMS cannot be introduced or changed for good results unless it is widely shared and users educated.
8. PMS can be handled by agents.
9. A performance contract should be signed by each individual at the beginning of his tenure in an organization.
10. Whenever civil servants leave, they should be assessed on their performance contract.
11. In the event of their not completing a full year, an assessment should be made for the period completed (not less than six months). During evaluation, allowance should be made for a person with a short tenure, since any individual needs a familiarization or induction period.
12. Competencies should be made known to the individual at the beginning of the year and the performance contract should cover identification of competency or critical indicators.
13. Every individual should be assessed in relation to the performance contract that may be in terms of key performance goals or targets to be achieved.
14. Assessment should be done by a committee consisting of a reporting officer, reviewing officer and an external expert.
15. The committee should take into consideration input from an individual's self-assessment, 360 degree assessment, the confidential assessment of his/her boss, and objective data on the success the performance contract.

Tenure should be fixed for each civil servant. There should not be frequent transfers. Adequate tome should be given to jobs that require a sustained impact and need familiarity with the region and people. For example, district collectors should be posted for a minimum period during which they should not be disturbed.

Performance contracts, highlighting the indicators, should be signed at the time of the posting.

Stakeholders' involvement in assessing the performance of a civil servant may include modified forms of 360 degree feedback. The stakeholders should be identified. If communities are involved, they should be appointed at the time of appraisal. The candidate as well as his/her seniors should also have a say. The stakeholders may include the community the department of the person is expected to serve as well as a few key beneficiary or target groups, seniors, juniors and colleagues, departments, and internal customers.

The individual's performance should be assessed on these parameters.

Accountability of time is an important part of PMS. Every officer should be able to account for 2500 hours of his/her time in a year, or for 200 hours a month. This accountability should form a part of the performance plan.

## PERFORMANCE-LINKED SALARY: RECOMMENDATIONS FOR CIVIL SERVICES (RAO, T. V., 2007)

There are many political issues in performance-related salaries. The experience of European economies in this matter has not been good. Incentives have had a great role to play. The philosophy is important. Organizations should be constantly innovating various methods of motivating people. These innovations should focus on ways of motivating them rather than on saving tax. With changes made in the Indian taxation system, it is time we focus our attention on incentives that encourage accountability, productivity, efficiency, effectiveness, output, retention, loyalty, innovations, teamwork, efficiency, a competitive advantage, and so forth, rather than tax savings and other incentives that yield benefits in the long term.

1. A well-defined PMS should be put in place as a precondition to performance-related pay (PRP).
2. A high value PRP is divisive and is likely to create new cadre classification values as civil servants start valuing high-paying services.
3. Salary rationalization should precede introduction of PRP. Currently, comparison of intelligent and bright civil servants

with corporate sector managers disappoints the former and is causing motivational issues. For example, in a state such as Gujarat, many IAS officers prefer to leave the service and join private sector organizations. This trend is expected to continue with the civil services failing to attract competent candidates due to private sector jobs having become more attractive.

4. PRP should be limited to around 25 percent of the basic salary (or CTC).

5. It should be treated as a form of recognition rather than as a financial incentive. This should be the main purpose rather than financial compensation for good performance.

6. Other financial incentives for extraordinary performance should be encouraged such as one-time payments, which could be of lump sum value.

7. Determination of performance incentives should be de-centralized to the respective departments, which should be encouraged to work out innovative systems.

8. Group incentives should be encouraged.

9. Every department in the Government should have a PRP budget.

10. Freedom should be given to profit-making and revenue-generating departments and public enterprises to have their own PRP systems with no ceiling on amounts to be distributed as PLP.

11. Freedom should also be given to civil servants to join other high-paying organizations for certain periods of time and rejoin the service back. This could be for one year to five year periods.

12. Civil servants should be encouraged to take up high paying international jobs wherever possible. Sponsoring them should be an incentive for high performers.

13. Group incentives play an important role in creating a team culture. Teamwork and collaboration are much needed in India. In order to promote synergy and teamwork, it is useful to have team incentives.

14. Team incentives can be in the form of celebrations, group picnics and awards, movies, parties, and so forth.

# 360 Degree Feedback

Many countries are using or are contemplating the use of 360 degree feedback in their civil services (Morgan et al., 2005). They include Australia, the UK, some countries in the EU, New Zealand, Canada, Korea, and others. The key driver of the introduction of a performance feedback process into the UK's civil service was Sir Richard Wilson's report on civil service reform, which specifically suggested the introduction of 360 degree feedback for senior civil servants by the end of 2001 (Cabinet Office, 1999). The underpinning assumption for this was that a key criterion for good leadership is self-awareness (Cabinet Office, 1999) and that "if done well, it is a very powerful tool of management and a very good way of helping people improve their own performance" (Wilson, cited in Moore, 2000, p. 15).

The role of 360 degree feedback as an element of "new public management" is designed to objectify, make known and measure performance (Townley, 1993). Yet this is not free of the attendant pressures that arise due to the "relatively diffuse nature of management authority", which is captured imperfectly by a "strategic choice framework which may exaggerate the scope for autonomous management action" (Bach and Della Rocca, 2000).

In a case study, Arthur Morgan et al. demonstrated the positive results of 360 degree feedback, although the results indicated its motivational value as being questionable (only 12 out of 21 civil servants found it having a motivational value, and 13 reported that it helped them in their professional development).

# PMS for the Civil Services in Other Countries

The following description of PAS systems in Singapore, Thailand, and the Philippines is based on a paper by Sarah Vallance (1999).

1. *Singapore:* In Singapore, PAS for civil servants is based on the Shell System, which has two parts. The first, called "work

review," requires a qualitative description and comment on an individual's work. It also focuses on training needs, and is open for dialogue with the assessee. The focus of this part is on the contributions of the appraisee. The second part deals with the developmental assessment of an employee on 10 qualities. The supervisor is required to rate the employee on these 10 qualities on a four-point scale (high, exceeding, meets, below), and also to rank the qualities. The appraiser also rates the individual in terms of his/her currently estimated potential (Sarah Vallance, 1999).

2. *Thailand:* In Thailand, ministries have been given the freedom to have their own appraisal systems to promote efficiency and effectiveness in job performance, and aid decisions on promotion, salary increases, motivation, training, and dismissal. They should, however, focus on output of work and ability to perform and manage work. The Civil Services Commission suggests that a number of factors should be taken into consideration in appraisals. These include: (a) quality, quantity, and application of work output; (b) the ability to plan and implement, direct and make decisions including deadlines being met, coordination with other departments, taking control, solving problems, resolution of conflicts, and help provided in accomplishment an organization's goals; and (c) the ability to improve work and services, including demonstration of new ideas and solutions, identification and addressing of problems, and efficient and effective performance of work. In addition, an appraiser is expected to comment on the employee's ability to utilize the staff and develop manpower resources to match people to skills, ensure maximization of skills, and encourage staff to be adaptable, acquire knowledge, and contribute to achievement of organizational goals. The guidelines recommend that appraisers to develop agreements in terms of the mission, results, objectives, standards, and desired outputs. The organization should choose one of the four methods: self rating, supervisor rating, committee rating, or a combination of the three. Employees' performance should be appraised twice a year and maintained by the department.

3. *Philippines:* In the Philippines, subordinate rating accounts for 22 percent and superior's rating 78 percent. Subordinates' rating is not available for officers when their superiors' ratings are discussed with them. The superior's rating form consists of three sections: evaluation of accomplishments, managerial competence, and of training and development needs. The first part assesses the extent to which performance objectives in the contract were met, individuals' performance in comparison with their peers, and qualitative assessment of the extent to which these were met.

Managerial competencies include management of work, people, resources, linkages, constraints and innovativeness. The assessors choose between the five rating levels. A subordinate's rating is similar to that of his/her boss.

4. *Laos:* Laos has been planning to introduce a new appraisal system for its civil servants with help from the UNDP and the Swiss Agency for Development Cooperation. This will involve individual self-evaluation, which will then be presented to the team in a group discussion. In this meeting, colleagues will also provide performance-related feedback to each other. Subsequently, the superior will evaluate individuals' performance, taking into account the information gathered in the group meeting. This new PMS is dependent on introduction of job descriptions that specify the tasks individuals are expected to undertake, against which they can be evaluated. Prior to implementation, the Government has strongly emphasized the importance of job descriptions as part of its "rightsizing" policy (Keopanya, 2004).

### 5. PMS in ASEAN (Surapong Malee, 2005)

• *Brunei:* This performance appraisal system was introduced in 1998 to create an economically effective and efficient civil service, and to continuously improve performance and the quality of service. It provides information that can be used to improve employees' performance in carrying out their duties and responsibilities, and supporting management in planning and monitoring their career path and potential development. It is also used for rewards, promotion, training, motivation, and communication. However, despite having had the system in place since 1998, the Brunei Civil Service has been driven by the continuing pace of globalization to achieve a higher performing organization, and move the system from a process-oriented one to a more strategic one, linking individual performance to organizational goals. Performance plans need to be developed and more reliable assessment tools created to ensure effective management of underperforming staff. This envisages a closer link between performance appraisal and training and development programs as one way forward (Malee, 2005).

• *Cambodia:* The Cambodian Civil Service has adopted talent development as a crucial way of improving individual and organizational performance. It believes that individual performance can be enhanced by developing skills and knowledge, and has identified a strong need for development of a long-term human resource development strategy to strengthen the capacity of the country's Civil Service. This capacity-building approach concentrates on development of training programs for potential graduates and existing leaders and executives in the Civil Service. The programs are delivered at various institutions, including the Royal School of Administration, the training institutes of ministries and departments, universities, and through other methods of learning. These intensive training programs have a tough entry criteria, and are geared toward increasing the performance capacity of participating civil servants (Surapong Malee, 2005).

• *Indonesia:* The Indonesian Civil Service's PMS is designed to respond to a globalized world and is an attempt to create a clean and stable civil service, develop career paths, and be an aid to promotion and an increase in salaries. The system stresses that the practice of work performance management must be based on merit principles. It is an evidence-based evaluation, since information on staff performance needs to be gathered to make decisions on promotion and salary increases. Although the criteria used for assessing performance are mainly personal characteristics or non-performance-based criteria, there is also a job achievement criterion, which measures individual contributions against job standards. In Indonesia, the major use of performance appraisal is for increasing salaries rather than performance or quality of service. This is largely because Civil Service salaries are low, which gives scope for corruption. To cope with these challenges, the Indonesian Civil Service has been working toward implementation of a new performance management framework and a set of regulations based on measurable criteria and accountability (Surapong Malee, 2005).

- *Malaysia:* In Malaysia, PMS for the country's Civil Service concentrates on the Government's performance as one of the administrative strategies that enables the former to meet the challenge of globalization, innovate and improve service delivery, as well as enhance the overall performance of departments to carry out the Government's strategic goals and objectives. The PMS attempts to align the five components of performance management, including strategic direction, organizational capacity, people potential, workforce performance, and work culture. Performance measures are cascaded from the strategic federal level to departmental, divisional, and individual levels. The PMS provides the overall framework for managing performance in the Civil Service, and the new system is designed as a tool to ensure the productivity and quality of service. The country's Civil Service has also introduced a scheme for measuring the outcomes of work performance, based on four strategic areas: customers, employer-employee relations, performance management, and recognition and rewards. Challenges faced by the Malaysian Civil Service relate to achievement of efficient and effective performance goals, accountability, customer focus, cooperation, flexibility, a performance-oriented workforce, and secured recruitment to the Civil Service. As in most ASEAN civil services, the way forward to improve strategic management of human resources and performance management is to devise performance indicators, develop a collaborative approach among departments, establish review processes, provide leadership training, and eradicate corruption (Surapong Malee, 2005).

In the fall of 2002, the Corporate Leadership Council in the USA published *Building the High-Performance Workforce: A Quantitative Analysis of the Effectiveness of Performance Management Strategies.* Quantifying the impact of more than 100 performance management strategies on employees' performance, this research uncovered vital information on which strategies enhance (or diminish) their performance and by precisely how much.

In a subsequent work, *Benchmarking the High-Performance Organization,* the Corporate Leadership Council used the same sample of more than 19,000 employees and managers from 34 organizations across seven industry groups and 29 countries. This study addressed the frequency and effectiveness with which performance management strategies are implemented in organizations today. The intention was to help members locate "mismatches" between the amount of resources allocated to a given strategy and the return on employees' performance. With unparalleled precision, members can then reallocate scarce resources—money and time—to implement strategies that not only have the most impact on employees' performance, but are also most likely to be ineffectively administered or absent. In this extensive study on best practices on PMS, the Conference Board observed the following:

1. Many performance management strategies that can improve employees' performance by more than 25 percent were underutilized or ineffectively administered in practice.
2. Some organizations significantly outperformed others in the use and implementation of several high impact performance strategies.

3. Eighty-three percent of employees recognized the importance of their day-to-day work in the success of their business units and organizations, and 59 percent understood the connection between their projects and assignments and their organizations' overall strategies. However, some organizations were significantly better than others at ensuring that their employees recognize this link.

4. Overall, 57 percent of employees reported that they enjoyed their projects and assignments, and more than three-quarter of the employees recognized the importance of their projects in their personal development and long-term careers.

5. Only 10 percent of the employees had a full 360 degree formal performance Review with three or more sources of feedback. However, even in companies that most frequently use 360 degree feedback, only about one-third of the employees had a comprehensive review. Organizations had a sizeable opportunity to positively impact their employees' performance by providing more than one source of feedback during performance reviews.

6. On an average, about one-third of the employees reported that their managers voluntarily gave them informal feedback without their having to ask for it. Employees typically had to wait more than a week after completing a project or assignment before receiving informal feedback.

7. Only about one-third of the employees in an average company received a written development plan during their most recent formal performance reviews. Out of the employees who had a development plan, only one-third reported that their plans were challenging and applicable to their daily work.

8. Nearly a quarter of the employees reported that their managers made fundamental changes to their projects and assignments at least once a week. According to another quarter of the employees, their managers made changes to their projects one to three times a month.

9. Employees were skeptical about being rewarded for successful completion of their projects. Less than 40 percent of them believed that if they performed well on their projects

and assignments, they would be rewarded with a higher performance rating, a merit increase, annual bonus, or raise in base salary. Only 16 percent of the employees saw the link between strong performance on their projects and the likelihood of their being promoted.

10. Only 31 percent of employees in an average company reported that the training they received was effective.

How can organizations drive results through PMS? The following are some of the conclusions drawn by the Conference Board from their studies.

Organizations are changing the breadth and focus of their PMS approach. These changes include:

1. From managing system to managing performance.
2. By offering a clear business case for managing performance.
3. By providing the tools required to perform effectively.
4. By realizing that even the best intentioned managers cannot overcome subjectivity and/or focus on immediate goals.
5. By leveraging collaborative goal-setting and team-based performance management.
6. By targeting activities and individuals that will have a great impact on financial performance.

The five key imperatives identified for the success of PMS are:

1. Establishing performance management as an organizational priority.
2. Upskilling managers to improve their performance.
3. Expanding lines of performance accountability.
4. Aligning with business drivers.
5. Managing employees' goal realization.

The five problems in PMS include:

1. Inadequate manager focus: Many factors affect devotion of time and effort on PMS.

2. Insufficient manager skills to improve performance.
3. Narrowly defined ownership: Requires multiple owners of individual performance.
4. Disconnection with strategy: Inadequate linkage with business drivers.
5. Failure to execute: Lack of efficient execution across business units.

On the basis of various recommendations made by the author of this book, the Administrative Reforms Commission made the following observations in its recommendations on PMS for civil servants in India (see http://indiagovernance.gov.in/files/personnel_administration10.pdf, for more details):

> Performance management is the systematic process by which the organization involves its employees, as individuals and members of a group, in improving organizational effectiveness in the accomplishment of organizational mission and goals. Performance management is a holistic process bringing together many activities which collectively contribute to the effective management of individuals and teams in order to achieve high levels of organizational performance. Performance management is strategic in that it is about broader issues and long term goals and integrated as it links various aspects of the business, people management, individuals and teams. To strengthen both, individual effectiveness by recognition of the importance to the employee and the institution of relating work performance to the strategic or long-term and overarching mission of the organization as a whole. Employees' goals and objectives are derived from their departments, which in turn support the mission and goals of the organization. (pp. 228–229)

The report further observes:

> Performance Management is the essence of managing, and the primary "vehicle" for getting the desired results through employees at all levels in the organization. The performance

management process provides an opportunity for the employee and performance manager to discuss development goals and jointly create a plan for achieving those goals. Development plans should contribute to organizational goals and the professional growth of the employee. In the absence of such a system, staff members are unclear as to the employer's expectations regarding performance objectives and standards/targets, leading to low productivity, costly mistakes, stress, de-motivation, and conflict. Sound Performance Management Systems subscribe to the crucial Principle: "What gets measured gets done". The days of having a "one-set-of-measures-fits-all" Performance Management System are inherently flawed and long gone. Performance objectives and measures need to be specific to job categories and individual roles. (p. 229)

# 9

# Managing Motivation through Rewards and Recognition
## *Best Practices**

In the earlier chapters, we have discussed that performance depends on competence, commitment, culture, ability, motivation, and support. While performance, competence, and support can be defined through planning and communication, motivation or commitment are more complex phenomena. For long, it has been assumed that incentives motivate employees to perform well. Many organizational thinkers, such as Chris Argyris, have pointed out that incentives and other forms of extrinsic motivation factors are not in the best interest of either organizations or individuals. It seems as though people come to work for incentives, birthday parties, picnics, chairmen's dinners, and other celebrations that are promoted as incentives for good performance. By now, literature on motivation has made clear the following:

1. Different factors motivate different people at different points of time. Abraham Maslow's theory of need hierarchy outlined how motivational actors are organized hierarchically. Herzberg differentiated factors that cause motivation or satisfaction (motivators) from factors that cause work dissatisfaction (hygienes). McClelland and several other psychologists outlined the role played by family and society

---

* A large part of this chapter, reviewing incentive schemes of various organizations, is reproduced with permission from *HR Best Practices: Manufacturing Sector in India* by Nisha Nair, Neharika Vohra, T. V. Rao, and Atul Srivastava, New Delhi: Steel Authority of India, 2010.

in developing motivation including achievement, power, affiliation, and so forth.

2. Extrinsic motivators such as incentives (financial or non-financial) play a limited role.

3. Many factors, internal or external to the organization, individual, and the environment influence motivation. For example, some individuals are workaholics and what disturbs some others may not disturb them, and they continue to work hard if they are given the jobs they like.

4. In the long run, organizations should focus on intrinsic motivators and make work enjoyable by giving people the right kind of work that utilizes and develops their talent. A clear understanding of the purpose of the work, meaningful work, significance given to individuals and their work, the company or department's vision, job rotation, increased responsibilities, addition of challenging assignments, change of tasks and/or scenarios, good bosses, supportive climate, continuing or periodic recognition of contributions, and so forth, play a significant motivational role. These play a critical role in developing employees' motivation.

5. Extrinsic factors may sometimes act in the reverse direction if not managed appropriately.

Given the understanding we have gained in the last few decades on factors affecting motivation (an individual's personality, family, neighborhood, organizational culture, personnel policies, boss, company values, organizational practices, etc.), it is clear that an organization can only manage motivation to a certain extent. The extent to which extrinsic motivators provide motivation cannot be totally ignored. It is with this intention that some the organizations have tried out some mechanisms (mentioned earlier) in recent times. The reader may choose what suits his/her organization. Continuous change and experimentation is recommended. It should be remembered that in the final analysis, organizations should strive to increase intrinsic motivators. This can be achieved by focusing on KPAs or KRAs, tasks at hand, competency-building, listening, understanding, empathy on the part of reporting managers (as reflected in PCs and PRDs), and so forth.

Organizations choose between a variety of rewards to recognize desired behavior and boost employees' morale. These serve as a means to motivate employees, act as role models for emulation and inspiration, and raise standards of performance. This chapter attempts to synthesize what manufacturing organizations choose to reward and how they reward their employees. It is based on a survey conducted on best HR practices by IIMA for Steel Authority of India as part of its HR awards.

# Recognizing Individual Performance

Rewards for individual performance are a general feature in most organizations. They are referred to differently in different organizations. Systems for identifying talent also vary across organizations.

A scheme that aims to acknowledge the efforts of employees, who have displayed exemplary commitment in fulfillment of their objectives beyond their call of duty, is referred to as People Who Made the Difference (PWMD) at Schneider Electric India. The objective is to recognize and reward committed employees who have exerted exemplary efforts in their work. Akin to this, HPCL offers its Outstanding Achievers Award, which seeks to recognize the outstanding achievements of officers in junior grades who have displayed extraordinary commitment during a particular year in pursuance of its business interests across the company. Winners are awarded cash prizes along with silver plaques of high value. A notable feature of this award is that anyone can nominate an officer for an award. It could be his/her immediate supervisor, colleague or superior, or a colleague from any other department or location. An officer can also nominate himself/herself for an award, the process for which is completely online. Very similar to this, Honeywell India has a peer recognition award called the Bravo Award, which is again a reward, based on peers' recommendation for acknowledgement of good work. This is a cash reward and has various categories such as silver, golden, and platinum. Recipient employees are given Bravo Certificates along with the cash reward. One of the most prestigious awards in Honeywell is the Premium Achievement Award, which is given to very few employees, who have performed in an extraordinary or exemplary manner. For this reward, the recipient along with his/her spouse is invited to the USA, where they participate in and engage with senior leadership at team meetings. They are also sent on a sightseeing trip for a week. For its top performing individuals, Dabur India also sponsors annual foreign trips and has a Bulls Eye Award under which a laptop is given to top salespersons who achieve set targets.

Schneider Electric India presents a Rookie of the Year Award to its employees to build a culture of recognizing new entrants for their exceptional performance within the organization. Applicable to all graduate and management trainees, the award is given for the outstanding performance of new employees in areas including their taking the initiative to enhance their own knowledge and/or skills, contributing effectively to their team's success or bringing about process improvement in their work.

Employees demonstrating desired leadership behavior (as defined in their leadership framework) and those creating an impact on the organization through extraordinary efforts are rewarded by their line managers at Castrol India with a Spot Bonus Cash award. There is an organizational budget of 1 percent of fixed salaries for the spot bonus. Employees have been awarded as much as as ₹ 300,000 under it. A similar award has been instituted by NTPC, called the Performance Excellence Award for Regional Leadership (PEARL) award.

Honeywell India also has a star award, whereby employees contributing in a positive way beyond the call of duty are rewarded with stars. These are actual bronze stars that are given to such employees for their achievements. They can earn any number of stars, based on the achievements. These stars have points attached to them, and on their redemption, the employees can collect gift vouchers of the same denomination. Those who earn more than 15 stars in a year become members of the company's Star Club and are given various privileges for the next year. Along similar lines, Matrix Labs has a Matrix Achievers' Club, which has been instituted in recognition of the dedication and significant contributions of the company's employees. The award carries a certificate of membership, cash reward, trophy and an annual holiday. Star performers in ITW Signode are rewarded by being given first preference in their choice of their next assignment and location. In addition, they are promoted to the next level when they are 80 percent ready for this.

Extraordinary contributions are also rewarded on a periodical basis by different organizations. For example, Moser Baer has Employee of the Month and Employee of the Year awards to recognize individuals who have been consistent in achieving excellence in their work around the year. It also has an Outstanding Manager of the Year award. Tata Motors presents a Man of the Month award for consistent performance. The award winner is felicitated in front of all the employees. The Man of the Year is selected from all the Man of the Month awardees. An employee who has achieved one-time exemplary work is felicitated by a badge and certificate under the Exemplary Performance award. Similarly, JSPL has instituted a JEM scheme to recognize the efforts of individuals on a monthly basis. The company also presents a Business Executive of the Year award. The JEM award is based on nominations by heads of departments carried out through an evaluation sheet assessing areas including contribution to productivity, quality, cost, behavior, exceptional work done, discipline, punctuality, and so forth. The award displays the photograph of the winner on display boards located at prominent locations in the plant. The award winner is felicitated at the end of the year in a formal award ceremony.

In most organizations, there is an attempt to measure performance of outstanding achievers and reward them appropriately. Such practices help motivate people, and if the reward is fair and genuine, employees strive to become recipients of such rewards. The perception of these rewards being special and valuable is important for companies to maintain.

## Team Rewards

Most organizations offer team rewards in addition to individual rewards to promote teamwork and ensure energized, enthused, and motivated teams. Some team rewards instituted by organizations in the manufacturing sector include the following.

An award called Quest for Excellence has been instituted by Moser Baer to recognize outstanding achievement in business results and spur the spirit of healthy achievement as cross-functional teams. Tata Motors also offers quality-linked payment for achieving high productivity in the manufacture of vehicles. This is given in groups based on the ratings of cross-functional teams. For example, a team award was given when the truck ACE was produced in record time. The Trailblazer Team Award has been instituted by Dabur India for recognizing best performing teams, undertaking and completing difficult projects or performing exceptional acts. These teams are rewarded by citations and prizes. For example, in February 2009, the company recognized the good work done by its Jammu Unit team during the political and social turmoil which lasted for about two months. The team ensured that production schedules were adhered to consistently, despite the constraints, while ensuring the safety and security of the employees.

In order to give employees a chance to become an important part of the organization by seeing their ideas and thoughts being implemented in the areas they work in, JSPL has instituted a SMILE Award, which is given to teams from different units working in harmony to achieve the common goals of the organization. JSPL also has a project completion/production target achievement award that is a monetary benefit given to employees. This is in recognition of the extra effort put in by employees toward the profitability of the plant. TCG Lifesciences presents trophies to teams that have performed well in categories including good teamwork, best support team, and so forth. NTPC recognizes the best performance among its power plants/units and toward initiating healthy competition. An award ceremony is conducted at the corporate level, presided over by CMD and directors, and trophies are presented to the winning business unit heads in a formal ceremony. Honeywell India has a Line of the Month Award to promote team spirit and competitiveness among its various working teams. The best team is rewarded the award, based on its overall performance. All the team members are given gift vouchers. Bosch also recognizes outstanding teamwork on a regular monthly basis through its Team Effort Recognition Awards.

At NTPC, another initiative which is very popular (especially among young executives) is called Business Minds. This is a management game that develops executives' strategic thinking and decision-making capabilities by exposing participants to simulated real-life business situations that help them discover new skills. It is conducted in association with AIMA. Cross-functional teams participate in the game, since it is multidisciplinary in nature and reflects the real-life multifunctional role of business. The top eight winning teams from NTPC participate in the national-level management games conducted by AIMA. The winner and runners up at the company level receive cash prizes along with commendation letters and trophies. Business suits are gifted to all team members by NTPC for participating in the national-level round.

ITW Signode has a unique award called Dream Project to encourage employees, vendors, distributors, and other stakeholders of the organization to work on long-term prospects/strategic objectives beyond their current annual plans and to reward them commensurately for this. The minimum value of each Dream Project is ₹ 1 million for key accounts and equipment groups, and ₹ 500,000 for distribution. A reward is pegged at 2 percent of the value of the invoice.

It has been argued that it is inappropriate to reward behavior A, while hoping for people to show behavior B. Most organizations expect people to work in teams, but award only individual achievements. Thus, it is a welcome move among organizations to also explicitly reward and recognize team achievements.

# Rewards Linked to Performance

In addition to the various individual and team-based rewards, companies have specific reward schemes linked to performance at both workmen and officer levels. Moser Baer offers a plant production incentive linked to variable pay at all its manufacturing locations. It has formulated an incentive plan such that if employees work in line with the business targets, they gain tangible rewards every month. This incentive is based on production, customer delivery, and the quality of products manufactured by the employees. The company also has incentive plans for its sales teams. Variable pay is given to employees, based on their individual performance as well as that of the company. Variable pay, linked to output, is a common feature, as in Bosch, where it is paid on a monthly basis to recognize the good performance of workmen. The company's compensation package includes about 35 percent as variable pay linked to direct performance. In the event of early completion of projects, employees are rewarded in the form of additional payments at IFFCO. Specific measurable extraordinary performance by a group also receives cash awards.

The production incentive scheme in Indian Oil provides that every employee in the team of which he/she is a member is entitled to receive up to 15 percent of his/her base pay on achievement of targets against various well-defined and comprehensive parameters set at the beginning of the year. For officers, an incentive based on individual performance has recently been introduced, whereby they are rated on their achievements in various key result areas on a five-point scale. Based on this score, there is a payout ranging from 1 percent to 13 percent of the employee's base pay. Team performance and individual performance are in the ratio of 80:20. The team performance incentive for achieving 100 percent of a team's targets is pegged at 12 percent. The payout for individual performance is based on the individuals' rating on KPIs.

Based on the performance of the organization as a whole, NTPC's employees are paid an ex gratia/special incentive and annual performance-linked incentive. This scheme recognizes the higher degree of responsibility at higher levels, and accordingly, provides for progressively higher payments at higher grades. Employees in nonexecutive categories are also given special rewards, which are inclusive of ex gratia/bonus payable to them. Similarly, TCG Life Sciences offers various forms of bonuses, linked to performance, including (a) an association bonus to acknowledge consistent high performance for five years, (b) a contributory bonus for project delivery and achievement of milestone, (c) a special bonus to acknowledge outstanding performance, and (d) a recognition bonus (at senior levels) to acknowledge contribution to the organization.

One of the long-term incentives offered at Castrol India is a deferred cash bonus scheme for its managers. Under the scheme, managers can get as high as 50 percent of annual basic salary (approximately 15 percent of the individual's CTC) as Leave Travel Insurance (LTI). There needs to be a minimum period of three years of employment before employees can avail of the scheme. If their business performance exceeds certain targets, employees can get as high as 150 percent of the grant (approximately 22 percent of their CTC for superior performers) as LTI payouts. Similarly, the performance-linked component at Philips Electronics India comprises a productivity-linked bonus and team performance pay for both supervisory and management staff.

To promote a performance-driven culture, Maruti Suzuki rewards high performers in the organization under its Own Your Car scheme. The scheme facilitates 100 percent ownership of a Maruti car through third party financing for employees recognized as high performers. Those with consistent levels of high performance ratings in three consecutive years are eligible for car ownership under the scheme, which not only rewards performance, but also helps foster pride in the organization's product.

In HPCL, there are: (a) timely promotions on the merit route, (b) deputation/joint venture assignments, (c) higher positions with additional authority, (d) sponsorships to premier developmental programs, (e) executive MBA sponsorships, and so forth, for employees who are judged to be performing very well.

When a company does well and exceeds market expectation, one of the major factors that influence this performance is the hard work and involvement of its employees. It, therefore, makes ample sense for them to reward their employees, especially in years their profit margins are high. Many public sector organizations have limited headroom to reward their employees; therefore, linking of self-development rewards to excellence in performance is an innovation worth exploring.

# Rewards to Promote Desired Values/Attitudes/Behavior

Recognizing the importance of reinforcing and rewarding desirable behavior, many companies have instituted rewards for attendance, punctuality, living the organizations' values, adhering to safety, and so forth. Some such representative rewards are discussed in this section.

At Tata Motors, there is a Good Attendance Award given to employees who report to work for more than 265 days in a year. Bosch also recognizes and rewards regular attendance based on prespecified criteria.

In order to promote safety, HPCL has instituted a Safety Award for accident-free operations in its refineries. JSPL has a Best Safety Man Award for serving as an exemplar in maintaining the highest standards of safety, and Tata Motors has a Safety Award for safe work throughout the year.

There are also awards for specifically promoting organizational values. At Moser Baer, there is a novel TIPS Award that stands for the company's values—Teamwork, Integrity, Passion, and Speed. This particular award's objective is to celebrate the spirit of upholding and role modeling Moser Baer's values by rewarding those who consistently live out its core values of teamwork, integrity, passion, and speed in their day-to-day behavior. This is awarded once a quarter across the organization. There is one award per value. Another such award is Honeywell's Chairman's Award for the Everyday Hero under which its chairman presents the award to employees who support the company's five listed initiatives and 12 behaviors. Employees receive plaques and certificates, and their achievements and photographs are published in Honeywell's internal magazine. A cash reward of ₹25,000 is also given to the employee.

In order to instill pride in the national culture and language, HPCL has instituted a Hindi Incentive Scheme under which various awards are offered to promote the Rajbhasha (Hindi) among its employees. These include annual incentive schemes for Hindi correspondence courses and competitions among employees with awards earmarked for these.

Schneider Electric India offers various awards for promoting behavior deemed as valuable to the organization's success, such as (a) cost consciousness for conscious and optimum utilization of resources provided, (b) time management—effective and efficient management of time, (c) workspace management—management of work space assigned, (d) responsiveness—the quality or state of being responsive, (e) customer satisfaction—providing good service in a pleasant manner and meeting customers' expectations, (f) accessibility—easy to approach, reach, or speak with, and (g) adaptability and flexibility—able to adjust readily to different conditions or being responsive to change.

Among other awards, there is a Mentors Samman Award given in NTPC to encourage exemplary mentoring by senior employees. JSPL has initiated a Bravery and Courage Award to recognize employees exhibiting outstanding bravery. Schneider Electric India has an Office Etiquette Award for employees who best adhere to basic courtesy and also to the code of conduct defined in the HR policy of the organization. There are also awards for the most punctual, most energetic, and most methodical employees at Crystal Phosphates. Being the best attired is another award given in some companies such as Honeywell India, where the Best Attired Employee Award is given to employees in the operations team. A team that observes employees sends nominations for the best attired employee of the month. The winning employee receives a grooming kit or a gift voucher.

In order to enhance the commitment level of employees, companies have instituted service rewards on completion of milestone years of service. This aims to reward loyalty and express gratitude for employees' long association with the company. The practice of recognizing the long association of individuals with an organization for milestone years of service is followed by various companies such as Tata Motors, Bosch, NTPC, Moser Baer as well as others. HPCL rewards employees with more than 15 years, 25 years, 30 years, and 35 years of service and at their superannuation. Giving substantial awards such as gold coins is in practice. IFFCO presents service awards in the form of gold coins, cash, and to and fro airfare for employee and spouse to any destination (limited to ₹ 15,000). Schneider calls it the Hats Off Long Service Award and Tata Motors has a Retirement Award, a silver coin and plaque, to commemorate long years of service and commitment to the organization.

Attempts to make employees behave according to the values and norms of the organization can be called social engineering.

However, for organizations to foster desired behavior is a challenge, and innovative, noncoercive methods have to be thought through and implemented. Therefore, the various examples of companies rewarding desired behavior or internalization of values are worth thinking about and trying out.

# Rewards Linked to Quality and Improvement

For manufacturing organizations, where the quality of products is a critical factor for success, rewarding quality is all the more important. At NTPC, annual contests are organized at the project, regional, and company levels in which quality circles from across the company compete with each other. JSPL has a Best Quality Circle Award to reward best quality efforts. It has also instituted a Best Contractor Award for rewarding contractors who provide excellent services with a high quality of work. Regular quality and Kaizen competitions are organized at Philips Electronics India, and Bosch organizes programs and awards linked to Six Sigma to ensure high levels of quality. Tata Motors has an award called Gunwatta Rakshaks, which accords weekly recognition of employees detecting faults in quality coming in from suppliers. Those who receive this recognition the largest number of times are felicitated annually by top management.

Many organizations also have suggestion awards that serve as a step toward continuous improvement. JSPL has a suggestion scheme called Mera Sujhav, a way to reward any individual, irrespective of grade or group. The scheme provides an individual the opportunity to think out of the box and offer solutions where there can be a possibility of cost saving and other benefits to the organization. The company also has a Young Thinkers Award, which is presented to an employee giving the largest number of implementable suggestions. Similarly, Moser Baer, under its suggestion award, acknowledges employees for their suggestions that improve its productivity and quality, increases production, and saves time and material, leading to cost reduction. There is a similar quality suggestion scheme at HPCL, which recognizes and rewards the best suggestions. The National Open Competition for Executive Talent (NOCET) at NTPC is another such award, which is a three-tier theme-based team event held to solicit ideas on issues facing the organization. A theme for the competition is decided and a topic that is relevant to the organization is chosen. Three to four member teams compete at the unit, regional, and corporate levels. A panel of judges comprising top NTPC executives and external experts judge the teams on their concept. Trophies, cash, training of choice, and widescale publicity are awarded to the winners. Various companies such as Honeywell India and Moser Baer hold competitions around 5S to improve efficiency by eliminating waste and reducing unevenness of processes.

Another route to continuous improvement and growth in organizations is achieved by rewarding innovation and recognizing the creativity of employees. Moser Baers Innovation Award aims to recognize employees who have successfully converted their breakthrough ideas from concept to reality, and have tangible results to show for their creative efforts. Similarly, ABB offers patent money and rewards of ₹ 25,000 for every inventor after filing of a patent. A plaque is also issued for each filing, mentioning the title and the inventor's name.

Involvement of employees is not only to be found in the responsibilities assigned to them, but also in their suggestions and ideas for work or improvement. Employees who work day in and day out in an area have the best suggestions for improvement in these. Organizations would be well advised to have processes in place to set up mutually beneficial employee suggestion schemes.

## Low Cost, Token Appreciation Rewards

Not all rewards are monetary or incur a sizable cost to a company. There are many awards that are low cost and low value, but high in recognition and visibility. Companies often present rewards such as appreciation letters, publication in in-house journals, Star of the Month award, and so forth.

JSPL presents gift vouchers, appreciation cards, and certificates to deserving employees. Maruti Suzuki sends "Thank you" cards to signal appreciation of a job well done. There is also the practice of giving dinner coupons and movie tickets to around 8 percent of the best performers in each division/group in companies. Schneider Electric India has instituted a Moment of Fame Award to recognize professional attitude and behaviors that add value to employees, processes, and the organization. Dabur India also has a Hall/Wall of Fame. Special recognition such as appreciation letters by top management, dinner with family with heads of projects/HODs, coverage in cable networks, posters with pictures of award winners, and quality circle scarf/belt/cap are given by NTPC to its outstanding employees. The company also has a program called Guest of Honor, under which quality control team members with outstanding contributions visiting other stations are given guest of honor status by providing accommodation in the corporate guest house, hospitality facilities, free to and fro travel, etc.

In order to acknowledge and appreciate the effort put in by operations staff in the field to attain operational excellence, HPCL has a system of recognition called Celebrations of Small Wins at plants. Small wins are celebrated as and when there is outstanding performance/achievement by a team or individual members with regard to various operating parameters such as stock losses, scrap disposal, irregularities, innovations, and so forth. During such celebrations, all team members get together and relish the success of the team/colleagues. Similarly, at Philips Electronics India, sweets are frequently distributed across the company to celebrate outstanding performance by any department/team for a day or week. To promote an attitude of appreciation among its employees, Honeywell India has a Peer Appreciation Board, where any employee can post appreciation about any other employee. This has become a way of life in Honeywell and the board is full of appreciation every day. Another novel practice for celebrating good work followed at Tata Motors is WOW slips and "well done" cards, which are given to recognize and appreciate the work done by team members and subordinates.

Not all rewards need to be large or expensive. Even small but significant tokens can communicate to people that their work is being noticed and appreciated.

# Rewards Linked to Career Advancement/ Development

Some rewards are in the form of opportunities for career and professional advancement. TCG Life Sciences has a system of rewarding star performers with nomination for knowledge/skill enhancement training, and a PhD course. NTPC also encourages its employees to pursue higher education by suitably rewarding and providing monetary incentives and cash lump sum payment in recognition of employees acquiring higher educational qualifications. Furthermore, it offers special awards/recognition to members winning overall positions at company-level competitions by sponsoring the team for a study tour of reputed organizations/ power plants abroad/in the country. Any team winning the first position in the national convention organized for quality is also sponsored for a study tour abroad. In addition, there are sponsorships on offer for external training to deserving individuals/teams. At IFFCO, employees making extraordinary contributions are considered for foreign assignments/fast track promotion, including joint ventures (JVs), and their services are put at the disposal of the organization beyond their normal period of service. Good performers at *HPCL*, irrespective of the salary grade to which they belong, are provided with the opportunity for enhanced opportunities to learn by way of sponsorships to high-profile, high-value training programs in top-level institutes in India, such as the IIMs, and also abroad. It also nominates bright and good performers to JVs and on deputation for JVs/foreign assignments to provide them with the opportunity to have a varied experience. At ITW Signode, rewards are in the form of learning opportunities that include nomination to MDP programs in top business schools, financial assistance for tuition, training in new technology, and sponsorship for attendance at international seminars and conferences.

People feel that the company values their contribution when it makes long-term investments in their growth. Such investments, though not expensive, also benefit the company in the long run.

# Communication of Rewards

An important part of rewarding employees is timely and visible recognition for high impact. The manner in which rewards are announced or communicated adds much, if not more, to the value of the rewards themselves. Some practices with regard to announcement/delivery of rewards are highlighted below.

Moser Baer gives On the Spot awards to encourage and recognize any effort, stretch, or notable contributions made by employees within or outside their job responsibilities. In order to communicate the launch, process, or results of any scheme, various methods are used, such as puzzles, which generate curiosity among employees, on posters, the intranet, rewards and recognition boards, spreading awareness though departmental meetings, and the company newsletter. Public forums, such as open houses, are utilized to felicitate the awardees. Important members of the senior leadership team attend the event and employees are awarded among large groups of people. HPCL also sends formal emails through its public relations and corporate communications teams, outlining and commending the concerned individuals/teams for their efforts, and also by printing the names of the award winners in the annual report. Another practice followed by Honeywell India to recognize and make visible the contribution of employees is sending out a note of achievement along with their pictures to family members for every award they receive.

Some companies have annual days and formal award functions for recognizing significant achievements. At JSPL, all award winners are recognized publicly, either on August 15 or January 26 by the managing directors of their companies at an event where external dignitaries are also invited. Philips Electronics India also has an annual recognition day for felicitating best performers in the presence of the entire unit/organization.

It is not just the reward, but also the process of rewards that makes a difference. A reward that is delivered clandestinely may not make the awardee feel so good about the award or others finding out about it may think that something must be amiss. Proper and timely communication of rewards adds to their efficacy.

In some, there seems to be a lot of innovation in recognition and reward management systems. Given the ever-changing motivational pattern of people and the law of diminishing returns (nothing can motivate forever) that operate for human beings, this is one area where there will always be a need for more and more innovative thinking and experimentation. Indian organizations seem to be well on their path for such experimentation.

The Khandelwal Committee (HR Committee in PSBs appointed by the Ministry of Finance, Government of India) of which the author was a member, made the following observations on rewards and recognition:

> The Committee is of the considered view that the overall objective of any incentive scheme should be to promote a high performance culture through continuously raising the bar of performance of the organization, not only in terms of quantifiable business parameters but equally, in terms of improvement in qualitative aspects of productivity and efficiency. Employees making outstanding contribution through their performance toward these objectives should only be entitled to receive performance linked incentive. By its very nature, incentive therefore is not meant for distribution across all sections of employees but should be directly related to performance. Banks would thus be required to install and implement a strong and credible Performance Management System for effective implementation of the scheme and to avoid discontent in the larger section of performers.

With regard to this, the Committee recommended the following broad contours of the principles that can govern the performance-linked incentive schemes of PSBs:

1. An incentive scheme should aim at differentiating performance and rewarding the pivotal employees. This is with a view to retain employees in critical areas and build a future leadership pipeline.
2. The scheme should also positively incentivize potential business growth, and as such, it cannot be a general incentive

for distribution across the board. It should be linked to performance, which presupposes that objective and measurable performance parameters for every role are clearly spelt out.

3. Existing incentive schemes for mobilization of deposits, recovery, suggestions, and so forth should be dovetailed into the new incentive scheme.

4. The Steering Committee of the Board on HR should monitor formulation and implementation of the scheme in every bank.

5. The Committee also recommends that in tune with market trends, PSBs can also consider offering Employee Stock Option Plans (ESOPs) in the next few years as a measure to promote ownership in employees and also retain talented workforce.

6. Other forms of incentives should be encouraged by banks. These may include various forms such as team incentives, celebrations, CMD clubs, regional managers' clubs, GMs' or EDs' clubs, and so forth. Funds should be allocated for high-performing branches in different categories and innovative schemes encouraged without putting restrictions on them.

## Focusing on Team Performance and Team Incentives for Better Results

For several years, we have been focusing on performance management of individuals. We all know that results are achieved by team efforts, although individuals are also important. Indian culture is divisive and individual-focused performance systems will only perpetuate this divisiveness and the caste system, and may even hamper teamwork. In spite of this awareness, individualization is so predominant in our minds that we have not done anything beyond paying lip service to the need for promoting teamwork. We have been hell bent on differentiating people, rather than integrating their efforts. Hence, in the performance equation, KRAs, PRDs, ratings, performance linked pay, and everything we did, we focused on individuals.

The changed global scenario has brought in a new era in India, which may be called the competence era. This era is further perpetuating individual performance management rather than team performance management. This is because there is pressure to differentiate. The pressure comes from several sources. These include differentiated pay packets, the need for competent managers, the willingness of some organizations to pay any amount for competent individuals, enhanced salary structures that force organizations to compute the rate of interest (ROI) on each employee or value addition of each employee, and increasing proliferation of literature from the West (as well as Asia) in the recent past focusing on individual leaders and leadership. With all these influences, it is understandable that the corporate sector continues to focus on individual performance and ignores other realities.

The following realities indicate the need for refocusing performance management on group or team performance in addition to individual performance:

1. At higher levels of leadership, strategic thinking, employee motivation, development, and team management competencies are critical and make a significant difference. Performance management indicators are most often team performance-based, rather than based on individual performance. A team's performance or output is an indicator of an individual leader's competence, and there can be several cases where the team performs in spite of the leader and not necessarily due to him/her. In such cases, the team should be given adequate weightage and team performance should not merely be attributed to the leader.

2. At higher levels, it is very difficult to quantify and measure the performance of individual senior managers. Measuring instruments fail because performance indicators are qualitative and cannot be reduced to numbers.

3. According to managers frequent plea, they have done their best as individuals, but the team has not worked out. Some of them state that they have done their best, but there are many factors beyond their control.

4. Organizations need to create team chemistry and leadership to help in making this work. If team performance is focused, team chemistry can be managed relatively better. In focusing on team performance, an organization creates enablers for team leaders to be effective.

5. Synergy and outcomes are likely to be better if the focus is on the team rather than on the individual.

6. Measures are easily available for team performance and are more objective rather than for individuals at higher levels.

7. By focusing on team performance simultaneously, many dimensions can be tackled as compared to individual performance.

8. Team performance is always closer to organizational performance rather than individual performance to organizational performance.

9. In the past, top-level performance has been measured mainly in terms of team performance in most cases.

Given these considerations, and perhaps many more, it is necessary to recognize the importance of team performance management in addition to individual performance.

### THE IL&FS EXPERIENCE

Infrastructure Leasing and Financial Services (IL&FS) was one of the earliest to recognize all of this and put in place a PMS that combined the individual with team performance management and attempted to align both with organizational performance. About two decades ago, it designed a PMS that gave importance to team as well as individual performance. There were two separate systems. The individual performance management system was along traditional lines and required every employee to identify performance areas and set targets or goals wherever appropriate. Each team was also required to plan its performance by identifying the tasks it was expected to perform in a given year and assess its performance. The following are the highlights of the system designed at that time, which continues with some modification even today:

1. Individual performance is assessed on a performance appraisal format requiring the employee to plan his/her performance, and get it reviewed and rated by the reporting office at the end of the year.

2. A top-level review committee uses the individual appraisal data as input for determining the individual's performance pay at the end of the year. The amount depends on the performance of the organization as well as the performance of the individual during that year.

3. IL&FS has identified its own teams or departments, and each department is required to identify its own tasks and plan its performance at the beginning of the year. In planning performance, the requirements of internal customer departments are taken into consideration. The competencies or behaviors to be exhibited by members of a group as a team are also discussed and identified.

4. At the end of the year, there is self-assessment by the team on the parameters of performance, including those that may not have been identified or anticipated at the beginning of the year.

5. Self-assessment is conducted by the team as a whole or a group of representatives on the basis of the work done during the year. This is passed on to a top-level committee which reviews the performance of the team and provides feedback to it. During the review, they take into consideration internal customer services and other variables. The review team is not within the purview of the team appraisal and should therefore look beyond the department or team to which it belongs.

6. The performance-linked pay assigned to the group is determined by the performance category to which it belongs and its organizational performance during the year.

7. Every member of the group is assigned the same amount of pay in multiples of or fractions of his/her salary. For example, if a group is a high performer, everyone in it may receive 20 percent of his/her salary as a one-time payment for the year.

8. Organizational performance determines the amount of performance-linked pay. However, individual performance and team performance determine how much more the individual gets in addition to the amount he/she receives for the good performance of the organization.

Since the time IL&FS has introduced this system, many other organizations have adopted the model with modifications. The PMS worked out by the National Stock Exchange of India has improved it further by attempting to combine individual performance with group performance and integrate this into 360 degree feedback.

# 10

# Lessons from Experience
## *A New Look at Performance Management Systems**

Significant developments have taken place in concepts of performance management across the world in the last two decades. There
has been a realization that performance management is going to
be subjective, no matter how much we try to make them objective. This is because supervisors/managers always vary in their
standards, judgment, assimilation of information, and processing
abilities with respect to their performers as well as many other
parameters. However, performance is too important a matter to
be equated with annual appraisals. Annual appraisals and ratings
reduce the entire year's effort of an individual to a number, and the
numbers are assigned by appraisers, keeping in context the work
and performance of the individual. The numbers are used by some
high-level authorities without any awareness of the context in
which the ratings are assigned without understanding the individual. Thereafter, ratings lose the person and deal with numbers. This
is where serious injustice gets done to performers. Performance
management has to be looked at differently. It is not enough to
change the name. It is equally important to understand the nature,
potential, and complexities of PMS. CEOs need to be properly
guided and line managers to be assessed on how much time and
effort they put in for performance management and improvements.
The outlook needs to shift from PMS being an annual exercise to
ongoing activities. One way is to scrap performance management

* Reproduced with modifications from *Lessons from Experience: A New Look at Performance
Management Systems* by T.V. Rao, *Vikalpa*, 33(3), July 2008, 1–15.

and focus on performance improvements and move from KPAs to activities. This chapter suggests a number of changes required to make PMS more effective.

# Performance Appraisals 30 Years Ago

It is about 33 years ago that Larsen & Toubro (L&T) asked two of us from IIMA (Dr Udai Pareek and me) to examine the company's performance management system. We interviewed several managers at different levels. L&T's managers gave us a number of suggestions, which later became the base for our designing an integrated HRD system for L&T. A few years after that, we were associated with the State Bank of India, BEML, Crompton Greaves, the TVS Group, the Murugappa Group, Bajaj Auto, L&T ECC, Steel Authority of India, LIC of India, GIC, Canara Bank, Bank of Baroda, and a number of other organizations, which reviewed and redesigned their systems on similar lines with a development focus.

When I look back at my experiences during the last 33 years, I realize that we are still struggling with effective implementation of appraisal systems in our country. The issue comes up again and again, as performance-linked pay or variable pay and performance incentives have come under focus. The following are some of the suggestions I would like to make on the basis of this experience:

1. Change from appraisal to management and focus on improvements and development.
2. Recognize the comprehensiveness of PMS as a system.
3. Recognize the complexities of PMS. It has many dimensions.
4. Allocate adequate time and legislate this, and if required, plan it in the company's calendar.
5. Decentralize and shift management of PMS to line managers and unit heads.
6. Take HR managers out of PMS. Develop and employ a new category of managers called "performance managers," preferably from line jobs.

7. Make it a part of the budgeting process and integrate it with the company's other systems.

8. Create a new index called Performance Index for each employee and make this a quarterly and annual practice. It should be based on performance and potential. It should include 360 degree feedback (from juniors, internal customers, and so forth as well as bosses). The index should include weightage given to time allocated for managing the performance of self and juniors, interpersonal competence (dyadic relations), teamwork, and other organizational contributions through individuals' initiatives (contributions to intellectual capital and talent management). The index can be issued in the form of a certificate, converted into encashable points and used for recruitment, promotion purposes, and so forth.

9. Use technology to support your work.

10. Implement PMS rigorously and give it the seriousness it deserves.

These recommendations are explained below with reasoning.

1. Change from "appraisal" to "management" and focus on "contributions, and improvements: I have realized that one of the most significant mistakes we have made is in giving a name to the performance appraisal system. We have continued to use the term "performance appraisal." After serious reflection of this issue, I have come to the conclusion that it is high time we abandon the term.

   One may ask what is there in a name. This is what I kept asking and did not push for change for several years. I now realize that there is a lot in a name. It stresses that the purpose of the system is "appraisal," which means evaluation. It amounts to reducing an entire year or six months' work of an individual to a number. Numbers have some wonderful properties. They are intended to render so called objectivity and comparability. Unfortunately, it is this comparability and objectivity that has played havoc in the lives of many employees. It has caused some people to get promoted (and some of them undeservingly), some others to leave their jobs, and yet others to walk into office every day with low interest and satisfaction and carry on with their jobs half-heartedly.

No two numbers are comparable in appraisals. The numbers in performance appraisals do not follow any rules except those of nominal scales. However an organization may try to promote objectivity, it should be recognized that at best the numbers assigned by appraisers follow "ordinal scales." We cannot say with confidence that a rating of 4, assigned on a 5-point scale by a production chief, is indicative of the same performance level as a rating of 4 assigned by the marketing chief, or for that matter two marketing chiefs operating in two regions for their juniors. The ratings depend on so many factors—the supervisor or rater; his/her previous background, personality, expectations, and background; the way goals are set; the level of the goals, expectations of the assessor from the performer; the chemistry with which setting goals was initiated; the culture of the organization, and so forth. No two numbers are comparable. We cannot say that a person who gets a 68 rating on a 100-point system is definitely superior to another who gets a rating of 64, and especially if the 64 is from a setting where the performer had significant odds to surmount (including that of his supervisor perhaps). Yet, we treat it as sacred and use it to fit into normal probability, add, subtract, multiply, calculate incentives, and so forth. I think this is a fundamentally wrong attempt to fit qualities in quantities and use them for anything beyond a discussion or analysis.

By reflecting on this and various other experiences in my work on performance appraisals, I would like to suggest the following:

- Ratings in appraisals are notional and at best should be used for discussion to integrate performance on a number of non-additive parameters (adding his achievement of sales targets, percentage increase in customer base, with how well he has developed his juniors, and how much he has followed the various systems for a regional sales executive). They cannot and should not be used to be force fit into normal curve blindly or determine incentives mathematically. At best, they can be used for discussion and review of performance. Ratings are "poison," but may be inevitable by-products of the performance process. They should not, however, become the primary pre-occupation of appraisals.

- Performance should be assessed against expectations, which can be changed during the course of performance with availability of new information, data, and challenges. Expectation-sharing and reviewing constitute the most important part of performance management.
- It is high time we drop the term appraisal and use ones such as "management." Management is broader and encompasses many factors in a system. It includes planning, development, improvements, recognition, and so forth. Those who prefer to be even more focused can use terms such as PMS, Performance Development System (PDS), Performance Improvement Program (PIP), and so forth. (See Appendix A, Chapter 10 for a comparison between PAS and PMS from my book on the topic, Rao, 2003.)
- However, merely changing the term does not help, but the spirit needs to be promoted. This can be done by taking a new look at the potential of PMS and using it for objectives other than appraisals and generating numbers in percentages, and so forth.
- Good performance should be rewarded. But, what good performance is should be understood from the beginning by each individual, and there should be a shared understanding of what constitutes rewardable performance and what is not by performers and their superiors. This understanding should be there at the beginning of the performance period and not at the time of deciding on rewards.
- Small rewards and recognition should be encouraged and supervisors should have adequate autonomy to

recognize and reward the performance of their performing employees. This reward could constitute a significant part of the CTC (around 5 percent to 10 percent) of juniors. Recognition should take place all through the performance period and should not be limited to annual stock-taking or performance reviews.

• Annual reviews of performance should be conducted using innovative methods and should become a part of corporate life. Such reviews need not necessarily result in numbers being assigned to individuals.

This is not a complete list of suggestions, but a mere glimpse into the way we need to think.

I would like to illustrate the basis of this thinking by a simple illustration of how we have been promoting a new way of looking at performance planning. The following is a new way of looking at performance planning and goal-setting.

We have demonstrated that by viewing performance review discussions as learning opportunities for seniors to learn from their juniors, we have changed the meaning of coaching and mentoring to great extent. PRD and coaching sessions are meant to develop coaches as much as performers. In fact, I am now of the view that PMS is a learning opportunity.

2. Recognize the comprehensiveness of PMS as a system: PMS can have multiple objectives. These include the following:

• Continuous performance improvements in employees.
• Development of a discipline of planning work and managing time and talent.
• Ensuring role clarity.
• Recognition of strengths and areas needing improvement in relation to performance identification of development needs for performance enhancement.
• Competence-building among individuals, teams, and organization as a whole.

- Database for rewards, promotions, recognition, and motivation.
- Insights into self—self-awareness, which is essential for enhanced leadership and managerial effectiveness.
- Development of mutuality and respect among seniors and juniors and bosses and subordinates.
- Development of problem-solving capabilities among employees.
- Inculcation of a learning culture.
- Seniors being enabled to learn from juniors, and vice versa.
- Provision of mentoring and coaching support to employees on performance improvements.
- Employees prepared for competition and continuous change.
- Objective assessment of performance of each employee and generation of data on them for various HR decisions such as rewards, rotation, recognition, higher responsibilities, and so forth.
- Integration and alignment of the work of individuals and their teams with organizational goals and tasks.

These are not mutually exclusive and may overlap. However, organizations often tend to emphasize nonessentials and understandably stress on the short term rather than the long term. There is often an undue emphasis on objectivity and rewards as though employees only work all the year round for annual rewards and recognition. By linking PMS with rewards and recognition, most organizations undervalue individuals' interest in work and create "politics" among their employees. In fact, PMS seems to frequently lead to politics and demotivation—the reverse of what it is intended to create. This is due to a few people being selectively rewarded and most ignored, making the rewards once a year rather than a continuous function, and taking away power and authority from supervising line managers and concentrating it in the hands of a few (HR managers and top management). This has done the greatest damage to the cause of good PMS.

I have come to the conclusion that the most important objectives of PMS should be the following:

To enable employees to plan their work for the entire year (or a part of it), and ensure that they engage in productive activities, utilize their competencies in the best possible manner, and contribute to the achievement of departmental or organizational goals and results, while at the same time, constantly learning and developing their own capabilities and enjoying their work.

The most important parts of this objective are the following:

- Work planning and accountability: If you plan your work, you will be more accountable for it. You are also likely to enjoy it due to your accomplishments. Work planning also ensures alignment with organizational goals, since individuals plan their work in the context of organizational priorities.
- Competency utilization: You are able to undertake work or at least give adequate opportunities to yourself to utilize your competencies.
- Work place learning as a tool for continuous learning and development: This is the greatest reward you can get from your work. When you learn and grow, your competencies are built and you enhance your own brand value. If you grow beyond your role and if your organization cannot accommodate, you can always find other opportunities.
- Building mutuality, teamwork, work satisfaction, motivation, and self-respect: These are all imperative for all employees.

The process of implementing PMS may also ensure that additional objectives are met. It should include the following:

- Participative planning.
- Periodic planning and review.
- Periodic analysis of performance blocks and opportunities.

- Collective planning.
- Collective ownership where required.
- Promotion of competencies, values, and desired culture by making it a part of planning.
- Participative review and learning from each other.
- Establishment of a mechanism for monitoring performance and implementation plans, and ensuring organizational support.

Therefore, PMS can be a great tool if designed comprehensively and implemented in all earnestness. It should have little place for politics and manipulation.

3. Recognize the complexities of PMS with its many dimensions: In the fall of 2002, the Corporate Leadership Council in the USA published *Building the High-Performance Workforce: A Quantitative Analysis of the Effectiveness of Performance Management Strategies.* Quantifying the impact of more than 100 PMS strategies on employees' performance, this research uncovered vital information on which strategies enhance (or diminish) employees' performance and by precisely how much.

In a subsequent work, *Benchmarking the High-performance Organization,* the Corporate Leadership Council used the same sample of more than 19,000 employees and managers from 34 organizations across seven industry groups and 29 countries. This study addresses the frequency and effectiveness with which performance management strategies are implemented in organizations today. The intention was to help members locate "mismatches" between the resources allocated to a given strategy and their return on employees' performance. With unparalleled precision, members can then reallocate scarce resources—money and time—to implement the strategies that not only make the most impact on employees' performance, but on those that are also most likely to be ineffectively administered or absent. In this extensive study of best practices in PMS, the Conference Board observed the following:

- Many performance management strategies that can improve employees' performance by more than 25 percent are underutilized or ineffectively administered in practice.
- Some organizations were significantly outperforming others in use and implementation of several high-impact performance strategies.
- Among employees, 83 percent recognized the importance of their day-to-day work to the success of their business unit and organization, and 59 percent understood the connection between their projects and assignments, and the organization's overall strategy. However, some organizations were significantly better than others at ensuring that their employees recognize this link.
- Overall, 57 percent of employees reported that they enjoy their projects and assignments, and more than three-quarters of them recognize the importance of their projects for their personal development and long-term careers.
- Only 10 percent of the employees undergo a complete 360 degree formal performance review with three or more sources of feedback. Even in companies that most frequently conduct 360 degree reviews, only about one-third of the employees undergo comprehensive reviews. Organizations have a sizeable opportunity to positively affect their employees' performance by providing more than one source of feedback during performance reviews.
- On an average, about one-third of employees reported that their managers voluntarily give them informal feedback without their having to ask for it. Employees typically had to wait more than a week after completing a project or assignment before receiving informal feedback.
- Only about one-third of employees in an average company received a written development plan during their most recent formal performance review. Out of those who received a development plan, only one-third reported that their plans were challenging and applicable to their daily work.
- Nearly a quarter of all employees reported that their managers made fundamental changes to their projects and

assignments at least once a week. Another quarter of the employees' managers made changes to their projects one to three times a month.

- Employees were skeptical that they would be rewarded for successful completion of their projects. Less than 40 percent believed that if they performed well on their projects and assignments, they would be rewarded with a higher performance rating, a merit increase, an annual bonus, or a raise in their base salary. And only 16 percent saw the link between strong performance on their projects and the likelihood of their being promoted.
- Only 31 percent of the employees in an average company reported that the training they received was effective.

How can organizations derive results through PMS? The following are some of the conclusions drawn by the Conference Board from its studies:

Organizations are changing the breadth and focus of their PMS approaches. These changes include:

- From managing system to managing performance.
- By offering a clear business plan for managing performance.
- By providing tools required for employees to perform effectively.
- By realizing that even the best intentioned managers cannot overcome subjectivity and/or focus on immediate goals.
- By leveraging collaborative goal-setting and team-based performance management.
- Targeting activities and individuals who will make a significant impact on the organization's financial performance.

The Conference Board has identified the following five key imperatives for success of PMS:

- Establishment of performance management as an organizational priority.

- Upskilling of managers at improving their performance.
- Expansion of lines of performance accountability.
- Alignment with business drivers.
- Management of employees' goal realization.

The five problems in PMS the Board identifies include:

- Inadequate manager focus: Many factors affect devotion of time and effort to PMS.
- Insufficient manager skills: These are inadequate for improving their juniors' performance.
- Narrowly defined ownership: Multiple owners are required for individual's performance.
- Disconnect with strategy: There is inadequate linkage to business drivers.
- Failure to execute: There is lack of efficient execution across business units.

The findings of the Conference Board clearly bring out the complexity of PMS. By its nature, performance management is a complex process. It involves continuous dialogue, discussion, and debate at different levels between individuals, teams, and the organization. It cannot, therefore, be reduced to an annual exercise to which less than a few hours are devoted and great results expected. The complexity of PMS comes from that of defining performance.

4. Allocate and legislate adequate time, and if required, plan it on the company's calendar: In most of my PMS programs, I have been asking managers about how much time they spend on PMS. The usual responses are anywhere between 2 hours to 10 hours in a year. Rarely did I get answers of more than 10 hours a year. A large part of this time seems to be spent on self-appraisal and identification of KPAs or KRAs for self or juniors.

On an average, every manager is expected to put in about 2000 to 2400 hours of work annually. This amounts to about 180 to 200 hours a month. In most metropolitan cities, managers spend about two hours a day in commuting from home to office and back and/or for meetings elsewhere on an average. This amounts to about 400 to 500 hours or at least 20 percent of their time. Consequently, the time spent on PMS is not even 1 percent and is often 0.5 percent. What objectives can then be achieved?

When I ask managers to think a little more and estimate the time they spend on departmental plans, budgets, reviews, and solving problems, the figure changes. Some of them spend as much as 30–40 percent of the time in managing the performance of their departments or units. All their morning meetings as well as problem-solving meetings seem to be performance planning meetings. It is their inability to link performance management with performance appraisals that causes the problem. When I point this out to managers in some of the organizations, they immediately come up with the issue of how much of their time is wasted in meetings.

Unfortunately, the problem is that only once a year do we focus on individual employees because of rewards and promotions, and during the rest of the year, we forget that it is the individual who contributes. We do not focus adequately on the individuals, and as a result, they sometimes get away without being accountable for their work.

What is the way out? Recognize that individual performance management is as much of an imperative as that of departmental performance, and ensure that departmental budgets and plans are immediately followed up by individual plans and performance contributions. Every individual should be required to plan his/her 2,000 or 2,400 hours of work annually, quarterly, or monthly. This should be done as an individual discipline under the guidance of his/her seniors and needs at least 5 percent of the person's time to be devoted to such planning. This works out to be a day in a month or at least half a day during the month. It can be done by designating every first day of the month as the individual planning and review day. If organizations implement this, they will go a long way in making improvements in their performance.

5. Decentralize and shift management of PMS to line managers and unit heads:

• Take HR managers out of PMS and develop a new category of managers called "performance managers," preferably from line jobs.
• Make this a part of the budgeting process and integrate it with company's other systems.

PMS has been managed by HR managers till now. In many organizations, they derive their power from the controls they have. They spend their time issuing and collecting forms, tabulating trends, normalizing data, convening committees, announcing rewards, pacifying those who are not rewarded, communicating polices, and so forth. In other words, they spend most of the time trying to convince themselves and the line manager community about the objectivity of top management's decisions. Their preoccupation with this determines the issues with which line managers are preoccupied. Most HR managers keep changing PMS periodically and keep conducting orientation workshops. They suddenly become silent, immediately after these orientation workshops are over. Their lack of business orientation sometimes makes them hesitant to reach out to line managers and find out their difficulties.

This has gone on for too long. It is high time we get out of this vicious circle. I have been struggling for the last 10 years with a large number of HR managers, trying to convince them of the need for them to spend more time on coaching and mentoring line managers, discussing with them and understanding their difficulties, tabulating and sharing company-wide difficulties, and planning mechanisms to review problems, for example, e-PMS as an upward communication tool. In most cases, results have been disappointing. Doing a good job of implementing PMS requires a different level of competencies in HR facilitators. These include first and foremost an understanding of the business, followed by empathy, credibility, and OD or behavioral skills required to help professionals. Unfortunately, most top-level HR managers either do not have the time for this or are ill-equipped with the requisite skills. Therefore, it has rarely worked. As a result, most line managers continue to be disappointed with their PMS and the role played by HR. Consequently, HR departments have been mainly serving as punching bags for line managers.

It is high time PMS is taken out of HR managers' hands and is given to line managers. This requires planning, reviewing, and improving performance to be transferred to strategic business unit (SBU) heads and heads of departments (HoDs).

Decentralization involves the following:

PMS of employees becomes the responsibility of departmental heads or SBU heads, who decide departmental budgets such as performance strategies, individual plans, reviews, rewards, and celebrations. They should have the scope to decide their performance planning as long as they define the performance index of individual employees and provide relevant information to their centralized Human Resources Information System (HRIS).

They will be encouraged to have their own structures of the PMS mechanisms that suit their requirements. Corporate guidelines, if any, can be followed with a substantial degree of freedom.

Performance monitoring and rewards as well as support requirements will all be decentralized. In the case of small organizations, such decentralization may result in freedom and autonomy for departmental heads as well as the responsibility of ensuring that employees' performance is planned, aligned, recognized, and developed.

HR managers should be taken out of PMS management, and if necessary, a new category of managers (performance managers) be appointed. These can be line managers who spend part of their full time responsibilities on this.

6. Create a new quarterly and annual index called a Performance Index for employees, based on their performance and potential, including 360 degree feedback from juniors, internal and external customers, and so forth, as well as bosses: An Annual Performance Index (API) is an index of the annual performance of individual employees. It should indicate their contributions to achievement of departmental and organizational goals through their activities and competencies. The composition of the index or its components may vary from organization to organization and should be defined by each, depending on its requirements and context. For example, it may include the results obtained by individuals as well as their efforts, competencies, contribution to teams or departments, and the values and culture of organizations. Results and efforts in terms of KPAs, KRAs, and so forth, may be measured quarterly or monthly, depending on the nature of the organization (for example, IT companies may have a quarterly assessment or project-based assessments).

Some of the components recommended for inclusion in the Annual Performance Index are suggested in Table 10.1.

The index should include weightage given to time allocated for managing the performance of self and juniors, interpersonal competence (dyadic relations), teamwork, and other organizational contributions through one's initiative (contribution to intellectual capital and talent management). The index can be issued in the form of a certificate, converted into encashable points, used for recruitment and promotion purposes, and so forth.

7. Use technology to support your work. Developments in information technology (IT) and communications have made life simple. Now, performance planning, review discussions, and assessments can all take place online. Using in-house networks or web-based support will go a long way in having conversations on performance planning and performance reviews.

Performance plans can be made and reviewed online. Performance development needs can be identified and even

**TABLE 10.1**

Suggested Components of Annual Performance Index to Be Made for Each Individual

| S. no | Component and weightage range | What is to be included | Methodology and components |
|---|---|---|---|
| 1. | Individual performance: results (20%) | Extent to which measurable targets have been achieved. | Assess KRAs and output-related activities. Use measures of performance in terms of finances, customers, internal systems and processes, and learning. Use Balanced Score Card measures. Assess quarterly and finalize annually. Factor self-assessment and boss-assessment into process. |
| 2. | Individual performance: effort (20%) | Level and quality of work effort put in by individual. | Nature of activities planned and carried out. Way time was used and spent. Process achieved. Involvement in work. Initiative levels. Self-assessment and boss-assessment factored into process. |
| 3. | Individual performance: competencies, culture, and values (15%) | Talent utilization. | Extent to which various competencies are used for effective performance. Demonstrated competencies and qualities valued by organization, which contribute to formation of intellectual capital. |
| 4. | Group performance (15%) | Achievement of measurable departmental goals. | Assessment by top management of departmental or team performance using results achieved on various parameters; contributions of individuals factored in. |
| 5. | Internal customer service (15%) | Internal customer assessments using 360 degree feedback. | Use of simple assessment tool with relevant items dealing with internal customer support, problem-solving, and contribution to work; assessment by internal customers. |
| 6. | Development of juniors (15%) | Time spent on developing juniors and managing their performance. | Time spent on PMS, motivation, and leadership-building of juniors; use of simple assessment tool; assessment by juniors. |

*Source:* Author.

met online. There are many online training packages, which can be linked with development needs. Such needs need to be identified at the beginning of the year along with performance plans, rather than at the end of the year on the basis of performance reviews.

The following is a system recommended for online performance management.

Step 1: The company should formulate its annual plan online on the basis of a review of its last year's performance, and its business opportunities and aspirations for the subsequent year.

Step 2: It should communicate this to all its employees online.

Step 3: Each department or work team should plan its goals in alignment with the company's goals and plans along with departmental plans and budgeting exercises.

Step 4: Individuals should plan their own work input and results in terms of KPAs, KRAs, activities, and time allocations, and post these online.

Step 5: Individual development needs should be identified and posted along with performance plans online to be accessed. In addition, intervention planning should be initiated by concerned entities including departmental heads, the HR department, or the training center.

Step 6: Performance plans should then be accessed and approved by seniors and reporting officers online.

Step 7: The HR department will then communicate plans for training and development interventions to concerned individuals and departments.

Step 8: There is a quarterly review of performance in relation to the performance plans and quarterly accomplishments of individual performers and simultaneous assessment by reporting officers. Assessments should be made in confidence and revealed to candidates after self-assessment and boss's assessment are complete. It should be designed to facilitate the process.

Step 9: Performance plans should be modified and reviewed at the departmental and individual levels on the basis of the quarterly performance review of the organization, department or team, and employees.

Step 10: The process should continue for second and third quarters as in Step 9.

Step 11: Annual individual performance reviews should be conducted after departmental reviews and assessments are shared online in lines similar to those explained in Step 8.

Step 12: Annual assessment of company's internal customer service should be assessed online by a simple assessment tool, with the online system not taking more than 5 to 10 minutes per assessment. Assessments should be made by all internal customers, individually and anonymously.

Step 13: There should be an anonymous annual assessment of the performance of individual managers by their next in-line juniors on parameters including time spent in developing them, support provided to them, efforts made to utilize their talent and develop these, and so forth.

Step 14: An annual performance index should be computed with assistance from the company's IT department.

The technology should be developed to suit the organization's PMS philosophy and requirements, rather than to adapt PMS in sync with its technological capabilities. In recent times, organizations, such as the Steel Authority of India, have demonstrated how indigenously developed IT support can be of use in implementing good PMS.

8. Implement PMS rigorously and accord it the seriousness it deserves: The success of PMS lies in its implementation. CEOs and top management need to give it the importance due to it. The moment it is recognized as being synonymous with an organization's performance management rather than mere assignment of ratings to individual employees, half the battle is won.

# Appendix A

## PERFORMANCE APPRAISAL SYSTEM (PAS) AND PERFORMANCE MANAGEMENT SYSTEM (PMS): A COMPARISON (RAO, 2003)

The new language of performance appraisal uses the term "performance management" rather than "appraisal." Appraisal is an annual affair, while performance management is a year round one.

Appraisal focuses on ratings and improvements on work, the stakeholders, service levels, productivity, the motivation effort, and all such performance-related variables.

The following table depicts the differences between performance appraisal and management:

Therefore, the main difference between the performance management and appraisal systems is their emphasis and spirit. In the past, good organizations have used their performance appraisal systems as PMS. They may have used the traditional title, which seems to mean a lot in communicating the appropriateness of the system and its emphasis.

**TABLE 10A.1**

**Differences between Performance Appraisal and Management**

| Performance appraisal systems | Performance management systems |
| --- | --- |
| Similarities and Differences | |
| Focus on performance appraisal and generation of ratings. | Focus on performance management. |
| Emphasis on relative evaluation of individuals. | Emphasis on performance improvements of individuals and their department or team's performance. |
| An annual exercise—normally though periodic evaluation. | Continuous process with quarterly or periodic performance review discussions. |
| Emphasis on ratings and evaluation. | Emphasis on performance planning, analysis, review, development, and improvements. |
| Rewards for and recognition of good performance an important component of process. | Performance rewards may or may not be an integral part of process; defining and setting performance standards an integral part. |
| Designed and monitored by personnel/administration department. | Designed by personnel/HR department, but can be monitored by respective departments themselves. |
| Ownership mainly with administration/personnel department. | Ownership with line managers, with personnel/administration facilitating implementation. |
| KPAs and KRAs used to bring in objectivity. | KPAs or KRAs used as planning mechanisms. |
| Developmental needs identified at the end of the year on the basis of appraisal of competency gaps. | Developmental needs identified at the beginning of the year on the basis of competency requirements for the coming year. |
| Review mechanisms put in place to ensure objectivity in ratings. | Review mechanisms implemented to bring about performance improvements. |
| A system with deadlines, meetings, input, output, and format. | A system with deadlines, meetings, input, output, and format. |
| Format driven with emphasis on process. | Process driven with emphasis on format as an aid. |
| Linked to promotions, rewards, training and development interventions, placements, and so forth. | Linked to performance improvements and through these to other career decisions, as and when required. |

*Source:* Author.

# Appendix B

## PERFORMANCE MANAGEMENT DATA FROM THREE INDUSTRIES FROM INDIA AND ABROAD

**TABLE 10B.1**

**Responses of Managers of Three Corporations on Performance-related Questions**

| Question | Responses of participants | | | | | | | | | | | | | | |
|---|---|---|---|---|---|---|---|---|---|---|---|---|---|---|---|
| | 100% | | | 75% | | | 50% | | | 25% | | | 0% | | |
| | A | B | C | A | B | C | A | B | C | A | B | C | A | B | C |
| 1. To what extent did you have a clearly set work plan for the last six months? | 7 | 11 | 4 | 20 | 59 | 14 | 14 | 10 | 10 | 0 | 5 | 0 | 0 | 0 | 0 |
| 2. To what extent did your seniors with whom you worked share your understanding of your work plan and priorities in the last six months? | 7 | 20 | 3 | 18 | 32 | 12 | 12 | 20 | 9 | 3 | 9 | 4 | 1 | 1 | 0 |
| 3. To what extent were you able to put to use most of your capabilities in the last six months? | 6 | 11 | 5 | 19 | 39 | 16 | 13 | 28 | 6 | 3 | 5 | 0 | 0 | 0 | 1 |
| 4. To what extent are you clear about your work plan and priorities for the next six months? | 11 | 26 | 1 | 18 | 38 | 18 | 10 | 16 | 9 | 2 | 3 | 0 | 0 | 0 | 0 |

*Source:* Workshop Survey by Author.

*Notes:* A = senior managers from a family-owned business conglomerate = 41; B= middle and senior managers of professionally managed company in Gulf region = 85; C = top management of MNC in India = 28.

## TABLE 10B.2

### Wastage due to Lack of Proper Implementation of PMS by Various Categories of Managers in Four Organizations

| | Senior and middle managers: Professionally managed (N = 85) | Family business: Senior managers (N = 41) | Top management of MNC (N = 28) | HR managers from another organization (N = 17) |
|---|---|---|---|---|
| Unplanned work or time wasted due to lack of clarity | 28% or 14 person years wasted due to unplanned work. | 29% or 14 person years of unplanned work. | 30% or 15 person years of unplanned work. | 27% |
| Lack of congruence in priorities of boss and performer | 31% | 34% | 38% | 32% |
| Unutilized competencies | 33% | 32% | 29% | 34% |
| Lack of clarity of priorities for the next six months | 24% | 27% | 32% | 21% |

Source: Workshop Survey by Author.

# 11

# 360 Degree Feedback as a
# Performance Management Tool

## Introduction

In recent years, 360 degree feedback has become very popular. It has been felt for long that one person's assessment of another cannot be free from bias. In addition, with the focus on customers (both internal and external) and emphasis on the softer dimensions of performance (leadership, innovation, teamwork, initiative, emotional intelligence, entrepreneurship, and so forth), it has become necessary to get multiple assessments for a more objective assessment. The Multirater Assessment and Feedback System (MAFS), which involves 360 degree appraisals, is used by almost every Fortune 500 company in some form or the other. In this system, a candidate is assessed periodically (once in a year and sometimes even half yearly) by a number of assessors, including his/her boss, immediate subordinates, colleagues, and internal and external customers. The assessment is made on a questionnaire that is specially designed to measure behavior considered critical for performance. The appraisal is conducted anonymously by others and is collected by an external agent (consultant) or specially designated internal agent (for example, the HRD department). The assessment is consolidated; feedback profiles are prepared and given to the participant after a workshop or directly by his/her boss or the HRD department in a performance review discussion session.

This chapter focuses on applications of 360 degree or multirater feedback as a performance management tool. Those interested in using 360 degree feedback as a leadership development tool could consult the book *The Power of 360 Degree Feedback* by T.V. Rao and Raju Rao (SAGE Response Books).

# Objectives of 360 Degree Feedback or MAFS

It is possible to aim at the following through 360 degree feedback or MAFS:

1. Providing insights into the strong and weak areas of the candidate in terms of his/her effective performance in roles, activities, styles, traits, qualities, competencies (knowledge, attitudes, and skills), and impact on others.
2. Identification of developmental needs and preparation of development plans more objectively in relation to current or future roles, and performance improvements for an individual or a group of individuals.
3. Reinforcement of other change management efforts and organizational effectiveness-directed interventions, which may include TQM-related efforts, customer-focused or internal customer satisfaction-enhancing interventions, flat structures, quality-enhancement and cost-reduction interventions, and decision-related process changes.
4. A basis for performance-linked pay or performance rewards.
5. Alignment of individual and group goals with organizational vision, values, and goals.
6. Culture-building.
7. Leadership development.
8. Potential appraisal and development.
9. Career planning and development.
10. Succession planning and development.
11. Team-building.
12. Planning of internal customer satisfaction improvement measures.
13. Role clarity and increased accountabilities.

# Advantages of 360 Degree Feedback or MAFS

The 360 degree feedback system has certain advantages, which are not substitutes for traditional appraisals but an addition to them. Normally, MAFS should be viewed as a supplement to regular KPA- or KRA-based appraisal systems, rather than as a replacement of these. The additional advantages offered by MAFS include the following:

1. It is more objective than a one-person assessment of traits and qualities.
2. It adds objectivity and supplements the traditional appraisal system.
3. It normally provides more acceptable feedback to employee.
4. It can serve all the purposes served by the traditional appraisal system, for example, by identifying developmental needs, rewarding management, and encouraging performance development.
5. It helps to enhance a focus on internal customer satisfaction.
6. It has the potential of pointing out supervisory biases in traditional appraisal systems.
7. It is an effective tool to enhance customer service and quality of input as well as service provided to internal customers.
8. It provides a scope for candidates to get multiple inputs to improve their roles, performance, styles, and ideas, and increases their acceptability.
9. It is more participative and enhances the quality of HR decisions.
10. It is suitable for new organizational cultures, including a participative culture, learning culture, quality culture, leadership culture, competency-based performance culture, empowering culture as well as teamwork, promoted by most world-class organizations.

## PREREQUISITES FOR PARTICIPATION IN 360 DEGREE FEEDBACK

The 360 degree system can, however, be a sensitive issue. It can throw a person who is not prepared for it off-balance. It can also create new issues in an organization. If not designed and conducted well, it has the potential danger of a candidate developing wrong perceptions or notions about one or more of his/her assessors and new attitudes toward them. It is, therefore, necessary and important to manage the process well and make it foolproof. The first step is to determine if the organization is ready for it. The second important step is to determine if the candidate is ready for it. The following are indicators of an organization's readiness for MAFS:

1. The top management of the organization is committed to developing the competencies of employees on a continuous basis.
2. There are a number of HRD systems operating in the organization and they are being seriously implemented.
3. The top management is serious about creating opportunities for employees to learn from each other and from their mistakes.
4. The top management is willing to invest time and effort in giving feedback to their subordinates.
5. The top management and senior managers take the current appraisal system seriously and do all that is required to ensure its effective implementation.
6. The top management and senior managers conduct performance review and counseling sessions regularly.
7. The top management is committed to competency-building through multirater feedback.
8. Members of the top management team are willing to subject themselves to an assessment by their subordinates and colleagues.
9. There are not too many status-related barriers and ego problems in the organization.
10. People take feedback in a supportive manner and use it for their development.
11. There is not too much politics in the organization.
12. People are not likely to use the feedback to "play politics."
13. There is a high degree of systems orientation being attempted by the organization.
14. The organization already is or is in the process of becoming customer-driven.

15. There is a high degree of emphasis on teamwork in the organization.
16. Its HR department has a high level of credibility.
17. Top management interventions are not looked at with suspicion by employees.
18. Managers are interested in learning about themselves.
19. There is a high degree of process orientation in the organization.
20. The organization is value-driven.
21. Softer issues of management, such as managing people, professionalism, development, and so forth, are emphasized in the organization.
22. Managers take their jobs seriously and are eager to learn.
23. There is a high degree of emphasis on competency-building.
24. The organization has a history of taking change management tools seriously and implementing these.
25. People in the organization take feedback seriously and try to benefit from it.

The following are indicators of the readiness of candidates for MAFS:

1. The candidates are keen to know about themselves through the eyes of others. They are willing to receive feedback from others and do not become over-defensive.
2. They desire to be better.
3. They are open to and known to respect the views of others.
4. The candidates are learning-oriented individuals.
5. They have a healthy attitude to competition.
6. They should have at least one-and-a-half years of experience (except in the case of management trainees).
7. They should have direct working relations with at least six individuals who can rate them.
8. The candidates should have no history of any previous psychological or psychiatric problems.

## RSDQ MODEL OF 360 DEGREE FEEDBACK

T.V. Rao Learning Systems (TVRLS) has developed a model for top and senior management to enhance their managerial and leadership competencies, which is known as the Roles, Styles, Delegation, and Qualities (RSDQ) model. This model of leadership and managerial effectiveness views effective management and leadership as a combination of four sets of variables. These include:

1. *Roles:* This is the extent to which an individual plays various leadership and managerial roles and activities. There are a number of roles, which have to be played by managers in order for them to be effective in their roles. These are transformation (leadership) and transactional (managerial) competencies and include:

   • Articulating and communicating vision and values.
   • Formulating long-term policies and strategies.
   • Introducing and managing new technologies and systems.
   • Inspiring, developing, and motivating juniors.
   • Managing juniors, colleagues, and seniors.
   • Building culture.
   • Managing internal customers.
   • Managing external customers.
   • Managing unions and associations.

2. *Styles:* While effective managers are aware of the leadership responsibilities and perform them well, it is not only roles or activities that determine their effectiveness, but also the way in which these are performed. The model envisages that managers may carry out most roles well, and devote time and effort to these, but they can be insensitive in the manner in which they carry out these activities. Leadership styles have been classified on the basis of earlier research on the following by the author at the Indian Institute of Management:

- One is a benevolent or paternalistic leadership style in which top-level managers believe that all their juniors should be constantly guided and treated with affection like parents treat their children. This style is relationship-oriented, where managers assign tasks on the basis of their likes and dislikes, constantly guide their juniors and protect them, understand their needs, salvage critical situations by actively involving themselves in resolving them, reward those who are loyal and obedient, and share information with those who are close to them.

- A critical leadership style is close to the Theory X belief pattern, where managers believe that their juniors should be closely and constantly supervised, directed, and reminded of their duties and responsibilities. Such managers are short-term goal-oriented, and cannot tolerate mistakes or conflicts among juniors. They are personal power-dominated, keep all information to themselves, work strictly according to rules and regulations, and are highly discipline-oriented.

- A developmental leadership style is characterized by managers empowering their juniors and developing their competencies, treating them as mature adults, and leaving them on their own most of the time. Such managers are long-term goal-oriented, and share information with their juniors, and thereby empower them further. They facilitate resolution of conflicts and mistakes made by their juniors with their own minimal involvement.

It has been found that the developmental mode is the most desired organization-building style. However, some individuals and situations require benevolent and critical styles at times. Research has shown that some managers are not aware of the predominant style they tend to use and the effect this has on their juniors.

3. *Delegation:* The RSDQ model considers the level of delegation as an important part of a senior executive's effectiveness. This dimension has been included because most senior

managers seem to have difficulties in delegating work, especially effective managers who get promotions rapidly in their career. Because of this, delegation has been isolated as an important variable of leadership. Those who delegate their work release their time to perform higher-level tasks and those who do not continue to do lower-level ones, and suppress their leadership qualities and managerial effectiveness.

4. *Qualities:* The model envisages that managers should exhibit the qualities (for example, proactive behavior, listening and communication skills, a positive approach, a participative nature, and quality orientation) of leaders and world-class managers. Such qualities not only affect the effectiveness with which they perform various roles, but also make an impact on their leadership style, and, therefore, are critical.

The TVRLS instrument for 360 degree feedback for managerial and leadership development is based on the RSDQ model. In the case of "managerial qualities," there are about 75 activities that have been identified under each of the roles mentioned earlier. An instrument (two versions—one consisting of 55 items for senior managers and another of 75 items for top-level managers) has been developed to assess these measures and the extent to which managers are perceived to be performing these roles effectively. In the case of "leadership styles," a 51-item instrument assesses the extent to which the styles mentioned earlier are demonstrated across 12 different situations or activities, and the impact such managers make on their subordinates in terms of five variables including feelings (dependence, incompetence, independence, interdependence, and resentment), job satisfaction, commitment to work, morale, and the extent of learning among their juniors. Through this instrument, participants get to know their styles, whether it is benevolent, critical, or developmental (dominant and backup), as well as the impact of this. The delegation questionnaire assesses the extent to which participants are delegating and releasing their own time to engage in higher-level roles and tasks.

There is a 10-item questionnaire that measures the various symptoms of delegation or non-delegation. In the case of behavioral qualities, 25 are included at present by using a semantic differential technique. Three open-ended questions at the end try to find out the most dominant strengths and weaknesses of the respondent along with suggestions for improvement.

The instruments developed on the basis of the RSDQ model are updated periodically, depending on dimensions important to top management roles and positions, with changes in the business environment. Details of this instrument for NGOs, schools, and colleges are available in the book by Rao and Rao (2014).

## Effectiveness of 360 Degree Feedback

Two months after a series of 360 degree feedback TVRLS sessions (see Rao and Rao, 2003) were held, a study was conducted on the effectiveness of a 360 degree feedback workshop. The line of inquiry was based on the aspect of gathering information on the impact of the workshop on people, changes observed as a result of it, actions adopted toward change, further support required, if any, and so on. The study covered 32 managers who had participated in the workshop. They were assessed through personal interviews and on one-to-one discussions. TVRLS reports the following:

1. Two months after the workshop, participants were still keeping the report and workbook within their easy reach for reference and reinforcement.
2. Out of the 32 managers interviewed, 24 shared the data and report, including their action plans, with their bosses, peers, and juniors to solicit their support in making positive changes.
3. The CEO of a multinational company, after attending the workshop, emailed the results of his profile and feedback to all his employees. He also made known his present focus area (based on scores in the report) and action plans for the future, and invited support as well as suggestions.

4. Many of the 32 managers started maintaining diaries to record their action plans and activities during the day or week.

5. Out of the 32 managers interviewed after the 360 degree feedback workshop, only two felt that it did not bring about any change in their actions or behavior. Incidentally, both quit their organizations!

6. Out of the 32 managers, seven took their reports home and shared the findings/data with their families, asking for their suggestions to enable further change in them. Not surprisingly, a high level of change was observed in all seven of the participants by their families, seniors, peers, and juniors in their work as well as individuals.

Out of the 32 managers interviewed, only one witnessed a negative repercussion in spite of his efforts to change his style. Open-ended feedback given to him had laid emphasis on his follow-up actions. His juniors had earlier felt that they would be able to function better if he stopped "breathing down their necks" after assigning tasks to them. After the workshop, he made a concerted effort to reduce his follow-up activities. Unfortunately, his subordinates started taking advantage of this and becoming even more irregular in their work.

In another study through a mailed questionnaire on TVRLS, responses were sought on the following:

1. Insights gained into roles, styles, delegation, and behavioral patterns, and whether the person discovered any dysfunctional aspects in these.

2. Changes brought about in roles, leadership styles, extent of delegation, behavioral patterns, and so forth.

3. Roles or activities on which the person specially focused after attending the workshop.

4. Results that seem to benefit him/her and the organization, and also if some things had not worked well.

5. The impact of the 360 degree feedback workshop on the person, his/her unit, and overall organization.

6. Suggestions to make such programs more useful and effective.

The participants were also given a separate questionnaire, which were to be distributed to "significant others" to gain their perception on changes observed. Feedback was sought on the following:

1. Predominant changes observed.
2. Changes observed in managerial roles, leadership styles, delegation patterns, and behavior.
3. Negative changes/No changes observed.
4. Suggestions for further improvement

The following most frequently mentioned changes in behavior demonstrated after the 360 degree feedback workshop included:

## MORE FOCUS ON LEADERSHIP ROLES

1. Articulation of vision.
2. More time spent on communicating vision and goal-setting.
3. Being more developmental as compared to benevolent or critical.
4. Paying attention to the needs of individuals rather than remaining preoccupied with oneself.

## INTERNAL CUSTOMER ORIENTATION

1. Better interaction with colleagues and subordinates.
2. Enhanced learning from colleagues and benefiting from their experience.
3. Increased rapport with seniors.

## INCREASED FOCUS ON FOSTERING TEAM SPIRIT

1. Setting of high goals for the team.
2. Participative management.
3. Conflict management.
4. Development of mutuality.
5. Sensitivity to others' feelings.
6. Development of a collaborative culture.
7. Establishment of a cross-functional review mechanism.

## MARKED INCREASE IN DELEGATION AND JUNIORS' DEVELOPMENT

1. Empowering subordinates to take increased responsibility.
2. Leaving routine decisions to juniors.
3. Not interfering in matters being handled by juniors.
4. Encouraging them to learn from their mistakes and being very patient with them.

## PREDOMINANT BEHAVIORAL CHANGES

1. Assertiveness.
2. Clear communication.
3. Initiative.
4. Patience.
5. Proactiveness.
6. Time management.

In terms of the impact on their unit/department/organization, the participants who responded felt that they had benefited from the feedback because it generated increased motivation, especially among their juniors. Moreover, their increased sensitivity to their managerial and leadership roles had resulted in better working relationships and a more congenial atmosphere at the workplace. According to most participants, the changes were brought about not only because the feedback came from people who knew them best at the workplace, but also because they were made aware of the differences between self-perception and reality.

TVRLS experiences in the area of 360 degree feedback (in actual workshops as well as post-feedback workshops) indicate the following (Rao and Rao, 2003):

1. Feedback from multiple sources has credibility because individual biases are minimized and a more complete picture is obtained.
2. 360 degree feedback is an efficient tool, mainly because it emphasizes the difference between self-perception and reality.
3. Feedback has a markedly positive effect.

4. Leadership competencies are strengthened.
5. Customer orientation is increased.
6. It leads to greater sensitivity.
7. There is increased team orientation.
8. 360 degree feedback does sometimes make a negative impact. One main reason for this is that people providing the feedback seem to feel that once the individual is made aware of his/her weaknesses, there will be dramatic improvements almost immediately. Automatically, others' expectations rise with respect to the individual's behavior and the increased sensitivity of the person may also be exploited.
9. Action plans are most effective when shared with other members in an organization. This is because changes desired in the individual to whom 360 degree feedback has been provided requires considerable organizational support. It would be useful for the organization to look at how it can support the person in terms of his/her action plans on improvement.

Rao (1999) made some useful observations on organizations planning to use 360 degree feedback and how they could go about this intervention. Some useful lessons that can be drawn from this include the following:

1. 360 degree feedback should be projected as a developmental tool before using it for appraisal. The most important aid in making it successful is to provide organizational support for planning and managing it as a change mechanism. Initially, it should be used for top management and then gradually at all managerial levels.
2. The system should be communicated across the organization. The objectives should be well defined. The HRD department can play a significant role in this. However, such a program cannot be implemented successfully unless all apprehensions are allayed.
3. Its effectiveness will be maximized by continuous organizational monitoring. Quarterly review of improvements after

the workshop is a good idea. Moreover, those who have received feedback can meet formally to discuss action plans and experiences.

4. Organizational support should be provided to aid individual development. This could be done by appointing seniors of the managers as mentors to continuously counsel and encourage them. A good way of integrating the system would be to add the change plan as a key result area in these managers' performance appraisal; action plans will be reviewed like any other task and target along with their regular performance appraisal. This is a good practice.

5. Convert normal appraisal into a 360 degree appraisal. This is the most logical step to take. This is especially applicable for those organizations that are looking for a 360 degree appraisal system. They may have some hesitation in starting an appraisal program and may only use the feedback as a starting point. In such cases, after the managers have been given feedback, their inhibitions and apprehensions may diminish. They will then be well prepared to receive feedback from others. Therefore, a logical extension of the program is to design a 360 degree appraisal program and make it a part of the company's annual appraisal process. The team that has gone through the program can design a simple format with the help of the in-house HR team or a 360 degree expert.

6. Conduct reassessments periodically. Some participants opt for resurveys using the same questionnaires after six months or a year. The RSDQ questionnaire is long and may pose problems for organization-wide reassessment on a continuous basis. Candidates who want to reassess their changes can use a shorter version of it.

7. Reward changes with the help of the reviewing officer. Another way of reinforcing the change process is to notice changes and reward these. This can be done in a systematic manner by instituting change awards or integrating into the reward or recognition system an element for change due to 360 degree feedback. Spread success stories, and document and reward successes.

8. Collect trends in commonly shared weaknesses and initiate training and other organizational actions. When a candidate goes through a 360 degree feedback program based on the RSDQ model, data about him/her is generated on nearly 165 dimensions. Benchmarking of data, which provides company-wide trends, is also enabled. Common observations are derived from such extensive data, which can be traced to certain organizational factors. This can help an organization develop an agenda for its training and other organizational development plans.

9. Use data for potential appraisal, career planning, and development. This is its most common use in Fortune 500 companies. In this case, it should be announced at the beginning and data made available to the organization. This data can be used for placement- and promotion-related decisions. However, since this is only additional data, it should not be the sole input. It can also be used for career counseling.

A change management 360 degree feedback program has significant potential. Our experience with TVRLS demonstrates this. It is hoped that many organizations will exploit the potential of this.

## HOW TO PREPARE FOR IMPLEMENTATION OF 360 DEGREE FEEDBACK

It takes considerable trust in an organization and much preparation before an organization can move from using 360 degree feedback strictly for development purposes to using it to take decisions on promotions and rewards. Many companies are just not ready for this. Most current literature on making 360 degree feedback effective as a tool for performance and leadership-style reviews recommend the following:

1. Begin with Development
   It is advisable to introduce 360 degree feedback as an internal tool for personal development and growth if your company has no experience in this intervention. This basic

change-management process is addressed by 360 degree feedback and can be frightening for many people who think that they will be rated by their juniors and coworkers. Most companies have at least a one-year program in place before linking it to performance reviews. GE pioneered the use of 360 degree feedback as a developmental tool for over three years, getting people used to it without seeing any change in the organization. The program has only taken root and begun to be seen as an integral part of the company's functions and value system in the last few years. A good alternative is to focus on a single department or division that seems the most ready for 360 degree feedback.

2. Link with Company Goal

   No program as unorthodox as 360 degree feedback should be taken lightly. It must be finally linked to a significant business reason that is plain for everyone to see. Is it the purpose of introducing 360 degree feedback to change the company's culture? Or is it to enhance its performance management system? Presumably, the reason is not because someone heard about or read about this new plaything.

3. Train Everyone

   TVRLS conducts training sessions for everyone who can complete a feedback questionnaire. Such consultancy firms address issues such as data quality, confidentiality, accessibility to reports, and their ultimate use. Trust is critical to the accuracy of data and one way to ensure this is through training. Do executives view this as a constructive or punitive process? It is human nature to rush to negative feedback. Training is required to focus on the positive because that is where the real leverage in improving performance lies.

4. Follow Up

   A feedback report should finally go into the action plan for an organization's improvement. The superior and the HR professional can help interpret the report so that the employee does not put in place a wrong action plan. The action plan, as in the case of several contemporary companies, must eventually be tied to results as well as to rewards and punishment systems of the organization. The focus is on individual accountability for bringing about the desired cultural change. If employees, especially at the top and senior leadership levels, are not held accountable for doing something with their 360 degree feedback, they can simply ignore the findings and allow perpetuation of negativity in the company.

5. Company Culture

If your culture is retaliatory and punitive, the 360 degree feedback process will not work well. In an atmosphere of downsizing, where everyone is afraid for their jobs, it can also poison people about 360 degree feedback, which they never want to use again. In fact, 360 degree feedback is most effective in a company that has a culture of learning and individual growth. If an executive is about to receive 360 degree feedback, but during the previous year he/she either (a) has not asked for feedback, (b) has not taken action on the feedback received, or (c) feels that some kind of retribution is going to take place, then by the time the 360 degree process gets going, there is already an atmosphere of mistrust and fear in the organization. Unless there is some other development input to create a positive climate, 360 degree feedback can add very limited value to the cultural change in the company.

In conclusion, it is important to note that 360 degree feedback can be a significant behavioral science intervention in bringing about cultural change in Indian corporations, which continue to be preoccupied with a top-down autocratic culture. Indian leadership at senior levels continues to demand obedience and gets it either through seductive or coercive means. Indian talent continues to flourish overseas or make unambiguous choices to work for MNCs, where a freer and more democratic climate prevails. The 360 degree feedback process, my experience leads me to believe, helps top and senior leadership break free from the decadent past and thereby develop competencies to attract and retain world-class talent so desperately needed for world-class business and organizational growth.

# 12

# Performance Management through Assessment and Development Centers

## Introduction

Assessment and Development Centers (ADCs), formerly known as Assessment Centers and/or Development Centers, have their origin in assessments conducted in the armed forces. These were initiated in US corporations such as AT&T in the mid-1950s and have become popular in India in the last decade and a half, especially in the public sector, which is starved for innovations in HR management. Most of them have begun to use ADCs as assessment and development tools with the pretention of developing competencies of the future. Systematic evaluation of the experiences indicates that ADCs have yet to establish their authentic utility as development tools in this scenario. There is fortunately some literature available to describe the current situation in various organizations (see publications on this theme by T.V. Rao Learning Systems at www.tvrls.com). In this chapter, we will first discuss the evolution and relevance of ADCs as potential appraisal tools and then establish how they can be used as performance management tools.

### ADCs AS POTENTIAL APPRAISAL AND COMPETENCY DEVELOPMENT TOOLS

In a competitive world, past achievements do not always guarantee future success. The risks of failure are high, especially for those who have been operating in a protected environment. Economic reforms are constantly exposing organizations to higher levels of competition. To face this, they need to advance at a high speed in all areas—technology, processes, management, finances, quality, costs, creation of new markets, new product inventories, and above all, increased efficiency, motivation, and productivity on the part of employees. Competing organizations from other countries have easy access to the best technologies, easy and unlimited finance, well-established management systems and practices, high-quality orientation, brand equity, and simple, flat, and cost-effective structures with fewer but very competent people to handle all of these. In such circumstances, they have no option but to become more technology-driven, market-sensitive, customer-focused, quality-centered, cost-effective, systems-driven, and managerially effective. However, to achieve these, it is necessary to have competent managers in strategic roles, so that organizations can gain a strategic advantage, without which they cannot survive for long.

Competent people should handle strategic and critical roles. Hence, there is a need to constantly identify such people. This need is what makes potential appraisal very significant.

To have competent people, we must know more about competency requirements. To know competency requirements, we must know the job profile or list of tasks to be performed. There should then be a reliable and valid method of assessing the extent to which a given employee has the competence to perform the new tasks. Potential appraisal entails assessment of the extent to which a given individual has the potential to perform the new task or job. Such an assessment can either be a simple or a complicated matter, depending on a number of factors.

It is simple if the employee is already performing most or all the tasks in his/her current job. In such cases, appraisal of his/her current performance is a good enough indicator of future potential. The performance appraisal period is an appropriate time to assess this potential. For example, if a deputy manager (production) needs to be promoted to the rank of a manager (production), most of his/her tasks will remain the same. Normally, such promotions are more a case of re-designation.

However, potential appraisal is complicated if the employee is to be considered for a new job or task. Here, one has to gather evidence of the person's potential to perform the new job, and past performance is not an adequate indicator of this. The best way to judge a person's potential and ability to succeed in the new role is to actually put the individual on the job and then assess him/her. However, there are many practical constraints. For one, the organization cannot afford to take such risks, and second, there are usually many aspirants for a particular post. The next best alternative in such situations is to simulate the job and observe the person's performance.

This is where ADC as a methodology gains in significance. ADCs are specially established centers that create simulated job conditions and observe a person's performance, thereby assessing his/her potential to occupy the position. Again, it is not necessary to simulate the entire job. In any case, in a promotion, 60–70 percent of the work can be handled well as a result of past experience. It is the remaining part that is critical and requires a different set of competencies. Therefore, this part of the job can be studied, competencies identified, and methods designed to evaluate these competencies.

Promotions should be preceded by thorough testing of competencies or potential for holding the position to which the employee is being promoted. It is here that ADC becomes relevant. It should communicate to employees that the organization is focusing on a performance and competency culture.

Most organizations include potential appraisal as a part of their performance management process. This has advantages, but also several disadvantages.

1. Potential is about the future, while performance deals with the past. Good performance in the past in a given job need not be a good indicator of likely performance in the future in a role that the individual has not performed.
2. The biases of the boss, who is just one level above, may creep into the potential appraisal.
3. Potential should relate to competencies, while performance pertains to KPAs and other tasks assigned to the individual. Potential is about assessing people against competencies required for higher level roles.

4. Performance on a given job is partly dependent on the support provided by the organization, including an individual's reporting officer and reviewing officer and their judgment may be more reflective of the situation in which the person has performed rather than his/her actual capabilities.

5. It is only fair to create the conditions under which the individual is likely to perform the new job and test him/her in relation to the situation as well as his/her competencies. This is how ADC becomes a relevant tool for promotion-related decisions.

Combining potential appraisal with performance appraisal may be appropriate under the following conditions:

1. There is no significant difference in the current job of the individual and the future job for which his/her potential is being tested.

2. The competencies required for the new job are the same as those needed by the current one.

3. The current job offers an adequate opportunity for the individual to demonstrate the competencies needed for the future one.

4. The reporting officer or the reviewing officer is experienced and unbiased and, therefore, able to accurately judge the potential of the individual.

It is, however, useful to supplement the data with 360 degree feedback and ADCs.

This chapter presents details of the ADC approach and generates some alternatives for organizations.

# Definition of an Assessment and Development Center (ADC)

An ADC is a comprehensive and standardized procedure in which multiple assessment techniques such as situational exercises and job simulation (business games, discussions, reports, and presentations) are used to evaluate employees for a variety of decisions and the feedback given to them, along with assistance on making and implementing a development plan.

ADCs normally follow the following steps:

1. Identification of competencies required to perform a given job or a set of jobs.
2. Development of competency frameworks for jobs, normally outlining a list of critical competencies needed for success in the organization across various levels and job categories.
3. Development of tools or multiple instruments, including psychometric tests, simulation games and exercises, role play, in-baskets, case studies, group discussions, team-assessment exercises, and competency-based interviews, specially designed by experts using Behavior Event Interviews started by David McClelland and team from Harvard University.
4. Appointment of trained assessors to run the development centers.
5. Execution or actual assessment of select candidates by several trained assessors using the competency framework and tools.
6. Generation of feedback reports on the basis of the tools.
7. Feedback given on the results of the ADC to the candidates and the organization, and facilitation of preparation of development plans through individual coaching.
8. Implementation of development plans.
9. Reassessment of the competencies enhanced on the job through follow-up interviews or ADCs.

Normally, steps 8 and 9 are not taken by most organizations, resulting in significant waste of ADC effort. Some organizations (particularly in the private sector and MNCs) use the data for promotion and placement decisions. In India, the public sector is shy of doing this for reasons relating to equality and insecurity or lack of confidence on the objectivity of assessments.

Most frequently, the approach is applied to individuals being considered for selection, promotion, placement, or special training and development in management. However, what is required is better performance management and development.

## TOOLS USED IN ADCs

As mentioned earlier, the main characteristics of ADCs are different methods of assessment using multiple assessors. The main assessment tools that are used include the following:

### PSYCHOMETRIC TESTS

In general, three types of tests or questionnaires can be used in ADCs—aptitude tests, ability tests, and personality tests. *Aptitude tests* attempt to evaluate verbal and numerical reasoning ability; *Ability tests* to measure awareness, knowledge, and other such aspects. They also measure simple skills such as an individual's problem-solving ability, etc. For example, a chapter pencil test can be administered to determine the familiarity or level of skill of the person in relation to computer literacy, financial management skills, and so forth. *Personality tests* are aimed at studying various dimensions of an individual's personality rather than his/her ability. MBTI and 16 PF are tests used in many organizations. While ability and aptitude tests have right or wrong answers, personality tests do not.

The tests selected for making an assessment take the following factors into consideration:

1. Objective—what needs to be measured?
2. Reliability and validity
3. Length of time required to administer the test
4. Availability of qualified experts to administer, score, and interpret the tests
5. The cost involved.

## INTERVIEWS—BACKGROUND INTERVIEWS, CRITICAL INCIDENTS/SITUATIONAL INTERVIEWS, BEHAVIOR EVENT INTERVIEWS

Generally, structured interviews are used in ADCs to increase inter-assessor reliability. Questions are decided on, and sample responses are formed and classified as good, bad, or average. This is used to rate a participant's response.

*Background interviews* are generally held if there is a possibility that participants' performance in their current and previous jobs could indicate their suitability for the roles for which they are being assessed. They are required to give specific examples of how they have performed in their jobs or handled job-related problems in the past.

In *situational interviews,* the following three types of questions are asked:

1. Situational (or hypothetical): The candidate is asked what he/she would do if faced with a particular situation in a job.
2. Job knowledge: This defines a term, explains a procedure, or demonstrates a skill.
3. Willingness to comply with job requirements.

The situations are based on critical incidents arising from an analysis of a job.

In the case of Behavior Event Interviews (BEIs), the objective is to obtain a detailed behavioral description of how a person goes about his/her work. The purpose is to find out what people actually do. As each situation is narrated by the interviewee, the focus is on what the situation was, who was involved, what did the interviewee do/say/want to accomplish, and what the outcome was. Therefore, a BEI is essentially an unstructured interview that focuses on asking an interviewee about specific incidents that reflect his/her behavior, thoughts, and actions in actual situations.

## LEADERLESS GROUP DISCUSSIONS (LGDS)

An LGD consists of a group of four to six participants who are given a problem (generally a real life one) to solve and are instructed to arrive at a group decision within a specified period. While various roles may or may not be assigned to the group, no one is designated as the chairperson. Assigned role LGDs simulate decision-making meetings at which resources need to be divided equitably. An LGD with no role assigned would be similar to ad hoc committees formed in organizations for specific purposes, for example, evaluating their marketing strategies, studying specific issues or problems they are facing, and so forth.

## IN-BASKET TECHNIQUES

An In-basket test is another form of a simulation exercise. The in-basket or in-tray represents day-to-day decision-making situations managers are likely to face in the written form from various sources. The in-basket contains a variety of material in the form of memos, correspondence, telephone messages, notes, requests, and so forth, for their attention. The contents are designed after a thorough job analysis—in terms of duties handled and competencies required. The participants are then asked to deal with each of them within a limited period, putting their reactions as much as possible in writing. Their general activity levels, problem analysis skills, planning and organization, time management, delegation, concern for priorities, and so forth can be assessed based on their reactions.

## MANAGEMENT GAMES/SIMULATION EXERCISES

A real life situation is simulated for an entire group in management games or simulations exercises, for example, running a manufacturing operation, trading in stocks, running a large multidivisional organization, etc. While the degree of complexity varies in these games, the common denominator is the relatively unstructured nature of interactions among the participants and the variety of actions that can be taken by them. As a complex game unfolds, it often reveals other exercises such as LGDs, role plays, problem analysis, and so forth. A computer program is frequently used to generate information and simulate a game. Participants are not allowed direct access to the computer, but a person acts as a mediator between it and the group. The mediator is a neutral observer who provides information that the participant group asks for and introduces various environmental factors such as the entry of competitors, recession scenarios, and so forth, as part of the simulation.

The interactive nature of the business game provides opportunities for assessment of participants' dimensions such as strategic planning, teamwork, team skills, leadership, analytical ability, etc. A great deal of expertise is required to run this game and assessor training is very extensive.

## ROLE PLAYS

Role playing is a method of adopting roles from real life, other than those being played by the person concerned and understanding the dynamics of the role. It can be described as the "method of studying the nature of certain roles by acting out its concrete details in a contrived situation that permits better and more objective observation" (Pareek and Rao, 1981). Role playing can be used as an evaluation technique because it helps gain insights into the various processes of human relations and also an individual's attitude and behavior in a particular role. Certain dimensions that can be evaluated with the aid of role play include conflict management, leadership skills, group problem-solving, team skills, verbal and nonverbal communication, interpersonal skills, flexibility, motivational style, etc. depending on the type of situation.

Role playing is especially effective as a technique in ADCs because it makes possible minimum distortion in real life situations and at the same time helps magnify these to focus on certain aspects. Even in the case of developmental aspects, giving feedback to people is relatively easier since they are able to accept feedback without any threat to their egos, and hence, do not become defensive.

## PRESENTATIONS

Individual presentations are extensively used in ADCs and take the form of an organization's vision, various organizational issues faced by it, case studies, and so forth.

# Use of 360 Degree Feedback as an Instrument in ADC

360 degree feedback can be used as a tool for assessment in ADC. It is a feedback mechanism, where assessees are provided feedback by the people with whom they interact at work, for example, their bosses, peers, juniors, and external customers. Feedback can be sought on various managerial and behavioral dimensions. This multirater feedback can then be compiled to prepare a profile of the assessee. Such a profile highlights the following:

1. How well individuals are performing in their managerial roles.
2. Their other strengths and areas needing improvement—as perceived by themselves and as perceived by others.

On the basis of this feedback, assessees can initiate and implement their action plans to improve their managerial effectiveness and make positive impact at the workplace.

## PERFORMANCE MANAGEMENT AND APPRAISAL SYSTEMS

The various benefits of 360 degree feedback are:

1. It is more objective and not very much affected due to individual bias.
2. It requires involvement and is participative.
3. It enables better planning of performance.
4. It provides individuals the opportunity to improve the quality of their input and services to internal customers.

5. It is a developmental tool, which helps to discover unknown and blind spots in people.
6. It provides a scope to get new ideas.

## PROCEDURE USED IN ADCS

The following procedure is generally followed in an ADC:

### Observation and Individual Assessor Rating

Generally, an assessor assesses two participants. However, the exercises are so designed that each of the participants is assessed by one assessor. During the actual exercise, only behavior is recorded and no final interpretations are arrived at.

Once all the exercises are over, each assessor is required to classify behavior observed into various dimensions according to a predefined list of competencies. Taking into account participants' performance in all the exercises and interviews, they are then rated on their competence using a five-point scale. The overall assessment is then prepared in the form of a report by the assessor for each of the participants, in which each of the participants' performance and observed behavior is described, the rating given, and reasons for the rating explained.

### Assessors' Discussions

Once individual assessors have prepared the reports, this is followed by an assessor discussion. Each assessor reads his/her report while other assessors make relevant recordings of each of the participants and give their own ratings. The assessor's judgment is not questioned or challenged; only clarifying questions can be asked. Once the preliminary rating by all the assessors is completed, a comparative analysis is carried out. A composite chart is prepared, recording each assessor's ratings. This chart provides a quick view of areas of agreement and disagreement. Ratings of each of the dimensions are discussed until a consensus is reached. Normally, the average is not taken because more insights can be obtained by discussing discrepancies.

Finally, an overall average rating is arrived at, which reflects a summary of the evaluation of a participant's performance in the

ADC. The overall rating is then supported by the final decision on the participant, which is the objective of the ADC—his/her suitability for a particular job, promotability, developmental needs, and so forth.

Thornton and Byham (1982) have laid down "certain basic principles that need to be adhered to in the ADC process, which when applied systematically, lead to accuracy of assessment and prediction of managerial performance." These include the following:

1. Assessment should be based on clearly-defined dimensions of managerial behavior.
2. Multiple assessment techniques should be used.
3. A variety of job sampling techniques should be used.
4. Assessors should know what it takes to succeed. They need to be familiar with the job and organization, and if possible, have experience in such a job.
5. Assessors should be thoroughly trained in ADC procedures.
6. Behavioral data should be observed, recorded, and communicated among the assessor team.
7. Group discussion processes should be used to integrate observations, rate dimensions, and make predictions.
8. The assessment process should be separated into stages that delay formation of general impressions, evaluation, overall ratings, or final predictions.
9. Assessees should be evaluated against a clearly understood norm—not against each other.
10. Prediction of managerial success must be judgmental.

### Consultant's Role

In case of the ADCs, the consultant's role is critical at the preliminary stages—the design and initial training phase. At the offset, the organization needs to clearly define the objectives of the ADC, what it plans to achieve, how the data will be used, and the kind of follow-up that will be done. Accordingly, the consultant can provide his/sher input in the following areas:

1. A job analysis exercise to identify the competencies required for a particular role.
2. Provision of conceptual input with respect to ADC methodology.
3. Designing of the ADC.
4. Preparation of various tests, exercises, and simulations to evaluate the participants.
5. Selection and training of assessors.
6. Assistance in conducting initial ADCs.
7. Assistance in organization's use of data generated.
8. Assistance in institutionalizing the concept and developing internal resources for use of the methodology for various personnel-related purposes.

## CEO's Role

The ADC concept is relatively new in Indian organizations. When introduced in any organization, there are bound to be doubts with respect to its utility and applicability. The roles of the CEO and top management are important in supporting and propagating the concept and ensuring that these are in line with the organization's objectives. The role of the CEO is important in terms of its doing the following:

1. Defining the objectives of the ADC.
2. Providing organizational resources that are needed for its effective implementation.
3. Ensuring that personnel data generated is not wrongly used.
4. Supporting interventions and processes that are undertaken after the workshop.
5. Implementing monitoring mechanisms to ensure improvements in workplace performance as a result of the ADC.
6. Ensuring and providing support for implementation of development plans and making sure that the ADC experience is reviewed and improvements undertaken.

**ADCs in India**

The first ADC in India was attempted by me in 1974 to select project leaders for the entrepreneurship development program in Gujarat. This was briefly mentioned in an article entitled "Role Set-based ADC Approach to Personnel Selection" (ASCI *Journal of Management*, 1975, 5[I], 10–16). Subsequently, efforts were made to introduce ADC in L&T, which intended to use it for promotion purposes. The company did significant work on job profiling, but never got to the stage of developing an ADC for potential appraisal of its senior executives. Crompton Greaves attempted to use an ADC approach to select its general managers from within the organization. This was again a one-time effort and was not repeated subsequently. Details of this effort in the early 1980s have been described by Susan Varghese. Subsequently, an attempt was made to introduce ADC in Ballarpur Industries (BILT) by Dr Anil Dixit with the help of the Behavioral Science Center. However, this did not happen due to resistance from line managers and change of leadership in HR.

It was only after liberalization in the 1990s that interest in ADCs was renewed. Many organizations began setting up ADCs. This was a natural response to their need to ensure competent people manning strategic positions.

It is estimated that over a 100 Indian companies have established ADCs and others are still exploring the idea. The companies that are trying this out include the RPG Group, Escorts, TISCO, the Aditya Birla Group, Eicher, Cadbury, Castrol (India), Glaxo, Grindwell Norton, ONGC, Mahindra & Mahindra, SAIL, Siemens, Wipro, Wockhardt, J&J, NTPC, Indian Oil, Engineers India, BPCL, HPCL, SAIL, HAL, BEML, BHEL, Cummins, Geometric, Mahindra and its Group companies, the Aditya Vikram Birla Group, Atul, and others. Many public sector organizations have gone for it in a big way. Different organizations have initiated ADCs for recruitment, selection, placement, promotion, career development, performance management, leadership development and grooming, succession planning and development including for identification of training needs, high-potential managers, and creation of a pool of managerial talent and multifunctional managers (who will be available across the group), recognition of employees, and fast growth.

The competencies that need to be measured are determined by each organization by using competency mapping methods and others such as job analysis, managerial aptitude profile surveys, identification of competencies in star performers, and so forth. A variety of assessment techniques are used such as in-basket and business simulation. The various tools used include questionnaires, group discussions, role plays, interviews, case studies, individual presentations, and so forth. While organizations feel the need to test the reliability and validity of the tools used, many of them are not doing so. Both internal and external assessors are used for the evaluation process. Assessor training is conducted either through in-house training programs or with the aid of external institutions such as the Academy of HRD (Hyderabad), SHL (UK), etc. Some Indian organizations have also sought assistance from organizations abroad such as GE, SUN, AT&T, NORTEL, CISCO, and Motorola that are using ADCs. With regard to employees who are eligible for ADCs, certain criteria are laid down such as minimum years of experience with the organization, proven track records, educational qualifications, and so forth. After the ADC, participants are provided with feedback, counseling, and other developmental input, as explained earlier, by using development centers.

However, there are certain issues with respect to ADCs that persist in Indian organizations such as:

1. Complexity of implementation.
2. Clear behavioral description of competencies.
3. Availability of assessors.
4. Assessor training.
5. Inter-rater reliability.
6. Appropriateness of selection tools.
7. Validity of exercises.
8. Organizational commitment in terms of time and resources.
9. Involvement of line managers.
10. Feedback to participants.
11. Data security.

Establishing an ADC is an investment. It will give adequate returns if it is a long-term investment, is carefully planned, and patiently executed. Any ambitious aim of accomplishing short-term objectives such as getting a mere objective assessment is likely to lead to more problems than appropriate returns. Sometimes organizations may be guided by a sense of frustration due to their past mistakes, current mismatches, or incompetence. While ADCs cannot undo past mistakes, they can do a lot in terms of creating a competence culture in organizations.

## ADCs and Performance Management

As mentioned earlier, a number of organizations have PMS that requires various degrees of assessment on competencies. Normal PMS focuses on performance of planned activities and exhibition of competencies identified by the organization and includes values such as customer focus, cost control, quality orientation, integrity, ethical standards, and so forth. It is in assessing and developing these competencies that most managers face challenges.

Seniors do not have adequate time to observe and guide their juniors. Most of the time, development of people to enable them to perform better is ignored by default. Biases are enhanced if competencies are given higher weightage and not enough is done to develop them. Hence the need for ADCs. They are robust tools for assessment of competency. Use them for appraising the performance of select candidates on the competency framework your company has evolved.

In using ADCs for performance management, the following points need to be remembered:

1. ADC is a tool or a system that tests the individual in simulated settings and by using multiple methods provides an understanding of the competencies demonstrated in the tests.
2. It ensures that the competencies assessed have relevance to individuals' success in their organizations at their current levels.
3. It ensures that candidates understand the competencies required, since these are normally printed in PMS formats.

Definitions or indicators of each competency are supplied to every manager.

4. It explains the purpose of the ADC in advance and provides feedback at the end.
5. It ensures that developmental plans are prepared by the individuals with clear specifications about what they plan to do and the support needed for their growth.
6. It makes sure that development plans are shared with seniors or reporting managers, and decisions taken to support these.

It recommends review of progress made as part of PMS quarterly or half-yearly assessments once ADC data are provided to the candidates.

# BIBLIOGRAPHY

Armstrong, M. and A. Baron. 2002. *Performance Management: The New Realities.* Mumbai: Jaico.

Balfour, P.L. 1992. "Impact of agency—Investment in the Implementation of Performance Appraisals," *Public Personnel Management Journal,* 21(1): 1–15.

Bernardin, H.J. 1977. "Behavioural Expectation Scale versus Summated Scales: A Fairer Comparison," *Journal of Applied Psychology,* 62: 422–28.

Bernardin, H.J. and P.C. Smith. 1981. "A Clarification on Some Issues Regarding the Development and Use of Behaviourally Anchored Rating Scales (BARS)," *Journal of Applied Psychology,* 66(4): 458–63.

Bernardin, H.J. and R.L. Cardy. 1982. "Appraisal Accuracy—The Ability and Motivation to Remember the Past," *Public Personnel Management Journal,* 11(4): 352–57.

Bernardin, H.J., R.L. Cardy, and J.J. Carlyle. 1982. "Cognitive Complexity and Appraisal Effectiveness: Back to the Drawing Board," *Journal of Applied Psychology,* 67(2): 151–60.

Borman, W. 1979. "Format and Training Effects on Rater Accuracy and Rater Errors," *Journal of Applied Psychology,* 64: 410–21.

Bracken, D.W. and C.W. Timmreck. 1999. "Guidelines for Multisource Feedback When Used for Decision-making," *The Industrial-Organizational Psychologist* (TIP), 36(4): 64–74.

Bretz, R.D., G.T. Milkovich, and W. Read. 1992. "The Current Status of Performance Appraisal Research and Practice: Concerns, Directions and Implications," *Journal of Management,* 18(2): 321–52.

Cabinet Office. 1999. "Setting the Agenda for the Civil Service of the Future." Press Release, CAB 307/99, December 15, 1999. Available at: www.cabinetoffice.gov.uk/news/1999/991215_civilservice.asp (accessed August 21, 2003).

———. 2004a. "Delivery and Reform Online." Available at: www.civil-service.gov.uk/reform/about_delivery/about_delivery.asp (accessed June 1, 2004).

———. 2004b. "Performance Management. Civil Service Performance and Reward Division." Available at: www.cabinet-office.gov.uk/civilservice/performanceandreward/performance.htm (accessed June 1, 2004).

Campbell, R.B. and L.M. Garfinkel. 1996. "Strategies of Success," *HR Magazine,* July, pp. 98–104.

Cantor, N. and W. Mischel. 1977. "Traits as Prototypes: Effects on Recognition Memory," *Journal of Personality and Social Psychology,* 35: 38–48.

Conger, J.A.D. Finegold and E.E. Lawler. 1998. "Appraising Boardroom Performance," *Harvard Business Review,* January–February.

Cooper, C.L. and C. Argyris, 1998. "The concise Blackwell encyclopedia of management," Massachusetts: Blackwell Business, Retrieved on 02 September 2010 (as cited in *Australian Journal of Basic and Applied Sciences*, 5(6): 1581–193, 2011ISSN 1991–8178).

Corporate Leadership Council. 2002. "Building the High-Performance Workforce: A Quantitative Analysis of the Effectiveness of Performance Management Strategies." Corporate Leadership Council, Pennsylvania Avenue NW, Washington, D.C.

Corporate Leadership Council. 2003. "Benchmarking the High-Performance Organization: A Quantitative Analysis of the Implementation of High-Impact Performance Management Strategies." Corporate Leadership Council, Pennsylvania Avenue NW, Washington, D.C.

Decotiis, T. and A. Petit 1978. "The Performance Appraisal Process: A Model and Some Testable Propositions," *Academy of Management Review*, 63: 635–46.

Donald, J. 1996. "Compensation: The Link to Customer Satisfaction." *HR Focus*, 1–6.

Drucker, Peter F. 1999/2005. "Managing Yourself," *Harvard Business Review*, pp. 1–11.

Duchi, W.G. 1982. *Theory Z*. New York: Avon Books.

Dunnet, M. and W. Borman. 1979. "Personnel Selection and Classification Systems," *Annual Review of Psychology*, 30: 477–525.

Edwards, M.R. and A.J. Ewen. 1996. *360 Degree Feedback: The Powerful New Model for Employee Assessment and Performance Improvement*. USA: AMACOM, American Management Association.

English, G. 1991. "Tuning up for Performance Management," *Training and Development Journal*, 45(4), April: 56–60.

Feldman, J.M. 1981. "Beyond Attribution Theory: Cognitive Process in Performance Appraisal," *Journal of Applied Psychology*, 66(2): 127–48.

Goleman, Daniel. 1998. *Working with Emotional Intelligence*. USA: Bantam Books.

Flanders, N. 1970. *Analysing Teacher Behaviour*. Reading, MA: Addison Wesley.

Floury, L., R. Hansun, and J.H. McCaul. 1994. "Review System Supports Customer Focus," *HR Magazine*, 39(1), January: 66–69.

Friedman, B.A. and E.T. Cornelius. 1976. "Effects of Rater Participation in Scale Construction on Psychometric Characteristics of the Rating Scale Formats," *Journal of Applied Psychology*, 61: 210–16.

Gangotra, V.A. 1983. "Study of Performance Appraisal in Jyoti Limited." Unpublished Report, Jyoti Ltd, HRD Department, Baroda.

Gillespie, T. L. 2005, Spring. "Internationalizing 360-Degree Feedback: Are Subordinate Ratings Comparable?" *Journal of Business and Psychology*, 19(3): 361–82. DOI: 10.1007/s10869-004-2233-z.

Goodson, J.R. and G.W. McGee. 1992. "Enhancing Individual Perception of Objectivity in Performance Appraisals," *Journal of Business Research*, June: 291–93.

Government of India. 2007, March. Ministry of Personnel, Public Grievances and Pensions. AIS (PAR) Rules 2007, All India Services Rules, 1970.

————. 2008, March. Report of the Sixth Pay Commission, New Delhi.

Harvey, R.J. 1982. "The Future of Partial Correlations as a Means to Reduce Halo in Performance Ratings," *Journal of Applied Psychology*, 67(2): 171–76.

Havard, B. 2002. "Performance Appraisals," Kogan Page, *Sunday Times Series*, London.

Holzbach, R.L. 1978. "Rater Bias in Performance Ratings: Superior, Self and Peer Ratings," *Journal of Applied Psychology*, 63: 579–88.

Hom, P.W., A.S. DeNishi, A.J. Kinicki, and B.D. Bannister. 1982. "Effectiveness of Performance Feedback from Behaviourally Anchored Rating Scales," *Journal of Applied Psychology*, 67(5): 568–76.

Hyde, A.C. and M.A. Smith. 1982. "Performance Appraisal and Training: Objectives, a Model for Change and a Note of Rebuttal," *Public Personnel Management Journal*, 11(4): 358–65.

Jacobs, R., D. Kafry, and S. Zedeck. 1980. "Expectations of Behaviourally Anchored Rating Scales," *Personnel Psychology*, 33: 595–640.

Katz, R. 1974. "Skills of an Effective Administrator," *Harvard Business Review*, September–52, October: 90–102.

Kay, I.T. and D. Lerner. 1995. "What is Good for the Parts may Hurt the Whole," *HR Magazine*, September: 71–75.

Kearney, W.J. 1978. "Improving Work Performance through Appraisal," *Human Resources Management*, 17: 15–23.

Keopanya, Nisith. 2004. "Reforming Performance Management procedures in the Civil Service in Lao PDR: Case Study." 2004, Commonwealth Advanced Seminar–2004, Wellington, New Zealand, February 15–27.

Kingstrom, P. and A.A. Bass. 1981. "Critical Analysis of Studies Comparing Behavioural Anchored Ratings Scales (BARS) and other Ratings Formats," *Personnel Psychology*, 34: 263–89.

Kipnis, D. (1972), "Does Power Corrupt?" *Journal of Personality and Social Psychology*, 24: 33–41.

Kulkarni, S.S., K.R. Nagia, and R. Prakasam. 1980. "A Nationwide Survey of Bank Employees Opinion Regarding Personnel Policies and Practices (1980-81)," Working Paper No. 4. National Institute of Bank Management, Bombay.

Landy, F.J. and J.L. Farr. 1980. "Performance Rating," *Psychological Bulletin*, 87: 72–107.

Landy, F.J., R.J. Vance, J.L. Barnes-Farrell, and J.W. Streele 1980. "Statistical Control of Halo Error in Performance Ratings," *Journal of Applied Psychology*, 65: 501–06.

Levinson, H.A. 1962. "Psychologist Looks at Executive Development," *Harvard Business Review*, 40: 69–75.

Loriann, R. 1993. "Self-Appraisals and Perceptions of Appraisal Discussions—A Field Experience," *National Productivity Review*, Summer: 129–42.

Love, K.G. 1981. "Comparison of Peer Assessment Methods: Reliability, Validity, Friendship Bias and User Reaction," *Journal of Applied Psychology*, 66(4): 45–157.

Luft, J. 1970. *Group Processes: An Introduction to Group Dynamics (second edition)*. Palo Alto, CA: National Press Books.

Luft, J. and H. Ingham 1955. *The Johari Window: A Graphic Model for Interpersonal Relations*. University of California Western Training Lab.

Malee, Surapong. 2005. "Performance Management in ASEAN Public Services: Driving Government Performance through Strategic HRM," Compendium Preparation Meeting of the ASEAN Civil Service HR Working Group held in Bangkok, Thailand, August 18–19, 2005.

McArthur, L.Z. and D.L. Post. 1977. "Figural Emphasis and Person Perception," *Journal of Experimental Social Psychology*, 13: 520–35.

McClelland, D.G. 1976. "Power is the Great Motivator," *Harvard Business Review*, 54(2): 100–10.

Milliman, J., S. Nason, C. Zhu, and H.E. Cieri. 2002. "An Exploratory Assessment of the Purposes of Performance Appraisals in North and Central America and the Pacific Rim," *Human Resource Management*, Spring: 87–102.

Mitchell, T.R. and L.S. Kalb. 1982a. "Effects of Job Experience on Superior Attributions for a Subordinate's Poor Performance," *Journal of Applied Psychology*, 67(2): 18188.

———. 1982b. "Effects of Outcome Knowledge and Outcome Valence on Supervisors Evaluations," *Journal of Applied Psychology*, 66(5): 604–12.

Morgan, Arthur et al. 2005. "360 Degree Feedback: A Critical Enquiry." Arthur Morgan and Kath Cannan University of the Glamorgan Business School, Pontypridd, UK, and Joanne Cullinane University of Greenwich Business School, Greenwich, UK, *Personnel Review*, 34(6): 663–80.

Morrisay, G.L. 1972. *Appraisal and Development through Objectives and Results*. Reading, MA: Addison Wesley.

Murphy, K.J. 1993. "Performance Measurement and Appraisals—Merck Tries to Motivate Managers to Do it Right," *Employment Relations Today*, 20(1), Spring: 47–62.

Nagabrahmam, D. 1981. "Adoption of Management System in Indian Organisation." Unpublished Phd Thesis in Management, Indian Institute of Management, Ahmedabad.

Neary, D.B. 2002. "Creating a Company Wide, On-line, Performance Management System: A Case Study at TRW Inc." *Human Resource Management*, Winter: 491–98.

Neisser, U. 1976. *Cognition and Reality*. San Fransisco: W.H. Freeman & Co.

Nisbett, R.E. and T.D. Wilson. 1977. "The Halo Effect: Evidence for Unconscious Alteration of Judgements," *Journal of Personality and Social Psychology*, 35: 250–56.

Novack, K.M. 1993. "360 Degree Feedback: The Whole Story," *Training and Development*, January: 69–72.

Pareek, U. 1977. *Interpersonal Feedback for Effectiveness*. New Delhi: Learning Systems (CR Reading 16).

Pareek, U. 2002. *Training Instruments in HRD & OD* (2nd Edition). New Delhi: Tata Mc Graw-Hill Publishing Company Limited.

Pareek, U. and T.V. Rao. 1971. "Motivation Training for Mental Health: A Study of Teacher Behaviour and Student Mental Health." National Institute of Health Administration and Education, New Delhi.

Pareek, U. and T.V. Rao. 1981. *Designing and Managing Human Resource Systems.* New Delhi: Oxford & IBH.

Pascale, R.T. and A.G. Athos. 1982. *The Art of Japanese Management.* London: Penguin Books.

Rao, T.V. 1982. "HRD Practices in Indian Industry." *Lok Udyog,* March 5–15.

———. 1999. "Making 360 Degree Feedback Work," *Human Capital,* August: 26–51.

———. 2001. *Performance Planning and Review Skills Book.* TVRLS, Ahmedabad.

———. 2003. *Performance Management and Appraisal System.* New Delhi: SAGE Publications.

———. 2004. *Performance Management and Appraisal Systems: HR Tools for Global Competitiveness.* New Delhi: SAGE Publications.

———. 2004. *Performance Management and Appraisal Systems: HR Tools for Global Competitiveness.* New Delhi: SAGE Publications.

———. 2008. July–September. "Lessons From Experience: A New Look at Performance Management Ssystems," *Vikalpa,* 33(3): 1–15.

———. *Personal Effectiveness Manuals.* T.V. Rao Learning Systems Pvt. Ltd., Ahmedabad.

Rao, T.V. and M. Iqbal. 1982. "HRD Practices in Malaysian Banks," *Banker's Journal Malaysia,* 14: 24–27.

Rao, T.V. and R. Rao. 2003. *360 Degree Feedback and Performance Management Systems.* New Delhi: Excel Publications.

———. 2005. *The Power of 360 Degree Feedback.* New Delhi: SAGE Publications.

Rao, T.V. and U. Pareek. 1978. *Performance Appraisal and Review: Operating Manual.* New Delhi: Learning Systems.

———. 1996. *Redesigning Performance Appraisal Systems.* New Delhi: Tata McGraw-Hill.

Rao, T.V., G. Mahapatra, R. Rao, and N. Chawla. 2002. *360 Degree Feedback and Performance Management Systems.* New Delhi: Excel Publications.

Richl, H. 1996. "A Skillful Approach to High Productivity," *HR Magazine,* August: 97–102.

Rosinger, G., L.B. Myers, G.W. Levy, M. Loar, S.A. Mohrman, and J.R. Stock. 1982. "Development of a Behaviourally-Based Performance Appraisal System," *Personnel Psychology,* 35(1): 75–88.

Schneier, C.E. 1977. "Operational Utility and Psychometric Characteristics of Behavioural Expectation Scales: A Cognitive Reinterpretation," *Journal of Applied Psychology,* 62: 541–48.

Sharma, R. 2002. *360 Degree Feedback: Competency Mapping and Assessment Centers.* New Delhi: Tata McGraw-Hill.

Singh, Dalip. 2001. *Emotional Intelligence at Work.* New Delhi: SAGE Publications.

Skinner, B.F. 1971. *Beyond Freedom and Dignity,* New York: Knoff.

Smith, P.C. and L.M. Kendall. 1963. "Retranslation of Expectations: An Approach to the Construction of Unambiguous Anchors for Rating Scales," *Journal of Applied Psychology,* 47: 149–55.

Snyder, M. and W.B. Swann. 1978. "Hypothesis—Testing, Processes in Social Interaction," *Journal of Personality and Social Psychology,* 36: 1202–12.

Sperry, Len and L.R. Hess. 1974. *Contract Counselling.* Reading, MA: Addition Wesley.

Starling, G. 1982. "Performance Appraisal in the Z Organisation," *Public Personnel Management Journal,* 11(4): 343–51.

Thornton, G.C. and W.C. Byham 1982. *Assessment Centers and Managerial Performance.* New York: Academic Press.

Tornow, W.W., M. London, and CCI Associates. 1998. *Maximising the Value of 360- Degree Feedback.* North Carolina: Jossey-Bass Inc.

Townley, B. (1993), Performance Appraisal and the Emergence of Management, *Journal of Management Studies,* 30(2), 221–38.

Tversky, A. and D. Kahneman. 1974. "Judgement under Uncertainty: Henristics and Biases," *Science,* 185: 1124–31.

Vallance, Sarah. 1999. "Performance Appraisal in Singapore, Thailand and Philippines: A Cultural Perspective," *Australian Journal of Public Administration,* 58(3): 78–95.

Warmke, D.L. and R.S. Billings. 1979. "Comparison of Training Methods for Improving the Psycho-Metric Quality of Experimental and Administrative Performance Ratings," *Journal of Applied Psychology,* 64: 124–31.

Yakavac, M. 1996. "Paying for Satisfaction," *HR Focus,* June: 10–11.

2nd Administrative Reforms Commission Report: Civil Services Reforms, Report 10. Available at http://indiagovernance.gov.in/files/personnel_administration10.pdf (accessed on July 5, 2015).

Report of the Committee on HR Issues of Public Sector Banks. Available at http://financialservices.gov.in/reports/HRIssuesOfPSBs.pdf (accessed on October 30, 2015).

# Index

360 degree feedback, 59, 187, 192, 194,
    200, 225, 228, 241–242, 249–265,
    262–263
    advantages, 250–251
    as an instrument in ADC, 269–271
    effectiveness, 257–259
    implementation, 263–265
    objectives, 250
    prerequisites for participation,
        251–253
    RSDQ model, 254–257
ABB, 216
ability factors, 77
absenteeism, 81, 119
acceptance, 45, 106, 122, 135, 145,
    149–150, 153
accomplishment, 11–12, 28, 54, 71–74,
    88, 108, 156, 195–196, 202, 233,
    243
accountability, 33, 80, 88, 185, 188–189,
    192, 198, 201, 233, 237, 265
accuracy of performance appraisals, 116
action planning, action plans, 134,
    136–137, 149, 152
Aditya Birla Group, 279
administrative actions, 157
advanced training and development
    opportunities, 163, 166–167
advances to clients, 47
aggression, 145
announcement in newsletters, journals
    etc, 168–172
    procedures, 271
    tools used, 271
annual operating plans, 35
annual performance awards, 163–164
annual review discussion, 12
appearance, 64
reporting manager and performer, 6–7
relationship, 23–24, 147

appreciation letters
    and certificates, 163, 168
approachability, 80
asking questions and responding, 141
assertiveness, 260
ADCs, 266–282
    objectives, 271
ASEAN, 196–203
assessor training, 274, 280
assessors discussions, 276–277
assimilation effect, 95–96
AT&T, 266, 280
attending, 16–17
attitudes, 54, 57, 212–215
attribution, attributes, 7–9, 109, 120
authority system, 122
autonomy, 99, 145–146
averaging, 26, 110
awareness, 57, 59, 63, 82–83, 87, 143

Bajaj Auto Limited, 227
Ballarpur Industries (BILT), 279
Bank of Baroda (BoB), 227
banks, performance appraisal prac-
    tices, 183–187, 220–221
BARS. See behaviorally anchored
    rating scales
behavioral dimension, behavior, 3, 8, 54,
    56, 61, 63–64, 93, 104, 106, 108,
    110–121, 124–125, 138, 142,
    144–146, 148–149, 157, 159, 163,
    176–177, 179–180, 206–207,
    210, 212–215, 224, 240, 249, 256,
    258, 274, 276
    changes, 260–260
behavior event interviews (BEI), 272
behaviorally anchored rating scales
    (BARS) 110–114, 119–120,
    122–123, 125
    effectiveness, 113–114

Bell curve, 126–129
BEML, 227, 279
benchmarking, 128, 199, 234, 263
Bharat Petroleum Corporation
    Limited, 2
biases in performance ratings,158, 176,
    178, 249, 251, 260, 281
    reducing, 103–131
bonus negotiation, 25
Bosch, 209, 211, 213–215
boss and subordinate, relationship,
    25–26, 28, 33, 44, 47, 60, 66, 72,
    81, 87, 99–100, 129, 134, 196,
    232, 242, 268
budget statements, 35

Cadbury, 279
calibration, 29, 178–179
Canara Bank, 227
capabilities, 13, 22, 24, 37, 39, 43–44,
    47, 59, 63, 70–71, 73, 81
capability gaps, 157–159
capability indicators, 70
capacity building, 197
capacity limitation, 22
career counselling, 113
career development, 156, 161, 279
career planning and development,
    250, 263
cash management, 130
Castrol (India), 179, 207, 211, 279
categorization, 81–82, 92, 115,
    118–119, 130, 186
CEO's role in ADC, 278
changed responsibilities and status, 166
civil services, 187–194
clinical counseling, 134–135
coaching, 14, 17–18, 75–76, 87, 134,
    136, 231–232, 239, 270
cognitive compatibility, 120
cognitive complexity, 119, 125
cognitive flexibility, 126
cognitive process, 118–119

collaboration, 80, 99, 101, 129, 171, 193
commitment, 12, 14, 30–31, 54, 56,
    63, 65, 93, 132, 149, 174, 204,
    206, 214, 256, 280
committees, role in performance
    review,14, 102, 161, 183–186,
    239, 273
communication process, 12–13, 55,
    59, 61, 68, 79, 92, 101, 130,
    133–134, 139–145, 155, 177,
    197, 204, 219–221, 239, 241,
    256, 260, 274
company culture, 265
company goals, 264
comparisons, 113, 156, 172
compatibility theory of performance
    appraisal, 120
compensation, 86, 193, 211
competence, competencies, 7–9, 11,
    13–15, 19, 32, 54–73, 84, 88–89,
    93, 96–97, 122, 132, 136–137,
    176, 180–182, 189–191, 196, 222,
    224, 233–234, 240–242, 250,
    252, 254–255, 261, 265–266,
    268–270, 273, 276, 278, 280–281
    building, 231
    lack in HR department, 99
competency mapping exercise, 8, 180,
    191, 280
competency model, 8
competency utilization, 88, 132, 233
competition, 32, 52, 87, 100, 129–130,
    163, 209, 213, 215–216, 218,
    232, 253, 266
competitive advantage, 192
competitive relationships, 151
complexities, 24, 226–227, 234
concern, 56, 68, 93, 125, 139, 147,
    150, 184, 273
confidence, 62, 55, 88, 105, 149, 229,
    243, 270
confidential assessment system, 191
confidentiality, 107, 125, 136, 264

conflict management, 259, 274
consciousness, conscientiousness,
    110–111, 172, 213
consistency, 43, 58
consultant's role in ADC, 277–278
control systems, 80
controlling, 94, 98, 134
cooperation, 81, 132, 151, 198
coordination, 100
cost-reduction, 250
counselling. *See* performance
    counselling
creativity, 54, 56, 58, 93, 143, 159, 216
credibility, 102, 182, 240, 253, 260
crisis management competence, 33
criticism, 61, 134, 141, 145, 172
Crompton Greaves Limited (CGL),
    227, 279
Crystal Phosphates, 214
culture building, 250
Currently Estimated Potential (CEP),
    195
customer focus/orientation, 56, 93, 198,
    250, 267, 281
customer satisfaction, 28, 48, 214,
    250–251
cynicism, 145

Dabur India, 175, 179, 182, 207, 209,
    217
data security, 280
decision-making, 80–81, 97–99, 101,
    130, 152, 210, 273
Defining Performance, 1–2, 24, 77,
    177, 237
delegation, 80, 98, 100–101, 156, 161,
    254–260
demoralization, 169, 171
demotivating influence, 26
dependency needs, 146
deposit mobilization, 46–47
developing performance, 13–14,
    175–178

development, 11, 24, 29, 39–40,
    43–44, 113, 116, 137
    vs. administrative decisions, perfor-
        mance ratings for, 124–126
    decisions, 109, 157, 159
    plan, 183, 200, 235, 270
development needs, 13–14, 24, 44, 49,
    69, 71, 82–83, 87, 147–148
    identification, 147–148
development-oriented performance
    appraisal system, 12, 46, 72,
    108, 124–125
diagnosis of problem, 151
Direct 2000, 89–92
direction, direction-setting mecha-
    nisms, 37
discipline, 3, 73, 87, 172, 186, 208, 231,
    238
displacement, 144
dissatisfaction, 108, 204
Dixit, Anil, 279
dual process system, 118
dyadic performance, 3, 25–27
dyadic relationship, 126, 136

effectiveness, 59–60, 63–64, 72–73,
    257–259
efficiency, 172, 174, 192, 195, 216,
    220, 267
ego problems, 33, 252
Eicher, 279
emotional intelligence, 63, 249
emotions, 63–64
empathy, 64, 137, 139, 144, 147, 149,
    206
employee development, 14, 68, 116, 182
employee-job matching, 167
employee satisfaction, 28
entrepreneurship, 249, 279
environmental factors, 77, 121, 274
Escorts, 279
evaluation, 92, 122, 142, 177
evolution, 266

expectations, 2–3, 7, 10, 12, 31, 38, 62, 72, 79, 83, 85–86, 96, 106, 110, 112, 125, 153, 155, 174–175, 203, 214
experimenting, 59–60
exploration, 69, 142, 144–146, 149–152
eye contact, 150

facilitating factors of performance analysis, 80, 82, 100f
failures, 10–11, 44, 70–72, 82, 103, 120
fairness, 187–189
feasibility, 152
feedback. *See* performance feedback
flexibility, 38, 126, 198, 214, 274
focus dimension, 23
follow up and monitoring, 14, 48, 94, 152–153, 258, 264–265
   lack of on part of HR department, 14
forced distribution, 103–131
forced ranking system, 130
freedom, 12, 69, 99–101, 145, 193, 195
friendship bias, 114
frustration, 281

gender bias in performance rating, 115
generalization, 145
genuineness, 129, 147
GIC, 227
Glaxo, 279
goal setting, goals, 36, 174–175, 188, 201
   and performance review, 174–175
grievances, 49, 52, 130
Grindwell, 279
groups, 35, 40–42, 61, 101, 111–112, 130, 156, 159
growth, 5, 38, 47, 61, 63, 65–66, 69–70
guidance, 26–27, 40, 76, 80–81, 83, 133

halo effect, 110, 120, 122–123
helping, helping attitude, 137
hindering factors in performance analysis, 78, 80, 97–98, 141

Honeywell India, 175–176, 179, 181, 206–207, 209, 214, 216–217, 219
housekeeping, 52
Houston, United States of America, 161
HPCL, 175, 178–180, 206, 212–215, 217–219, 279
human capital building, 84, 102
human information processing, 115
humor, 145

idiosyncratic biases, 119
IFFCO, 176, 211, 214, 218
in-basket techniques of assessment, 273
Indian Institute of Management, Ahmedabad, 254
Indian Oil, 174, 211, 279
individual assessor rating, 276
individual development plans (IDPs), 13–14, 175
individual effectiveness feedback (IEF), 202
individual performance, 21, 27, 34–36, 123, 171, 174, 197, 202, 206–208, 211, 222–225, 238, 242, 244
   inefficiencies, 33
   planning review and assessment, 240–241
   through performance appraisal, 24, 29
Indonesia, 197–198
influencing, 119, 139, 145–147
information, 3, 13, 20, 40, 46, 72, 94–95, 106, 133, 141, 151, 154, 156, 196–197, 199, 226, 230, 255, 257, 274
information processing, 108–109, 115–117, 119
information technology, 240–241
Infosys, performance management, 187
Infrastructure Leasing and Financial Services (IL&FS), 223–225
inhibiting factors, 74–83, 101, 106, 157, 159, 186

initiative, 3, 9, 54, 59–60, 62, 68–69, 80, 93, 124, 135, 146, 159, 175, 177, 187, 207, 210, 213, 228, 241, 249, 260
innovation, 55, 60, 62, 93, 172, 192, 212, 216–217, 220, 249, 266
input-output relationship, 23–24
inputs dimension, 20
insecurity, 270
insights, 44, 57, 83, 91, 136, 155–157, 232, 250, 258, 274, 276
integration, 95–96
integrity, 56, 93, 213, 281
internal customer assessment, 242
inter-personal competence, 136
inter-personal skills, 148
interviews, 152, 180, 257, 270, 272
invest twenty, 89–92
ITW Signode, 178, 180, 208, 210, 218

Japan: performance management system and appraisal, 150–153
Jindal Steel&Power Limited, 174
job context, 118
job knowledge, 177, 272
job rotation, 14, 49, 59, 83, 152, 156, 160, 183, 205
job satisfaction, 256
job training, 83
*Journal of Applied Psychology*, 109
JSPL, 174, 178–179, 181, 208–209, 213–216, 219

key performance areas (KPAs), 1–2, 4–10, 15–19, 24, 30–31, 36, 39–56, 69, 71, 74–75, 78–80, 84, 105–106, 108, 124, 130, 132, 157, 158, 186, 188–189, 205, 227, 237, 241, 243, 251, 268
components, 253–254
examples, 39–40, 47–53, 157, 177
and the performance planning, 4–9, 84

as mechanism of role clarity and development, 39–40
identification, 55, 77–78, 157–158, 237
orientation, 7, 37
key result areas (KRAs), 1–2, 4–7, 9–10, 12, 19, 30–31, 36, 54–56, 69, 84, 132, 174–175, 177, 186, 188, 205, 211, 221, 237, 241, 243, 246, 251
Khandelwal Committee, 173, 220

L&T ECC, 227
Larsen & Toubro (L&T), 227, 279
leaderless group discussions (LGD), 273–274
leadership, 4, 55, 87
competencies, 176, 183
development, 92, 187
and managerial role, 254, 259
qualities, 256
style, 254–256, 258–259, 263
learning, 13–14, 16–17, 20, 23, 25, 67, 70, 75, 84, 87–89, 94–95, 117, 158, 174, 197, 218, 231–234, 251, 254, 256, 259, 266
leniency effect, 110
liberalization, 81, 279
Life Insurance Corporation of India(LIC), 227
line managers, sense of ownership, 246
listening, 3, 55, 65, 93, 139–140, 143, 145, 149–150, 256

Mafatlal Group, 269
Mahindra & Mahindra, 279
Malaysia, performance management system and appraisal, 198–199
managerial effectiveness, 59, 61, 68–69, 71–73, 87, 232, 254, 256, 275
managerial hierarchy, 125
managerial performance, 6, 22, 105, 277
manpower requirement and redeployment, 97, 195
Maruti Suzuki, 212, 216

Matrix Labs, 207
methodology for performance analysis, 79–82
milestones, 211, 214
misunderstanding, 153
Mixed Standard Scale, 113–114
monitoring and follow up. *See* follow up and monitoring motivation,
Moser Baer, 174, 182, 108, 210–216, 219
Motherson Automotive Technologies & Engineering, 181
motivational values, 26, 166, 194
Motorola, 280
multiple objectives of PMS, 87–89
multirater assessment and feedback systems (MAFS), 249
  advantages, 250–251
  effectiveness, 257–259
  objectives, 250
  prerequisites for participation, 251–254
Murugappa Group, 227
mutuality, 13, 25, 43, 67–68, 87, 89, 134–137, 139–141, 143–144, 147–149, 232, 259

National Stock Exchange of India, 225
negative connotations, 134
new appraisal systems, 196
nominal scales of performance rating, 85, 104, 229
normal probability curve, 127
NORTEL, 280
Norton, 279
NTPC, 178, 180, 183, 207, 209, 211–218, 279

objectives of performance appraisal and analysis, 36–38, 54, 67, 101, 169, 176, 210, 226, 239, 300
objectivity, 36–37, 44–47, 85, 88, 103, 105, 108, 125, 187, 228–229, 232, 239, 246, 251, 270
observability, 122

observation-inference-scaling-recording and summary rating, 113
OD, 96–98
Oil and Natural Gas Commission (ONGC), 279
on-boarding, 95–96
open system, openness, 43, 56, 67, 93, 106–107, 135, 137, 149–150
open-ended questions, 257
opportunity cost, 32, 90
organizational culture, 205, 251
organization development, 75–102
organizational growth and dynamism, 265
organizational hierarchy, 114, 135
organizational plans and goals, 2, 35, 87–88, 155, 174, 184, 186, 195, 197, 203, 232–233, 241
organizational performance, 3–4, 92, 172, 197, 202, 223–225
organizational support, 10, 20, 30–32, 54, 76–77, 89, 97–98, 132, 137, 173, 234, 261–262
outputs and results dimension, 19–20

partialing, effectiveness of, 123
peers and subordinate, 183, 206, 257–258, 275
  assessment by, 114
perceptions, 12, 83, 110, 149, 251
performance analysis, 9–11, 14, 69, 71, 76–77, 79–80, 82, 120, 155, 157, 159–160, 186, 189
  factors, 52–54
  for counselling and identification of development needs, 82–83
performance appraisals, 24, 29, 85, 103–105, 116, 130, 157, 160
  components used by different organization, 127–129
  to performance management, shift, 227

role in performance management, 13–14
to planning, analysis and development, 184–188
practices, 126–129
ratings, 64, 66–67, 70, 178, 246–247
factors effecting, 108–109
theoretical considerations, 75–81
performance appraisal systems, 1, 84, 160, 187, 245–246
complexity, 109, 119, 121, 125, 135, 237
effectiveness, 109
four phases, 82
performance assessment, 137, 202
to performance development, 187
(see also ADCs)
performance conversations, 132–154
performance culture, 83, 92, 185, 220, 251
performance and development review (PDR), 174
performance and rewards, linking, 138
performance enhancement, 15, 29, 231
performance equation, 9, 20, 30–31, 76–78, 132, 134, 221
performance feedback, feedback mechanism, 113, 194
negative, 58, 134, 264
performance improvement, 29, 71, 77, 86, 92, 103, 133–134, 137, 155–172, 250
performance linked pay, 221, 224–225, 227, 251
performance management, management systems, 172–203, 226–248
difference from appraisal systems, 189–192
dimensions, 16–29
neglected, 25–27
performance planning, 4–7, 10, 13, 33–38, 69, 84–92, 94, 173, 186, 189, 231, 238, 240–241

performance rating, 26, 44, 92, 108
dimension-wise, 124
errors, statistical control, 123–124
generation process, 103
quality, 120
scales, 109–114
standards, availability, 116, 118
performance review, review systems, 39, 72, 82, 86, 92, 106, 138, 176, 181, 185, 231, 241, 243–244, 252, 264
feedback, 200, 235
performance review discussion (PRD), 11, 24, 71, 84, 94–95, 128, 132–136, 186, 189, 231, 249
conditions for effective, 9, 137–138
constituents, 138–152
objectives, 136–137
sequential process, 148–149
performance rewards, 156, 162–164
mechanisms, 163
performance targets, objectivity, 44–47
perseverance, 97
personal development, 179, 200, 235, 263
Personnel/HRD department's response to new appraisal systems, 161, 249
Philippines
performance management system and appraisal, 196
Philips Electronics India, 175, 179–180, 182–183, 212, 215, 217, 219
Philips leadership competencies and 360 degree appraisals, 176
placement decisions, 167–168, 270
planning orientation, 37
planning performance, 4–5, 7–9, 24, 40–47, 224. See also performance planning polarity, 82
positive reinforcement, 139–140, 146
potential appraisal, 184, 250, 263, 266–269, 279
power differentials, 122
power motivation, 146

priority areas, 37
PRD. *See* performance review discussion (PRD)
proactive behavior, 256
problem solving, 55, 87, 93, 133–134, 147, 153, 232, 238, 271, 274
process parameter, 25–27
productivity, 131, 162, 172, 175, 192, 198, 203, 208–209, 215, 220, 245, 267
professionalism, 99, 253
profits, 23
profitability, 209
projection, 144
promotions, 87, 108–109, 125, 129, 156, 165, 168, 175, 178, 183, 212, 232, 238, 256, 263, 267–268
prototype-generated false memories, 119
psychological maturity, 146
psychometric tests, 270–271
psychotherapy, 134
Public Sector Banks, 183–186
punctuality, 81, 119, 208, 213

quality, 9, 19–20, 23, 33–35, 56, 65, 93, 101, 104, 108–109, 112, 120, 132, 159, 175, 185, 195, 198, 208, 210, 214–216, 218, 250–251, 256, 264, 267, 281
quantification, 6, 36, 169

RPG Group, 279
RSDQ. *See* roles, styles, delegation, qualities rankings and ratings
rapport building, 149–152
rater, 85, 110–112, 114–115, 120–124, 129, 229
  ability, 115, 117
  biases, reducing, 121
  motivation, 115–117
  participation, 122
  training, 121–122
rating. *See* performance rating

ratio scales of performance rating, 105
recency effect, 110
recognition, 15, 82, 84, 86–88, 135, 150, 157, 162–164, 168–169, 193, 198, 202, 205–206, 211, 215–220, 230–232, 262
reliability of assessment, 114, 271–272, 280
reliability, 62, 113–114, 271–272, 280
responding, 139–143, 147–148
review. *See* performance review
reviewing performance, 9–13
rewards, 204–225
rewards and recognition. *See* performance rewards
rightsizing, 196
rivalry repression, 146
role clarity, 6–7, 37, 87, 91, 99–100, 152, 157, 231, 250
  key performance areas (KPAs) as mechanisms, 39–40
role incumbency, 124
role plays, 180, 274, 280
roles, role requirements, 4, 13, 28–29, 38–46, 55, 70, 93, 101, 111–112, 125, 132, 138, 150, 155, 161, 174, 250, 259–260, 267–268, 272–274, 278
roles, styles, delegation, qualities (RSDQ) model of 360 degree feedback, 254–265
  effectiveness, 257–259 (*see also* multitraiter assessment and feedback systems (MAFS))

salary and reward administration, 138, 161, 163–164, 168
Sanghi Industries, 177, 183
satisfaction, 7, 18, 28, 89, 137, 157, 187, 204, 214, 229, 233, 250–251, 256
scaling principles, 105
schemata, 115–116, 126

Schneider Electric, 175, 177, 180, 182, 206–207, 213–214, 217
searching, 57, 152
self-appraisal, 11, 69–72, 74, 84, 106–107, 157, 186, 190, 237
  for managerial effectiveness, 72–73
self-assessment, 11, 63, 107, 191, 224, 242, 244
self-awareness, 57, 59, 63–64, 69, 82–83, 87, 143, 194, 232
self-development, 57, 212
self-evaluation, 176–177, 196
self-realization, 153
self-review, 11
self-worth, 33, 61, 63
senior manager appraisal, 111, 170, 222, 252
sensitivity, 60, 64, 68, 259–261
setting standards, 53
severity effect, 110
sharing, 7, 13, 58, 79, 86, 106, 125, 133, 230, 239
Shell, Singapore, 194–195
Siemens, 279
Simple Graphic Scales, 114
simulation exercises, 273–274
sincerity, 60, 62, 76
Singapore: performance management system and appraisal, 194–195
SKF India, 180
skills, skill-based appraisals, 30, 54–55, 59, 63, 65–66, 68, 93, 122, 140, 146–148, 151, 165, 170, 177, 179, 190, 195, 197, 202, 207, 210, 218, 237, 240, 250, 256, 271, 274
  deficiency, 122
sociability, 54
softness, 98, 135
Sona Koyo Steering Systems, 177, 181
speed, 9, 101, 132, 213, 266
spirit, 86, 103, 159, 209, 213, 230, 245, 259
sponsorship, 152, 163, 166, 212, 218

staff management and control, 49
staff support, 80
State Bank of India (SBI), 186, 227
Steel Authority of India Ltd. (SAIL), 92, 173, 206, 227, 244
strengths and weaknesses, 57, 67–68, 70, 78, 108, 136, 143, 148, 157, 181, 257
subjectivity and errors in performance ratings, 7, 37, 77, 108–110, 125, 130, 169, 171–172, 176, 236
subordinates, subordinates' 10, 25, 40, 44, 47, 58, 72, 80–81, 110, 120, 124–125, 175, 183, 196, 217, 232, 252, 256, 258–259
  autonomy, 33
  behavior, 110, 121
  participation, 137–138
  success and failure, 43, 70
succession planning and development, 183, 250, 279
summarizing, 148
support, supporting, 5, 13, 20, 22, 30–32, 38, 43, 54, 67, 70, 76–78, 80–82, 87, 89, 91, 97–101, 119–120, 132, 137, 143, 148–149, 152, 157, 173, 189, 196, 204–205, 213, 228, 232, 234, 240–241, 244, 252, 257, 261–262, 269, 277
SWOT (strengths, weaknesses, opportunities, and threats) analysis, 76

TVRLS (T.V. Rao Learning Systems), 90–91, 254–259
talent utilization, 92–94
Tamil Nadu Newsprint and Papers Limited, 177
targets, target setting, 1, 37, 173, 189
task analysis and activity analysis, 36
Tata Iron and Steel Company (TISCO), 279

Tata Motors, 174, 179–181, 183, 208–209, 213–215, 217
TCG Life Sciences, 178–179, 182–183, 211, 218
team incentives, 221–223
team performance, 3, 27–29, 211–212, 221–223
   team appraisal, 224
team rewards, 208–210
team spirit, team building, 159, 209, 259
team work, 171, 192–193, 208–209, 213, 221, 228, 233, 241, 249, 251, 274
tensions, 137
time dimension, 20–22
time management, timeliness, 33–34, 213, 260, 273
time wastage, 62, 91
TNPL. *See* Tamil Nadu Newsprint and Papers Limited
top management, 179, 215, 217, 232, 239, 245, 252–253, 261, 277–278
total quality management (TQM), 177, 250
training, 13–14, 45, 83, 108, 119, 121–122, 125, 130, 166, 175
training needs, 117, 131, 136, 156–157, 178, 195, 279
   identification, 157–161
trait-based assessment, 7
transactional analysis approach, 147
transfers, 81, 108–109, 132, 156, 161, 163, 167–168, 191
transparency, 76, 92, 131, 182–183

trust in performance appraisal, 43, 60, 62, 66–67, 106–107, 115–116, 126, 134–135, 142, 147, 263–264

uncertainties, 34
understanding, 3–6, 9, 13, 24, 34, 39–40, 42–44, 64, 72, 76–79, 86, 91, 96, 109, 133, 135, 138, 143, 145, 157, 205, 206, 226, 230, 240, 274, 281
upward learning, 94–95
user reaction to performance ratings, 114

validity of performance assessment, 113–114, 271, 280
values, 3–4, 9, 11, 26, 30, 54, 56–57, 60, 62, 65–66, 84, 89, 93, 111, 115, 155, 164, 166, 168, 175, 182, 194, 212–215, 234, 241, 281

warmth, 148–149
weightages, 37, 41–42, 56
Wipro, 279
Wockhardt, 279
work culture, 198
work-oriented behavior, 138
work planning, 88, 233
working hard, 17, 75
working relationships, 66, 260

you-we technique, 148

Z organizations, 152–53
Zen philosophy of performance appraisal, 150

# ABOUT THE AUTHOR

**T.V. Rao** is currently the Chairman of T.V. Rao Learning Systems, Ahmedabad. He served as a Professor at the Indian Institute of Management, Ahmedabad (IIMA) for over two decades, starting from 1973. He is currently a member of the IIMA Society as well as its Board of Governors. Dr Rao is the founder and first President of the National HRD Network, the first Honorary Director of the Indian Academy of Human Resources Development, and has served as the President of the Indian Society for Applied Behavioral Science (ISABS).

A well-known consultant, Dr Rao has been a Consultant at the Commonwealth Secretariat (London), United Nations Industrial Development Organization, United Nations Educational, Scientific and Cultural Organization, United States Agency for International Development (Indonesia), and various other international bodies. He has also designed and assisted in implementing performance appraisal systems at several organizations in India and abroad, including in Larsen & Toubro (L&T), L&T ECC, National Thermal Power Corporation, Steel Authority of India Limited, State Bank of India, Bharat Earth Movers Limited, Bharat Petroleum Corporation Limited, EID Parry, Sundaram Fasteners, Mahindra & Mahindra, Sundaram Clayton, Crompton Greaves, Hindustan Lifecare Limited, National Organic Chemical Industries Limited, the National Stock Exchange of India, Titan, Color Chem, and Life Insurance Corporation of India.

A prolific writer, Dr Rao has published in diverse areas, such as HRD, education, entrepreneurship, health, population, and management training. He has also done work in 360 Degree Feedback Systems and in fact initiated this methodology at the IIMA in India, much before it came to be known as the 360 Degree Feedback System in the USA. Dr Rao has to his credit over 60 books, including *HRD Audit: Evaluating the Human Resource Function for Business Improvement* (SAGE); *Human Resources Development: Experiences, Interventions, Strategies* (SAGE); *HRD*

*Score Card 2500: Based on HRD Audit* (SAGE); *HRD Missionary, Designing and Managing HR Systems, Readings in HRD, Future of HRD,* and *Redesigning Performance Appraisals, 100 Managers in Action,* and *Managers who Make a Difference.* Dr Rao has assisted the Government of India in various capacities, such as being part of the HR Committee of Public Sector Banks and serving as a Consultant to the Administrative Reforms Commission.